NEVILLE
CHAMBERLAIN
and
APPEASEMENT

NEVILLE CHAMBERLAIN and APPEASEMENT

❧❧

A Study in the Politics of History

LARRY WILLIAM FUCHSER

W·W·Norton & Company

NEW YORK   LONDON

The text of this book is composed in 10/12 Palatino, with display type set in Craw Modern.
Manufacturing by The Maple-Vail Book Manufacturing Group.
Book design by Nancy Dale Muldoon.

First Edition

Library of Congress Cataloging in Publication Data
Fuchser, Larry William.
    Neville Chamberlain and appeasement.
    Bibliography: p.
    Includes index.
    1. Great Britain—Foreign relations—Germany.
2. Germany—Foreign relations—Great Britain.
3. Great Britain—Foreign relations—1936–1945.
4. Great Britain—Politics and government—
1936–1945.   5. Chamberlain, Neville, 1869–1940.
I. Title.
DA47.2.F8   1982   941.084   82-6417

ISBN 0-393-01607-2   AACR2

W. W. Norton & Company, Inc. 500 Fifth Avenue, New York, N.Y. 10110
W. W. Norton & Company, Ltd. 37 Great Russell Street, London WC1B 3NU

1 2 3 4 5 6 7 8 9 0

To M. M. M.

Contents

Preface and Acknowledgments

At the core of every political biography lies an essential and ineradicable paradox in that the politician is always both the maker and the product of history. Political action is both a manifestation of freedom and a product of necessity. In the events leading up to the second great war in modern times, Neville Chamberlain was both father and son of Clio, the muse of history.

The reality of this paradox is obscured for us because we can no longer see events of that war as they unfolded but only dimly through the haze of all that has passed between then and now. Our perception of the events leading to war is inevitably colored by images of Dresden, Hiroshima, and Auschwitz, and it is only with the greatest difficulty that we can perceive even the vaguest outline of events as they appeared at the time.

Yet World War II is a living reality in popular culture principally, of course, in an unending fascination with the demonic personality of Adolf Hitler. The drugstore paperback trade thrives on cheap thrillers about Hitler and the war; television documentaries and psychohistories dealing with Nazi Germany have become a major growth industry. In contrast, there has been relatively little popular or scholarly attention paid to Neville Chamberlain, Hitler's major antagonist in the events leading up to the Second World War.

Appeasement, the policy aimed at preventing war, was, of course, a tragic failure, and Chamberlain is remembered, if at all, as a pathetic old man, one of the great losers of history. Perhaps it is always true that the peacemaker is of less intrinsic interest than the conqueror, but in any case Chamberlain was an historical figure fated to deal with one of the most extraordinary dilemmas in modern history and as such he ought to command our attention, if not admiration. As prime minister, Chamberlain was committed, more than to anything else, to the avoidance of another war even as the German behemoth loomed ever more threateningly on the continental horizon. The present work began as a not unsympathetic reexamination of this popular image of Chamberlain as a weak and ineffectual old man feebly waving his unbrella, promising "peace in our time" while the Wehrmacht marched into the Rhineland, Austria, and Czechoslovakia.

A central purpose of this study was to illucidate as precisely as possible the particular combination of freedom and necessity in Chamberlain's pursuit of the appeasement of Europe. In this undertaking, Chamberlain's personal papers, which have only recently become available for general scholarly use, were of enormous importance. The present work is one of the first published works based on unrestricted access to these papers since Sir Keith Feiling's official biography in 1946. The papers are an extraordinary record of the private thoughts of a political leader as he rose from political obscurity to a position at the very center of world events. They are a truly unique source of documentation for a number of reasons, not the least of which is that Chamberlain habitually wrote detailed and revealing letters to his spinster sisters once each week for virtually the entire period he was in public life.[1] From these and other letters, from diaries, and from the official state papers of the Public Record Office we have an unusually rich and complete documentation from which it is possible to reconstruct a great deal of Chamberlain's private thoughts on events as they unfolded.

In general, Chamberlain was a much more powerful leader, both in his control over domestic affairs and in foreign policy, than has heretofore been indicated either by his critics or his apologists. It is important to recognize from the outset that Chamberlain saw appeasement not as the diplomacy of capitulation but as a dramatically positive effort to achieve a settlement of all the intransient issues which had plagued European politics since the signing of the Versailles treaty in 1919. As such, it was a policy conceived in the classic manner of nineteenth-century European diplomacy, a gentlemanly agreement to redraw the political map of Europe. Unfortunately, at least one of the partners to that agreement was not a gentleman!

Perhaps, even more significant than a reevaluation of Chamberlain's role in British politics, his papers reveal a great deal of what Erik Erikson has described as "life history and the historical moment." Political

---

[1] Unfortunately the custodians of the Chamberlain papers found themselves unable to grant the author permission to publish extracts from these papers. As a result, references to Chamberlain's letters and diaries are presented in paraphrased form. While every effort has been made to insure that the material presented in this book preserves as much as possible of Chamberlain's original meaning, certain distortions are, of course, inevitable. Readers wishing to compare the paraphrased material with the original can do so by obtaining a copy of the dissertation (with the same title) from which this book has evolved. The dissertation is available from University Microfilms, Ann Arbor, Michigan.

leaders bring with them, to every decision they make, not only the psychological baggage of their personal life history but also a particular understanding of their nation's collective past. It is the confluence of these two kinds of historical consciousness, or often unconsciousness, which constitutes a primary determinant of the boundary between freedom and necessity in political history.

As one reads Chamberlain's intimate diaries and letters, one is continually impressed by the degree to which historical memory, both personal and public, informed Chamberlain's perception of events in the years leading up to the Second World War. At the private level, an austere and, in some ways deprived, childhood produced a man of passionless rigidity, inordinately concerned to act in a manner of which "father would have approved." At the public level, Chamberlain was like most of his contemporaries, profoundly affected by the First World War, and he later entered politics with the conviction that, above all else, the mistakes of the past must not be repeated. So powerful were these historical memories that in 1938 at Munich, and in the months that followed, it was almost as if Chamberlain saw not Hitler and his unique threat to the peace of Europe, but rather the kaiser of 1914 repeating the same disastrous mistakes which had led to the "Great War."

Chamberlain believed that the alternative to coming to terms with Hitler would be another world war, infinitely more devastating than the last, and that therefore almost any act of political accommodation was fully justified, not only justified, but indeed the only conceivable course of moral action. It was these considerations rather than a belief that the Treaty of Versailles ought to be revised, or an appreciation of British weakness, or the need for domestic political unity, which were in the end decisive. As a result, Britain backed resolutely into war with Germany with her eyes focused doggedly on the past. The case of Neville Chamberlain and appeasement therefore illustrates, in a particularly poignant way, the dangers of making public policy on the basis of unexamined analogies with the past. It is a story which is not without relevance for contemporary political leaders.

This book is the product of several years of research, writing, and revision. The author wishes to express his deep gratitude to the many people who have contributed their time, advice, and wise counsel. Among them are Professor Henry Graff of Columbia University who originally stimulated my interest in diplomatic history, and Professors William T. R. Fox and Herbert Deane also of Columbia, as well as Professor Robert W. Cox of York University in Canada. In Britain, the help of the librarian and staff of the University of Birmingham is gratefully acknowledged as well as the assistance of the staff of the Public Record Office in London: Professor David Dilks and the Rt. Hon. The Lord

Boyle of Handsworth of the University of Leeds; and the various members of the Chamberlain, Kennrick, and Beale families who were graciously willing to speak to the author about their famous relative. The author wishes to express appreciation to his former colleagues at Williams College particularly Professor Kurt Tauber and Professor James MacGregor Burns and to Dr. Steven Cohen and Dr. Ann Fagan of New York City each of whom has made a particular contribution far greater than can be expressed in a single note of appreciation. The author is particularly indebted to Mr. George P. Brockway, chairman of W. W. Norton, for his patience and unfailing goodwill during an unusually protracted publication process. Finally, and most importantly, the author wishes to express his heartfelt thanks to Ms. Peggy Marble whose collaboration over many years has been beyond value. While many people have contributed to whatever merit the book contains the final responsibility for its excesses, errors, and omissions is, of course, the author's own.

Introduction[1]

THE lives of public personalities are of interest for a number of reasons not the least of which is the conviction that such leaders possess an indefinable almost mystical quality by which they are believed to command obedience and shape the course of history.[2] Private lives are examined by historians and biographers in an effort to understand the source of this presumed ability to command a center-stage position in the drama of world events. In an age mesmerized by psychoanalysis, we learn to look almost automatically behind the public facade for evidence of unconscious motivation, and we assume that behind that public mask there lies a great caldron of libidinal energy animating and controlling superficial reason.

As an historical personality, Chamberlain fails to measure up on either count. Not even his most ardent admirers have claimed that Chamberlain was charismatic. There was no magical magnetism in his leadership, only hard work and a dogged determination to get the job done. Moreover, Chamberlain's most intimate papers contain no great revelation of secret and sordid desire, no obvious pathology, and very little of the material of which psychohistories are usually made. Instead we find what looks, on the surface at least, to have been an uncommonly conventional and perfectly ordinary product of the late Victorian age. Although, as we shall see, even in the case of a personality such as Neville Chamberlain, reason had its secret passions.

Even though Neville Chamberlain is not a particularly attractive historical figure, he commands our attention because of his central role in the tragic events leading up to the Second World War. As prime min-

---

[1]The reader is advised that all bibliographical references are contained in the "Notes," beginning on page 203. A specific citation may be located under the appropriate chapter subheading.
[2]In the study of political leadership, the quest for a useful definition of the mystical quality usually labeled charisma is analogous to the quest for the philosopher's stone in medieval alchemy. This unending fascination has a long and respected tradition in the annals of liberal scholarship from Max Weber to the recent work of James MacGregor Burns.

ister, Chamberlain was the leading proponent of the policy of appeasement, a policy designed to avert another war with Germany. Chamberlain pursued that policy at a time when world peace was threatened by an unprecedented Nazi aggression, and as a result he is widely believed to bear a major responsibility for the coming of war by his alleged failure to stand up to Hitler. In the language of diplomacy, appeasement has become a metaphor for weakness and the cowardly abdication of power in the face of the malevolent.

In recent years, Munich, the most dramatic of Chamberlain's attempts to appease Hitler, has become a negative symbol for a policy which the judicious statesman should avoid at almost all costs.[3] As early as 1948, Churchill warned that the Soviet Union presented a threat analogous to that of Hitler in the 1930s. The leaders of the West, he said, "have only to repeat the same well-meaning, short sighted behaviour towards the problems which in singular resembalnce confront us today to bring about a third convulsion from which none may live to tell the tale." Anthony Eden later wrote that as prime minister in 1956, he had made the decision to intervene militarily in Suez partly because the policy of appeasement had "persuaded Hitler and Mussolini that the democracies had not the will to resist," and "that they could now march with certitude of success from signpost to signpost along the road which led to world dominion. . . . As my colleagues and I surveyed the scene in those autumn months of 1956," he wrote, "we were determined that the like should not come again."

It was, however, in the United States, heir to the political supremacy of the traditional European great powers, that the Munich analogy came to be most widely applied. American leaders, in the aftermath of the Second World War, needed no reminder that to give in to another "totalitarian"[4] might well lead to the same result as had Chamberlain's policy toward Hitler. They believed that since Chamberlain's attempts to appease Hitler had merely encouraged the dictator's appetite, it was necessary to hold a firm line against Stalin. As early as January 1946, James Forrestal stated his opposition to those who made light of communist ideology since, ". . . in the middle of that laughter we always should remember that we also laughed at Hitler." As one historian of the period, John Donovan, has noted, "In the face of Stalinist 'expansion' (as they regarded it), men like Rusk and Acheson were deter-

---

[3] It is perhaps worth noting that Martin Gilbert has made a distinction between appeasement in general, a policy of which he approves, and Munich, which he regards not as appeasement but as "surrender."

[4] It is interesting to note that the first *Oxford English Dictionary* citation for the word "totalitarian" is 1933. Herbert J. Spiro, in *The International Encyclopedia of the Social Sciences,* says that the term was never used until the late 1930s. It could be argued that the English-speaking public needed a term which covered both fascism and communism, and hence the term totalitarianism was created. This etymological phenomenon suggests that, at least in the eyes of some people, the distinction between the type of government of Hitler's Germany and that of Stalin's Russia had become diminished.

mined not to repeat the mistakes that had been made in the common Western failure of not resisting the Nazi aggressors."

President Truman repeatedly asserted his belief that the "lessons of history" offered clear guidelines for action. In his memoirs, Truman described his making of the decision, in 1950, to attack North Korea.

> In my generation, this was not the first occasion when the strong had attacked the weak. I recalled some earlier instances: Manchuria, Ethiopia, Austria. I remembered how each time that the democracies failed to act it had encouraged the aggressors to keep going ahead. Communism was acting in Korea just as Hitler, Mussolini, and the Japanese had acted then, fifteen years earlier . . . if this was allowed to go unchallenged, it would mean a third world war, just as similar incidents had brought on a second world war.

In fact, earlier military studies had indicated that Korea was of negligible importance and that a land war in Asia was to be avoided at all costs. Convinced that he saw another Hitler behind the North Korean aggression, Truman ordered an attack in the face of all military advice to the contrary.

Likewise, there were those who saw American involvement in Vietnam as analogous to Chamberlain's experience with Hitler. George Ball, for example, said:

> We have . . . come to realize from the experience of the past years that aggression must be dealt with wherever it occurs and no matter what mask it may wear. . . . In the 1930s Manchuria seemed a long way away. . . . Ethiopia seemed a long way away. The rearmament of the Rhineland was regarded as regretable but not worth a shooting war. Yet after that came Austria, and after Austria, Czechoslovakia. Then Poland. Then the Second World War.
>
> The central issue we face in South Vietnam . . . is whether a small state on the periphery of Communist power should be permitted to maintain its freedom. And that is an issue of vital importance to small states everywhere.

So it was that the Munich experience cast its long shadow over the postwar world. At virtually every juncture, decision-makers saw new Hitlers coming back to plague them, and were determined that Munich should not happen again.

Because of its symbolic meaning to a later generation of policymakers, it is important to reexamine the policy of appeasement to determine as precisely as possible exactly what that policy was and what it was not from the perspective of its most important architect: Neville Chamberlain. From this perspective, it is clear that appeasement was an altogether inappropriate, although perhaps inevitable, analogy for diplomats of the postwar era and, in sum, something quite different from what they believed it to be.

In the pages that follow, we shall demonstrate the dialectic opposite of Santayana's famous and by now banal maxim that "those who do not remember the past are condemned to repeat its mistakes." If anyone has had a special relationship to Clio, the muse of history, it is certainly not the politician.[5] Indeed, it would seem that the real "lesson" of appeasement, if there is one, is that it is precisely those who most vividly remember the past who are condemned to repeat its mistakes.

Yet, as one examines the historical and biographical literature on Chamberlain and appeasement, it becomes immediately clear that the ideal of dispassionate objectivity has seldom, if ever, been achieved, and we find instead a hopelessly partisan record of vilifications on the one hand and hagiography on the other. Indeed much of the literature of appeasement can be understood only in terms of the particular party identification of the authors involved. Responding to the national humiliation of Munich, critics have tended to see Chamberlain as a parochial merchant who naively believed Hitler would keep his promises. Often present in their works is the notion that the opposition had articulated an alternative policy which "recognized all along" that Hitler could not be trusted. Chamberlain's Tory defenders have stressed the realism of Chamberlain's actions, emphasizing such factors as the need to buy time to rearm and to overcome isolationist impulses in Britain as well as in the Dominions as explanations and, indeed, justifications, of appeasement. In their view, appeasement was a realistic and judicious policy reflecting Britain's diminished power position. In sum, writers on Neville Chamberlain and his policies tend to fall rather neatly into two categories: those who see Chamberlain as the arch-villain of modern British history and those who see him as a wise and gentle man of peace, facing an impossible situation.

Oddly enough, historians of appeasement have tended to base their analyses on what they believe were Hitler's intentions. Primarily, they

---

[5] Nor have scholars fared any better in distilling the "lessons" of Munich for the postwar world. The historian Hugh Trevor-Roper, for example, once wrote:

> Above all, it is certain that an aggressor can never be appeased. Appeasement has never succeeded in history. If Chamberlain knew no history, at least he supplies us with further proof of that certainty. From the debris of his disaster we may extract some comfort only if we can be sure Munich was the final end of appeasement.

Gabriel Almond, one of the leading American political scientists of the cold war era, constructed what he called "a typology of foreign policy deviations." Surely, it was no coincidence that Almond termed one of the categories of his typology, a type of behavior of which he clearly disapproved: "radical appeasement." In this regard, it is interesting to note that each of two major studies of appeasement done by Americans states very clearly that their purpose is to understand Munich and appeasement so that in dealing with another dictator, Stalin, for example, the same mistakes will not be made again.

In a somewhat specious proposal for correcting the problem of using false historical analogies in the making of policy, Ernest May has suggested that professional historians be formally made part of the decision-making structure.

see Hitler's policy as the fulfillment of a vast and insidious blueprint for world conquest which anyone who had read *Mein Kampf* could and should have known. They then compare the evolution of appeasement with what they regard as Hitler's step-by-step working out of a grand design aimed at global empire. The resulting conclusion has been that appeasement was the quintessence of naivete, if not abject stupidity. In recent years, the first assumption (i.e., that Hitler's foreign policy had been explicitly spelled out in *Mein Kampf*) has been increasingly brought into question, and it is now generally accepted that there were at least some elements of pragmatism in Hitler's aggressive policies. This revision of views as to Hitler's intentions has, it is believed, necessitated a revision of judgments of Chamberlain's policy. It is argued that if Hitler's policy represented a series of pragmatic aggressions and not a blueprint for world conquest, then Chamberlain's policy was more understandable if not justifiable.[6]

Simply because we now know, or believe we know, that Hitler's aggression was pragmatic rather than programmatic does not necessarily vindicate Chamberlain, nor does it necessarily vilify him. Recently there have been several notable efforts to move beyond the old stereotypes to a more complex understanding of the meaning and purposes of appeasement. There is, for that matter, much to applaud in recent Tory revisionism which seeks to credit Chamberlain with a greater measure of realism than had, at least popularly, been assumed. Indeed, there is much to be said in favor of the view that Chamberlain understood the dynamics of European affairs to a far greater degree than his much-maligned public image would indicate. It is certainly true that Chamberlain exerted a personal control over the machinery of state which was unprecedented in scale as well as in scope. Yet, such revisionism often fails to appreciate the historically conditioned parameters of Chamberlain's understanding of Hitler and appeasement.

To understand Chamberlain and his policies on their own terms we must seek to re-create events from the perspective of Chamberlain himself; as a first step, we must try to enter creatively into the world as it existed between the years 1919 and 1939 to determine the "unspoken assumptions" and the "bounded rationality" of the period. There are however inherent dangers in this approach, one being that it seems inevitably to lend credence to the "great men" view of history, a revival of Carlyle, and a misguided emphasis on the heroic. There are, of course, very good reasons why such naive notions have been consigned to the ash heap of scholarship. May they ever remain so. But with all our fas-

---

[6]Maurice Cowling's *The Impact of Hitler,* is the latest in a long series of apologia. Whether or not Cowling actually intended to argue that appeasement if pursued far enough (Chamberlain's crucial mistake being in giving an unequivocal guarantee to Poland in 1939) could have prevented British involvement in a war with Germany is a question which awaits the publication of a concordance to this highly documented but fundamentally incomprehensible work.

cination with material explanation and with sociological analysis, it is nevertheless true that individuals do, at times and under certain circumstances, exert a significant influence over the course of events.

To return then to the world of the interwar years is to try, and it is a nearly impossible task, to put aside all that we know about the events of World War II, to make an effort to suspend our most vivid historical imagery of Hiroshima, of Auschwitz, and of all the horrendous and tragic events of World War II, and to return to a world in which British Imperial might was the dominant force in world politics and in which "the Great War" was the paramount historical memory.

Few tasks are more difficult for those of us living in the latter quarter of the twentieth century than to understand the subjective meaning of the First World War for those who survived it. In Britain, six million men had been mobilized to fight that war. Of these, one in three was either wounded or killed: roughly three-quarters of a million dead and another million and a half wounded. All of the British lives lost in the hundred years before the war were but a tiny fraction of those lost in the 1914–19 war with Germany.

From every possible perspective and in the most literal possible sense, World War I was an unprecedented event in British history. In the postwar period, experience of that war informed almost every aspect of British life from literature and the arts to politics and diplomacy. Virtually nothing seemed as it had been before the events of August 1914. Many of these changes can be understood in terms of lessons believed to have been learned in the war and their projected application to future events. The misery, bloodshed, and death experienced directly by many, and vicariously by everyone, translated itself into a powerful anti-war movement dedicated to the proposition that the Great War must never happen again. To measure the precise influence of the peace movement on interwar politics and foreign policy is, of course, impossible; yet the living memory of the past was a profoundly important determinant of policy. No British diplomat could ever again contemplate using military power as an instrument of policy in the nineteenth-century manner, like the movement of pawns on the chessboard.

Few politicians were willing to renounce completely war as an instrument of national policy, but it was a tool which would never again be contemplated with the equanimity of former years. No longer was the meaning of war symbolized by the glory of Blenheim and Trafalgar, but by barbed wire, mustard gas, and the stench of rotting corpses in a tangle of muddy trenches. The twentieth century had become an era of total war, and it was widely believed that if ever again Britain were to become involved in a general continental war, the result would be beyond estimate, perhaps beyond the capability of Western civilization to survive. Churchill eloquently summarized this sentiment when he wrote:

. . . [the war had] established that henceforward whole populations will take part in war, all doing their utmost, all subjected to the fury of the enemy. It is established that nations who believe their life is at stake will not be restrained from using any means to secure their existence. It is probable—nay, certain—that among the means which will next time be at their disposal will be agencies and processes of destruction wholesale, unlimited and perhaps, once launched, uncontrollable.

Under such conditions no one could take lightly the possibility of another continental war.

For the professional military, the war had demonstrated the utility of an entirely new method of warfare. The dreadnought had been replaced, at least in part, by the airplane as the symbol par excellence of military might. The bomber, they believed, would always get through, and therefore the entire civilian population would be at the mercy of any determined aggressor.[7] In such circumstances, it is not difficult to see how Hitler could have been regarded as such an aggressor and how the temptation to come to terms with his demands might have seemed compelling.

On the diplomatic level, there was relative agreement as to the "lessons" of Sarajevo. For men like Chamberlain the war had come about because the world had become rigidly divided into two hostile blocs of rigid alliances, and that in these circumstances, a relatively unimportant event (such as the assassination at Sarajevo) could lead almost automatically to general war. Such analysis of the causes of war led necessarily to a great fear lest Europe ever again become divided into such a pattern of alliances. As Chamberlain surveyed the diplomatic horizon in the prewar years, he saw a re-creation of a familiar pattern— an awesome, frightening pattern which at times looked as if the tragic events leading to the 1914 war were happening all over again.

Indeed, as we intrude into the world of interwar political assumptions, it often seems as if the policy of appeasement was, in a sense, overdetermined by the weight of the past. Perhaps, it is always or almost always true that when we take on the full weight of assumptions held by historic personalities, history seems like a Greek play whose tragic conclusion is implied from the very beginning, and we can do no more than document the full measure of that tragedy. But perhaps we can also distinguish those options which were clearly beyond the realm of the possible from those which might conceivably have been tried; in sum to discover some measure of freedom within the realm of necessity.

---

[7]The obvious similarity between this situation of exaggerated fear of a new bomber technology and our own time in which the possible destructive capability of an all-out nuclear war, as yet untested, is an analogy which should be resisted at all costs.

≈1≈

Fathers and Sons

What greater ornament to a son than a father's glory, or to a father than a son's honorable conduct.

SOPHOCLES, *Antigone*

Most of us, at some point in our lives, nurture the fantasy that we are completely free agents of our own independent will: the private hero of a tale uniquely our own. It is a narcissistic illusion which we are quick to recognize in others, less so in ourselves. Under the influence of Freud and the psychoanalytic tradition, we have arrived at a new appreciation of the degree to which we are all self-deluded in the account we give of our motives for behaving as we do. In this sense at least, if not in its more esoteric formulations, psychoanalysis has altered our understanding of the historian's task. The writing of history is no longer simply the unproblematic task of uncovering "what actually happened." The historian attempts at the level of group behavior something of what the analyst strives for in a single individual: constructing a coherent account of the past. In this sense, history is always an act of interpretation and never the simple uncovering of facts. And we proceed on the assumption that the past, both personal and public, is an abiding influence which operates like the deus ex machina in ancient Greek drama, controlling our lives in ways of which we are often unaware.

For Neville Chamberlain this was most certainly the case. From the Chamberlain family, and particularly from his father Joseph, Neville inherited a legacy which he failed, in any significant way, to transcend, which was one of the major forces in his life, and which in the end became a kind of sacred trust to be preserved and perpetuated at all costs. To further his father's policies, wishes, and ambitions was for Neville one of the unquestioned assumptions around which he built his entire life, and, we might add, a significant determinant of his perception of Hitler.

There was, moreover, another level on which Clio, the muse of history, helped to shape Chamberlain's policy toward Nazi Germany. In addition to Chamberlain's largely unconscious formulation of his personal past, there was also his equally unconscious perception of the nation's collective past. In Chamberlain's private experience with the First World War, reinforced by a conventional understanding of the causes of that war, there was the conviction that, above all else, it was his destined role to insure that past mistakes must never, never be repeated. Thus the profound wish to act in a manner of which his father would have approved and the wish to avoid another Great War were two determinants of the policy of appeasement.

THE CHAMBERLAIN FAMILY IN POLITICS

To locate the Chamberlains of Birmingham within the complicated matrix of British politics and society is a difficult task partly because they belong to that ill-defined group known as the British middle class. We can, however, distinguish the Chamberlains from the older aristocratic ruling class on the one hand and the newer working-class political elite on the other. The Chamberlains clearly belong to neither of these groups, although in their basic attitudes and in the policies they propounded they were certainly much closer to the former than to the latter.

They were part of the new, relatively liberal governing elite whose position in British society derived from industrial, not landed, wealth. Like the Whigs before them, families such as the Chamberlains shared neither the values of landed wealth and the established church nor the ideals of working-class democracy. Joseph Chamberlain and his sons were not so wealthy that vast political power flowed almost automatically from their wealth, nor were they so poor as to be tied to their profession by the need to earn a living. Thus they were solidly middle class in the British but not in the American sense of that term.

The Chamberlains were further distinguished from the older British aristocracy by virtue of a radical tradition stemming in part from a Unitarian background. By the late nineteenth century, being a Unitarian, while it distinguished them from the Anglican majority, no longer carried the stigma it once had. And while they shared much with the older ruling classes, the Chamberlains were, by the standards of the time, rather independent thinkers deeply committed to the improvement of the lives of the laboring classes and to the politics of Liberal Unionism. They were a family accustomed to service in public causes and never doubted their right and responsibility to govern. Yet, from their private papers, one senses that political success was not necessarily accompanied by social acceptability, that the Chamberlains felt in a sense flattered by whatever measure of social acceptance they were able to achieve by holding office, and that they held the aristocracy in considerable awe.

However much they may have differed from families such as the Churchills or Cecils, the Chamberlains' politics were not, as certain critics have charged, simply the parochial views of middle-class merchants.[1] They were, like most of Britain's ruling elite, parochial in the sense that their world view was British-centered and empire-dominated, but not in the sense of knowing nothing at all of the world beyond their immediate concerns. In fact, Neville Chamberlain was widely traveled and could converse adequately both in French and in German. The term cosmopolitan is not, however, appropriate since the Chamberlains' world clearly centered on the English-speaking peoples of whom the British Empire was by far the most important part, and Britain was after all its center.

They were a part of the social and cultural milieu which we often associate with the late Victorian era and the height of Britain's imperial greatness. It was an ordered world in which the precepts of individual and class behavior were well understood and rigorously applied by those who occupied the higher reaches of government and society. While much has been written of Victorian standards of propriety (although much less than has been written about what future generations believed them to be), to families such as the Chamberlains they were standards as unquestioned as they were rigorous.

Of these characteristics, none was more significant than the peculiar Victorian notion of reason and its role in action. As a child, Chamberlain, like others of his class, learned that in a conflict between reason and passion the former must always prevail. For reasonable men endowed with a certain measure of goodwill, a solution to every human conflict was possible. For reasonable men sitting around a conference table a compromise satisfactory to all simply had to exist.

To Chamberlain, reason had a very clear meaning; it was the ability to eliminate all emotional content from one's decision-making calculations, to deny rather than coexist with the passions. Where a Medieval man might speak of "natural law" as an ultimate standard of human conduct, the Victorian would substitute the word "reason," and the result was probably much the same. Yet in denying their emotions, Chamberlain, and others like him, acted as men have always acted;

[1] Trevor-Roper has argued that, unlike the Churchills and Edens, the Chamberlains were "entirely parochial" and lacked "understanding of history or the world." Whatever may have been the class differences between the Chamberlains and the older British artistocracy, we shall demonstrate that Neville Chamberlain had had a relatively wide exposure to world affairs and that he was not *simply* a parochial merchant.

their decisions were an amalgam of complex and sometimes opposing passions. The difference is that while Chamberlain denied even to himself any motives for his conduct which he could not consider rational, reason became the obedient slave to unknown passion.

Chamberlain's official biographer has said that the Chamberlains "always repressed, since they despised, emotion, generations of enforced reserve having diluted and covered their passion with an ever exercised self-respect." This assessment, written by a man who by and large shared the Chamberlains' values, is a telling commentary on the degree to which the Chamberlains were distinguished even within their own social milieu. So tightly did Neville Chamberlain seek to control his emotional self that he could not admit intimate feelings even in the privacy of his own diary. Sir Keith Feiling, Chamberlain's biographer, noted that he "would not commit introspection to paper, and when he once did so [i.e., in his diary] during an unhappy time, he later cut out the page."[2] Chamberlain's inner life remained as hidden from those who would have been his friends as it was hidden from himself. It will become abundantly clear later on that the fact that feelings were carefully hidden did not mean they did not exist, nor did it mean that they were not a highly significant part of his perceptual framework. In fact, it might well be argued that *because* they were feelings hidden from his conscious self, they were an even more important determinant of his behavior. As his biographer admits, Chamberlain "was himself ruled by affections in the last resort."

At a very early age Chamberlain learned the canons of personal conduct acceptable for a person of his class and social position. These patterns of behavior were reinforced and accentuated by experiences in later years. The result was a personality of unusual severity, an individual ruthlessly and rigidly pursuing unquestioned goals. In so doing, the face which he presented to the world was almost always one of complete composure and rationality untouched by impassioned rhetoric or personal charm. This ultra-rationalist persona was a mask which he wore at all times, never allowing himself the luxury of an unbridled display of sentiment. While he was apparently never able to establish personal relationships on the basis of genuine human warmth and affection, he was capable of intense and malicious hatred of despised enemies. In fact few people could equal the sheer delight which Chamberlain took in showing the enemy to be a fool. It was an insidious if not pathological feature of his complex personality.

There were many other ways in which Joseph Chamberlain and his sons may be seen as characteristic products of the Victorian era. They accepted without question the standards of their social class, a belief in

[2] Another obvious reason was the fact that Chamberlain knew that his diary would be part of his justification before history and possibly wrote it accordingly.

a natural order of things, a social hierarchy based on a Darwinian view of both man and nature, a fundamental contempt for those unfortunate enough to have been born outside the Anglo-Saxon race (particularly those of Jewish origin), and an absolute faith in the moral rectitude of the British Empire.

Although it is perhaps important to distinguish the racial attitudes of the British ruling class in the late nineteenth and early twentieth century from those of continental Germany, families like the Chamberlains held attitudes which were unmistakably racist. Joseph Chamberlain is quoted as having said:

> I have been called the apostle of the Anglo-Saxon race, and I am proud of the title. I think the Anglo-Saxon race is as fine as any on earth. Not that I despise other races. They have their several virtues and aptitudes, though I admit that the aptitudes of my own race appeal to me most strongly. There is, in fact, only one race that I despise—the Jews, sir. They are physical cowards.

Such characteristic anti-Semitism was, in Britain, seldom carried to the extreme of sanctioning overt forms of persecution, but it may well have lessened sensitivity to those who did.

Joseph Chamberlain was one of the first British statesmen to see Zionism sympathetically, not as a humanitarian issue, but as a solution to the "Jewish problem" and a means of advancing British Imperial interests. In his general attitude toward Zionism and specifically in his negotiations with Theodor Herzl, Joseph Chamberlain established a precedent closely followed by his son Neville. When as prime minister the younger Chamberlain was forced to deal with the problem of Jewish refugees, his attitudes and proposed solutions bear a remarkable resemblance to those of his father.[3]

Joseph Chamberlain was the first of his family to earn a reputation as a politician of national let alone international standing. His was a spectacular career pursued with apparently limitless energy and marked with important triumphs and few significant failures. With no cause was the elder Chamberlain more closely identified than with the cause of imperial unity, and he led crusades on behalf of imperial tariff reform and in opposition to Gladstone's policy of home rule for Ireland.

In the early 1900s, Joseph became convinced that Britain's policy of "splendid isolation" was a bankrupt policy and that therefore Britain should come to terms with either Germany and Austro-Hungary on the one hand or France and Russia on the other. Since the imperial policies of the latter seemed the more immediate threat to British interests, Ger-

[3] See pp. 171–72 *supra*.

many seemed, to him, Britain's "most natural ally." Therefore Joseph Chamberlain devoted his energies to fashioning an Anglo-German alliance which was to be accompanied by a general understanding with the United States and an agreement with Japan. According to his biographer, Chamberlain's "long-term aim was nothing less than the adherence of the British Empire to the Triple Alliance."

For a variety of reasons the alliance was never brought to fruition, although the elder Chamberlain was successful in negotiating an Anglo-Japanese alliance in 1902. The German rebuke of Chamberlain's initiative led eventually to the formation of the Entente Cordiale between Britain and France, a diplomatic alignment of crucial significance in the events leading up to the First World War. Here again the influence of Joseph Chamberlain on his son is clear. The German initiative was most certainly a suggestive paradigm for Neville in his early excursions into foreign policy.[4]

However, the determining influence of a father on his son is more clearly and fundamentally demonstrated at the more basic level of family relationships. Joseph Chamberlain, in his early years as a rising Birmingham industrialist, married and had two children, a son, Austen, who would later become a distinguished statesman in his own right, and a daughter, Beatrice. When his first wife died, Chamberlain, after some years, remarried, this time to the sister of his first wife, and fathered another son, Neville, as well as three daughters: Ida, Hilda, and Ethyl. It is quite clear that Joseph Chamberlain was far more concerned with business and career than with home and children, although in later life, he would come to think of himself as the founder of a political dynasty. Children were thus of instrumental importance in a life euphemistically described as devoted to public service yet perhaps more realistically characterized as a life consumed by the quest for political power and public prestige.[5]

Therefore, the birth of Neville Chamberlain on 16 March 1869, was not one of the preeminent events in the life of his father. The emotional deprivation of a child born into a family in which the father was preoccupied with career was significantly heightened by the fact that Neville's mother died on the eve of his sixth birthday and the fact that two years later he was sent to the public school of Rugby. No matter how conventional these arrangements were in nineteenth-century terms, they must be regarded as developmentally significant; the remoteness of a father preoccupied with other things, the death of a mother at a relatively

[4]See p. 41 *supra*.

[5]Even if we make ample allowance for the conventions of British political biography it is quite clear that his children, at least in their early years, were of only peripheral interest to Joseph Chamberlain. Indeed, the birth of Neville and his younger sisters is not even recorded in a massive six-volume biography.

early age, and the loneliness and isolation of a public school could not but have had a significant effect on Chamberlain's mature personality.

Unfortunately, the little we know about the early life of Neville Chamberlain is based primarily on information supplied by his official biographer whose discretion was beyond question, but who nevertheless supplies us with the broad outlines of Chamberlain's childhood experiences. We know that outside the protective Chamberlain-Kennrick family he was plagued by an "accursed shyness" which was worsened at Rugby where he was badly bullied. He endured the humiliations of public school without breathing a word to his father, and just when he was beginning to adjust to his new and difficult life, his father, quite arbitrarily it seems, had him transferred. Feiling tells us that this "from the inscrutable working of a boy's pride always remained a rankling wound."

At some point during these years, Joseph Chamberlain made a second decision which would profoundly affect his son's life; both of his sons were to follow in his own footsteps, one to pursue his father's public career, while the other would be responsible for the family's economic security. Austen was to follow the statesman's calling while Neville was relegated to the less exalted role of maintaining the family business. Austen went on to the glories of a Cambridge education, followed by a brilliant diplomatic career, while Neville was sent to study metallurgy and science at the then quite modest institution of Mason College (later to become Birmingham University). Neville's academic career was marked neither by indolence nor intellectual brilliance. Rather, he seems to have been grimly resigned to do his father's bidding.

While it is manifestly clear that the bond between Neville Chamberlain and his father was never one of great intimacy, the older Chamberlain exerted a powerful influence on his son. In a rare moment of candor Neville admitted, "I respected him and feared him more than I loved him."[6] Nevertheless, the younger Chamberlain was always acutely aware that he was his father's son and in later life respected his father's memory "almost to the point of idolatry." To take but one example: in 1932, with the passage of the tariff bill, he spoke in the Commons of his great pride in being able to bring to fruition the aims of the protectionist cause which had been the great unfinished work of his father's career. Such statements recur again and again in Chamberlain's public speeches and to an even greater degree in his private papers. In his later career, Chamberlain could always raise himself to his greatest heights of rhetorical eloquence in public debate when he was expounding a view

[6] The author was unable to locate the source of this statement in the Chamberlain papers.

which he associated with his father. At virtually every juncture in his career, Chamberlain gave some indication that his was a course of action "of which father would have approved."

In 1890, Joseph Chamberlain made a third patriarchal decision of major importance in his son's life. Political connections led him to believe that a sisal plantation in the British West Indies could be a potentially lucrative means for replenishing sagging family fortunes. As the most dispensable member of the Chamberlain family, Neville was given the responsibility for making this enterprise an economically rewarding venture. At the age of twenty-one, Neville left England for Andros, a small remote island in the British Bahamas, to assume responsibility for the new plantation. In sending his son "to undertake on an island on the other side of the Atlantic an almost Crusoe-like attempt," the elder Chamberlain was repeating a family pattern since "in his own teens he had been bundled suddenly into a business of which he possessed at the moment not an iota of knowledge."

For a relatively young man of different childhood experiences, the Andros experience might have been a welcome opportunity to pursue private adventure away from repressive paternal authority which would lead eventually to a more independent identity. Indeed, to a limited extent it may have been exactly that, but in the main, the Andros years were a time of extreme loneliness and isolation in which Neville struggled valiantly to fulfill parental expectations. His letters reveal a grim and dogged determination to succeed and to overcome his feelings of loneliness and longing to return to the security of the family. Virtually cut off from the outside world, he lived for seven years in almost complete isolation, occupying his spare time with projects for civilizing the "darkies" and with private schemes of self-improvement.

Economically, the project was foredoomed by the soil and climatic conditions of the area; Andros was simply not a suitable site for the profitable production of sisal. The elder Chamberlain eventually came to recognize that "he had saddled his second boy with a hopeless task" and "he knew that it was all his own fault." This was not, however, a perception shared by his son. Neville assumed complete personal responsibility and on 28 August 1896 he wrote to his father that the failure of the venture was due solely to his lack of good business sense. The following year, the project was abandoned and an enterprise on which much hope had been placed became a heavy financial loss. Virtually all that remained was 7,000 acres of worthless land.

There can be no doubt that the Chamberlains sacrificed a great deal in terms of financial security for their participation in public life. In sharp contrast to, for example the career of Lloyd George, there was never any question of the Chamberlains using public position for private gain. We know that on Joseph Chamberlain's death there were insufficient funds to maintain the family home at Highbury, and that when public funds for its preservation failed to materialize, the house was in danger of being pulled down to make way for industrial expansion. Even as late as 1935, Austen wrote to his brother that he was experiencing grave financial difficulties, was almost without independent income, and was living almost exclusively on his meager salary. The persistent lack of financial security was one reason for Neville's often-stated reluctance to enter politics in the years following his return from Andros.

The cumulative result of Chamberlain's early life experiences, his isolation in boarding school and on Andros, was an extremely dour personality which one critic described as having been "weaned on a pickle." It was a sarcastic but not inaccurate characterization. Chamberlain had had virtually no experience with cooperative activity or with personal intimacy, and his future relationships would always be characterized more by manipulation and coercion than by collegial mutuality. He was not, as was often said, a "clubable" man. The Andros experience was the culminating failure in an early life unmarked by significant success, and he emerged from that experience with a renewed determination to succeed and to prove himself worthy of being his father's son.

NEVILLE CHAMBERLAIN'S EARLY CAREER

For Chamberlain, the years following his return to England were a time of great frustration bordering on despair but marked eventually by a reorientation of career from business to politics. The stigma of having failed to fulfill his father's wishes was an extremely difficult burden to overcome, and as late as 1902, he wrote that he hadn't yet discovered his goal in life and that bothered him a great deal. Eventually, however, Chamberlain would prove that his father's decision to relegate him to a business career had been a mistake.

But the onus of failure was a difficult burden to bear particularly since his half brother Austen was already at the height of his powers.[7] Chamberlain eventually overcame the failures of his early career, first by involvement in the family business in which he became quite successful, and eventually by participating in municipal politics. In business, he was determined to overcome the Andros failure, vowing to work as hard as was necessary to regain the lost capital. Family connections soon brought him to active and successful participation in a number of Birmingham manufacturing concerns. Political involvement beginning in small ways with various projects for community betterment came later. However, once he found a place for himself in public life, Chamberlain

[7] See 20–21 *supra*.

was determined to make up for lost time and to compensate for the lack of distinction in his early career.

The year 1911 marks a turning point in Chamberlain's life and political fortunes. It was the year, in which at the age of forty-two, he married and began his political career. Even in his choice of a wife, the younger Chamberlain followed a pattern established by his father. Joseph Chamberlain's third marriage, at age fifty-two, had been to a much younger woman of a temperament exactly opposite to that of her husband.[8] Anne Vere Cole, whom Neville married in January 1911, was in her late twenties and, like her mother-in-law, an uncommonly attractive woman. Also like her mother-in-law, the new Mrs. Chamberlain was a precise complement to her husband's personality. While he was stern, morose, and humorless, she was gay, vivacious, and sociable.

It would be unnecessarily harsh to claim that there was no love between Chamberlain and his new wife, but it was certainly not an emotional attachment springing from reciprocity between equals. In the first place, like many men of his class, Chamberlain picked his wife much as he would have selected new breeding stock for Highbury, although choosing a wife was, to be sure, of considerably greater importance. The difference, however, was a matter of degree not category. A proper wife was an extremely valuable possession and her qualities as a hostess could be potentially decisive in one's political career.

Like everything else in life, marriage was a contractual arrangement entered into with honor and of lifelong and unquestioned validity. Neville Chamberlain always regarded his wife with a kind of paternal condescension, a lesser partner in an unequal relationship, a woman to be carefully groomed for her future position as a statesman's wife. In a characteristic letter of 1918, Chamberlain chastised his wife for her foolish and outlandish behavior telling her that she was quite right to feel overwhelmed with shame at her lack of social tact. While there was often bitter criticism in these letters there was also avuncular praise when her conduct pleased him, and once he wrote that in the early days of their marriage he had been positively ashamed to receive her frivolous letters but that later they had often contained much useful information. In later years he was less critical and came to rely on her a great deal, but never did Neville's letters to his wife betray more than a touch of warmth or affection beyond the realm of the purely conventional. In fact, his praise and admiration for his wife were directly related to her contribution to his career. Even if one makes ample allowance for contemporary standards it was, from the husband's point of view, a relationship of great value but of primarily functional utility.

Marriage did not lead to a break in the pattern of emotional isolation

[8]On 15 November 1888, Joseph Chamberlain married Mary C. Endicott, an American. She was twenty four and, by all accounts, a strikingly beautiful woman.

so characteristic of Chamberlain's early life, but his relationship to his younger cousin Norman was becoming, in this period, one of increasing trust and mutual admiration. There can be no doubt that it was profoundly important to both of them. Norman Chamberlain was a dashing and ebullient figure in Birmingham society, tirelessly involving himself in projects for aiding the city's disadvantaged youth. Eventually, Norman would serve with Neville on the Birmingham City Council. Their shared social concern led to a close working relationship in which Norman became Neville's protégé and confidant. For Neville, the relationship bolstered his confidence and furthered his efforts to overcome the Andros failure and return to an active career. He was doing so with a vengeance.

Within four years from his election to the city council, Neville became lord mayor of Birmingham and quickly established himself as a municipal politician of great competence. Birmingham was then one of the leading industrial cities in England, and Chamberlain rapidly demonstrated a capacity to deal effectively with the problems of a burgeoning metropolis. His early efforts in the area of town planning were highly regarded and earned for him the beginning of a national political reputation.

As lord mayor he was remarkably successful in reconciling the interests of the various social classes while at the same time instituting progressive, if not radical measures for the city's poor. At this stage in his career, there was little evidence of the bitter estrangement which was later to poison his relations with the parliamentary Labor Party. In fact, he was reelected as Birmingham's mayor largely because of his good relations with organized labor.

Had it not been for momentous events on the international scene, Chamberlain might well have remained within the milieu of Birmingham politics. It was an environment in which he felt at home and in which he had been remarkably successful, and memories of the defeat at Andros had at last begun to pass away. But the requirements of a wartime economy were to bring Chamberlain out of the obscurity of Birmingham politics and into national affairs. Few people foresaw the magnitude and consequences of Britain's decision to join the coalition against Germany and the Austro-Hungarian Empire. Most believed that it would be a short war fought for limited objectives, the type of war reasonable and civilized men had come to expect. But the exigencies of modern technology were to make it a war quite different than anyone had expected.

In 1914, however, Chamberlain seems to have shared beliefs common to many of the governing classes. As early as 1908, he had favored British armament to meet the rising German threat. In August 1914, he noted in his diary that if Britain refused to join the coalition against

Germany, she would lose all political standing on the continent and he therefore fully supported the decision to go to war.

While he had little doubt as to the rectitude of British involvement in the war, he was quick to realize the consequences of the new type of warfare. In January 1916 Birmingham had its first air raid. Within three days, Chamberlain submitted a plan to the home secretary. It contained "in brief, all that are now considered the first elements of air-raid precautions—a zone of observation, preliminary warning, simultaneous signal, and extinction of lights." He realized that this new kind of warfare was one in which economics played a central role. "Victory," he said, "would go to the nation that produced the largest output at the lowest cost." His outspoken views on labor-capital relations, such as support for conscription of labor and limitations on profits, brought him more and more into the spotlight of national politics.

Joseph Chamberlain had been greatly incapacitated since his stroke in 1906, and with his death in 1914, the way was open for Neville to make the transition from municipal to national politics. His half brother Austen was instrumental in this transition. Between the two brothers there had always been a muted competition but Austen had always been ascendant. Austen admitted to feelings of jealousy over his brother's growing reputation as lord mayor, but he was nevertheless willing to work for Neville's political advancement.

At a time when the allied cause looked grim indeed, the problem of efficiently organizing Britain's manpower resources became increasingly crucial. In spite of his own distrust of the new Prime Minister, Lloyd George, Austen put forward his brother's name for the new position of director general of national service. Austen wrote of his anxiety over Neville and the new position but felt that he had an "excellent press" and "everyone's good will." While Neville felt the post to be an "appalling responsibility" he quickly decided to accept. "If it was only my own career at stake," he wrote, "I wouldn't care a rap, but the outcome of the war may depend on it." Despite the enthusiastic support of Labour, Chamberlain's tenure in the new post was to be as disastrous as it was short-lived.

No doubt he had been placed in a nearly impossible situation; the limits and responsibilities of his office were never defined, he was denied a seat in Parliament which deprived him of the opportunity to defend his actions before the Commons, and he was not given a senior civil servant to aid him in his work. Under such conditions failure to adequately centralize manpower recruitment was all but inevitable. He resigned in August 1917 after having served only seven months. To say that the experience permanently soured Chamberlain's relationship with Lloyd George is a gross understatement. It, in fact, led to a virulent hatred which Chamberlain assiduously cultivated for the next twenty-five years, relishing every opportunity to vent his malice. Chamberlain was determined "to enter Parliament but never to serve with Lloyd George again."

Lloyd George, in his memoirs, noted that Chamberlain was "a man of rigid competency" who "stubbornly resisted every proposal made to him for strengthening the Department in certain directions where it was patently inefficient." From the perspective of Chamberlain's later career, it seems that Lloyd George was surely right in attributing Chamberlain's failure in part to his lack of tact and inability to work cooperatively with others. The decisions leading up to the Munich meeting were in no respect collective decisions but were rather decisions imposed on and acquiesced to by members of the Government.

Chamberlain's failure as minister of national service is important in explaining his future behavior in at least two other respects: it made even more unpleasant his memories of the war and his personal involvement in it, and, moreover, when Chamberlain himself was to deal with the problems of peace and war, he was denied what might, at least potentially, have been the useful counsel and experience of Lloyd George, the only statesman who had firsthand experience in leading the British nation in war.

The period following his resignation was perhaps, from a personal point of view, the worst in Chamberlain's entire life. Steadily, and with a depressing regularity, came reports of greater and greater amounts of British blood and treasure poured into the trenches of France. The bitter taste of defeat in his first venture into national politics, rather than the conviction that he had been partly responsible for sending the flower of British youth to their death, helped make him depressed and morose. In October 1917, his diary records:

> Every now and then a feeling of almost irresistible nausea and revulsion comes over me at the thought of all the drudgery, the humiliation, the meanness and pettiness of that life, and of the hopeless impossibility of getting things done. And then I grind my teeth and think if it hadn't been for my d——d well meaning brother, I might still have been Lord Mayor of Birmingham, practically in control of the town and about to enter upon my third year of office.

He had risen, in only six years, from a life as an obscure Birmingham businessman to that of a cabinet minister with a national reputation, and now he was, once again, as he had been following his return from Andros, a broken and defeated man.

The pain of his experiences in the war was further compounded, in December 1917, by the news that his cousin Norman had been killed in

France.[9] Iain Macleod, one of Chamberlain's biographers, claims that Norman's death affected Neville "even more deeply than his own father's death had done, and sowed in him the seeds of his life-long hatred of the futility of war," and that "Neville's abiding hatred of war was born of the death in action of Norman Chamberlain."

The deeply personal impact of his cousin's death on Neville Chamberlain is difficult to overstate. He and Norman had served together on the Birmingham City Council and, despite a considerable difference in age, the two were very close. Chamberlain described his cousin Norman as "the most intimate friend I had," and said, ". . . I do not think that in his later years he [i.e., Norman] took any important decision which we had not previously discussed together." He saw in Norman the qualities he most admired. Of his cousin, Neville said, "He was redeemed from priggishness by a keen sense of humour, which caused him to recoil from anything approaching sloppy sentimentality or cant with positive horror."[10] Norman wrote on hearing of the death of their mutual cousin Johnnie, that the latter was, "like Neville one of the very few people who roused in me all the sensations of a willing and enthusiastic *follower*." The news of Norman's death was, for Neville, a devastating blow, the recollection of which was to remain with him for the rest of his life. His diary entries abound with painful memories of his dead cousin.

So significant was it that in those days of deep personal depression, Chamberlain made a trip to France to visit his cousin's grave. He spent four days visiting the battlefields of the war, from Rheims to the Somme and the Ypres salient. His diary records German prisoners "herded into their barbed wire cages in the evening . . . a humiliating spectacle for humanity, they looked like slaves, but I felt no sympathy for them,"

[9] In fact, Neville Chamberlain lost two cousins in the war; a cousin, Johnnie, was also killed in action.

It is interesting to note that Norman Chamberlain, in the last few months before his death, seems to have shared the feelings of disillusionment so characteristic of the generation of British youth who fought on the western front. In a letter to his mother he wrote:

It seems to me the country at large—and other advanced countries—have suddenly realised that the toleration and liberty and attempts at equality which had come to be accepted as normal and unexceptionable were very far from being accepted universally. . . . And now during the course of the war people have realised something else—not only were the tacitly accepted principles of more liberty, greater equality, nearer sympathy, rejected by the strongest organiser in the world, [i.e., Germany] but we discovered that they weren't really accepted as consciously and as widely as we thought at home.

Neville Chamberlain quoted this passage in *Norman Chamberlain*.

[10] In a letter to Norman of 24 April 1916 Neville wrote that Norman's letters gave him a satisfaction which he felt inadequate to describe and that receiving a letter from Norman lifted his mood for days thereafter. From this and other similar letters it is clear that his cousin aroused in Neville a depth of sentiment which was so unique in intensity that Neville was embarrassed and almost overwhelmed at the depth of his own passion. For a man of Chamberlain's disposition such emotion was literally without precedent.

and he added, "it makes one savage to think that their own country is untouched."

So deeply did Neville feel the loss of this cousin that he immersed himself in the only book he was ever to write: *Norman Chamberlain; a Memoir*, a project which, he said, "eased my conscience."[11] In it he quoted one of Norman's last letters from the front, which said, "Nothing but immeasurable improvements will ever justify all the damnable waste and unfairness of this war—I only hope those who are left will *never, never* forget at what sacrifice those improvements have been won." In one of Norman's letters, to be delivered to his mother in the event of his death (and quoted by Neville in his book), Norman wrote, ". . . it is the hope of a new England for which I'm not unwilling to sacrifice my life." In a sense, Chamberlain's subsequent career can be seen as a response to his cousin's plea.[12] It may possibly have been the decisive reason why he chose not to retire from politics after his defeat as minister of national service. In August 1917, he wrote that when he thought of his two dead cousins he simply knew that he would return to public service in one form or another. A diary entry of 13 April 1918 records that while Norman was still alive he, Neville, had not realized the unique beauty of a life such as Norman's, a life devoted to public service, and that compared to Norman his own life seemed petty and insignificant. In his address on being elected to Parliament Chamberlain said, as if in response to his cousin's plea, "I have repeatedly stated my conviction that we could best show our gratitude to those who have fought and died for England by making it a better place to live in. My sole reason for wishing to enter Parliament is my desire to assist in bringing about this transformation."

Chamberlain was among the millions in Britain who would remember the war not as a great crusade on behalf of the noble causes of human freedom and national self-determination, but as a fiery holocaust of death and destruction. Although he had been too old to have participated in

[11] The book is interesting for what it does not tell us about Neville Chamberlain. Although Neville professed great affection for his cousin, the book contains only a trace of the emotion we know him to have felt. For the most part the book is a collection of Norman's letters connected with minimal bits of dry commentary. The fact that even in a memorial book to be circulated only among members of the Chamberlain family Neville could not allow himself the luxury of emotional expression is an indication of how tight was his control over private feelings.

[12] It is of course difficult to prove that there was a connection between Chamberlain's memory of his fallen cousin and Neville's later political career, but there are significant parallels between the career that Norman had pursued and had hoped to continue and the causes which Neville later championed. The most obvious of these is a common concern with social welfare issues. Norman had been active in programs for the aid of indigent Birmingham young men. Neville continued this work. Some of the programs which Neville later instituted as minister of health bore a remarkable resemblance to what "Norman would have wanted." Norman had been defeated in his first bid for a parliamentary seat and would probably have stood again after the war. Neville was elected from a similar district in 1919. In a letter to his mother, Norman had written, "I feel certain I am the man to reorganize the Conservative party." On two occasions, in 1924 and in 1929, Neville was the acknowledged leader in successful campaigns to reunify the Tory party.

the actual combat, Chamberlain had served in a manner appropriate to a person of his class and political position, and he shared the sense of national disillusionment that came in its wake. To such feelings were added the humiliation of failure in national office and the deeply personal loss of his friend and cousin. These must indeed have been extremely painful memories.

When in 1938 as prime minister he bore responsibility for the alternatives of peace or war, he would remember what the last war had meant to him, and it must therefore have seemed as if almost anything would be better than a repetition of that experience. There was a direct relationship between Chamberlain's memory of his dead cousin and the policies he worked for as prime minister. It was a relationship of which observers at the time of Munich were not unaware. In a revealing newspaper article in the *Daily Mail*, written in the wake of Hitler's invasion of Austria it was noted:

> Those who have heard the Prime Minister's recent speeches have observed that when war has been mentioned, his voice acquires a deeper timbre. This is especially so when he is thinking of the sacrifice of youthful lives which war makes inevitable. Mr. Neville Chamberlain hates war as much as any peace pledger.
>
> The reason for the Prime Minister's obvious emotion on such occasions is found in a book, unknown to the public, entitled *Norman Chamberlain*.

Chamberlain's fear and loathing of war were compounded by the conventional understanding of military technology and strategy which seemed to indicate that a future war would be infinitely more terrible than the last. But these decisions and events were, in 1919, far in the future, and we must return to Chamberlain's early career for an understanding of how he arrived at the dilemmas of 1938.

Chamberlain as a National Politician

In the Coupon Election of December 1918, Chamberlain successfully stood for a parliamentary seat from his native Birmingham. Privately he wrote, that he did not anticipate his parliamentary career with much pleasure nor did he expect, at his advanced age and with the disaster as minister in the Lloyd George Government, to make a significant contribution. At fifty, he was older than any other British prime minister in beginning a parliamentary career. His friend Leo Amery said that Chamberlain chose to remain in national politics rather than return to the relative security of Birmingham, "largely to prove to himself and to the world that his failure as Minister of National Service in the war had been due to Lloyd George and not to himself." There was also much truth in his public explanation of why he had chosen to enter Parliament, namely to build a lasting memorial of social legislation to those who had fallen during the war. Characteristically, he wrote that the election campaign had helped him to overcome his debilitating depression by forcing him to transcend his purely private feelings of despair.

In spite of his age, Chamberlain began his parliamentary career with more advantages than the usual backbencher: his father's reputation was still highly regarded, his half brother Austen was chancellor of the Exchequer, and he himself had occupied a post of cabinet rank.[13] As long as Lloyd George was prime minister it was highly unlikely that Neville either would be offered or would have accepted another cabinet position. Therefore, when the wartime coalition collapsed in 1922, Chamberlain was offered the position of postmaster general in the Bonar Law Government. Austen was the recognized leader of the coalition Tories, and Neville believed that by accepting a cabinet post in the Bonar Law Government he could bring about a reconciliation of the two factions within the Conservative party. Austen at first opposed Neville's joining the Government, but when Neville offered to give up the post and his parliamentary career with it, Austen agreed. The episode demonstrates Chamberlain's emerging importance as an independent power within the party. In compensation for his not being offered the Ministry of Health, his first choice, Neville was given the sinecure post of paymaster general and became a privy councilor as well. From 1922 onward, Chamberlain held a cabinet post in every Conservative Government until his death in 1940. It was during this period that Chamberlain first made the acquaintance of Edward Halifax and Samuel Hoare. Both men were to be of crucial importance in his later career.

When in March 1923 Sir Robert Horne refused the Ministry of Health, the post was offered to Chamberlain, and he accepted on the sole condition that he be given a free hand: there was to be no repetition of the mistakes of the Lloyd George years. In May, Stanley Baldwin replaced the ailing Bonar Law as prime minister. Baldwin's original inclination had been that Chamberlain would retain the Ministry of Health, but since Baldwin could not find someone suitable for the Exchequer, Neville Chamberlain was persuaded to accept. Baldwin's first Government was, however, shortlived, and in January of 1924 the first socialist government in Britain's history was formed under the leadership of Ramsay MacDonald. Although ideologically opposed to socialism, Chamberlain was not among those who saw a frightening Bolshevik menace in the parliamentary Labour party, and he regarded the formation of a Labour

---

[13] Austen's standing as chancellor of the Exchequer was viewed by Neville as a mixed blessing. In a letter to his sister of 4 January 1919, Chamberlain admitted that his relations with Austen were somewhat troubled and that he believed Austen was overly conservative and out of step with the times. Moreover he believed that Austen saw him as something of a radical. There was, and perhaps had always been, a subtle although muted competition between the two brothers. Significantly, it was Neville's views which were closest to those of their father.

Government with relative equanimity. Chamberlain used what was to
be only a brief period out of office to complete his work toward party
reunification. This was accomplished at a party meeting of 11 February
1924. The way was now open for a Tory victory in the November 1924
General Election.

His work at party reunification gave Chamberlain new influence
within the party and when Baldwin was again asked to form a Government, Chamberlain had a major voice in determining the composition
of the Cabinet. He preferred to return to the Ministry of Health and
suggested that Churchill be given the Exchequer. Baldwin accepted the
suggestion and Churchill accepted the position. In the years that followed, as we shall see, Chamberlain and Churchill were to form a
remarkably effective working relationship.

To this period can also be traced the beginning of a rift between
Chamberlain and the Labour party. In 1918, he was prepared to work
for those Labour candidates whom he considered worthy of office, while
in the aftermath of the general strike of 1926, Chamberlain's relations
with Labour began to take on the mutually acrimonious character which
was to mark so much of Chamberlain's later career. In 1927, his diary
records a concern that his parliamentary speeches gave the impression
that he had nothing but contempt for the Labour party. His tenure as
minister of health was nevertheless one of the most productive in his
career. On 20 November 1924, he put before the Cabinet a list of twenty-
five measures dealing with health and welfare issues which he wanted
passed. Of these, twenty-one became law before he left the Ministry
and the remainder were eventually adopted. These were years of great
personal success and growing public popularity; he was indeed pushing forward his father's work. It may well have been the period of his
greatest personal happiness.

In his first ten years in Parliament, Chamberlain came to be regarded
as one of the very few dynamic forces in a party characterized by iner-
tia. Had the Conservatives won the General Election of 1929, Chamberlain would have been given the Colonial Office. As it was, Labour won
287 seats to the Tories' 261, and on 4 June 1929 MacDonald was again
asked to form a government. Chamberlain used this period of opposition for working out a colonial policy which would reconcile the Beaverbrook and Baldwin factions within the party. Lord Beaverbrook, in
his dissatisfaction with what he saw as the do-nothing policy of Stanley
Baldwin, had founded the United Empire party to work for the cause of
empire free trade. To accomplish the task of reconciliation, Chamberlain assumed the leadership of the Conservative research department,
a position which put him in control of the party's policy planning appa-
ratus.

Meanwhile, the world economic crisis which had begun in America was threatening the pillars of international economic stability. No country was immune from its effects, and no country had a greater stake in the existing system than Great Britain. In May of 1931, the Credit Anstalt of Austria fell and the Bank of England came to its aid. In July, the London Conference was convened in an effort to deal with a worsening German financial crisis. The Conference produced no results. Britain was losing gold reserves at the rate of £2½ million per day. Although he was in opposition when it began, the financial crisis was to bring Chamberlain closer to the center of real political power. On 30 July, he spoke in Parliament, drawing attention to the seriousness of the British position and the Government's inability to deal effectively with the crisis. In August, Chamberlain took a leading part in negotiations with the opposition, and by the end of the month a National Government under the leadership of Ramsay MacDonald was formed. Its only clear mandate was to secure a balanced budget.

Within three months a second National Government was formed and Chamberlain moved from the Ministry of Health to the Exchequer. In his new post, Chamberlain acted quickly to institute measures he had long advocated in an effort to stem the worsening crisis. Free trade, the very basis of international economic liberalism, he believed had to be replaced with protection as official Government policy. In February of 1932, Chamberlain was able to secure passage of the Tariff Reform Bill. The bill, which he regarded as one of the greatest of his growing list of parliamentary successes, called for an across-the-board tariff of ten percent except for certain items specifically excluded. Dominion imports were to be excluded pending the outcome of the Ottawa Conference scheduled for July 1933. The Tariff Bill, as we have seen, was the triumphant culmination of a crusade begun by his father on behalf of protectionism and represented the reversal of a time-honored and ideologically-sacred tenet of British economic liberalism.

His years at the Exchequer brought Chamberlain to the very center of political power, and he was increasingly viewed as a statesman whose support was to be sought on virtually every important issue, including those issues normally outside the competence of the Exchequer. Chamberlain liked to think of himself as one who never greedily sought political power for its own sake but rather one who reluctantly accepted it when duty called. The reality was quite the opposite. Indeed, as we shall see, Chamberlain positively thrived on the type of power which entails the coercion and manipulation of the enemy. Increasingly, the area in which he felt qualified to act came to include almost all areas of public policy and, as we shall see, expert opinion and administrative jurisdiction counted for very little.

❧ 2 ❧

The Struggle for Power: 1931–35

THE portrait which emerges from an analysis of Chamberlain's early years as a cabinet minister and rising national politician is that of a man highly competent and efficient in the art of public administration, a man seeking to compensate for earlier failures, and a man relentlessly bent on the aggrandizement of his personal power. The move from the Ministry of Health to the Exchequer was, for Chamberlain, an important step upward in the hierarchy of power and influence. Thus far he had good reason to be pleased with his step-by-step progress up the political ladder toward the ultimate goal, the goal which had eluded both his brother Austen and his father: that of becoming prime minister.

Chamberlain was never the sort of person to admit that his sights were set on the nation's highest political office or that he desired power for its own sake. To have done so would have constituted a clear violation of the mores of the governing class, a class which had long preferred to cloak the naked pursuit of power in the euphemism of "doing one's duty." Chamberlain's private papers betray him, and we find that behind this facade of selfless service to king and country there was a man cynically, even ruthlessly, striving to increase his personal dominion over British society.

As early as 1930, he participated in an attempt to unseat Stanley Baldwin as head of the Tory party. Baldwin survived the challenge to his leadership, the coup failed, and Chamberlain's hopes were, at least temporarily, frustrated. From that point onward in Chamberlain's letters, Baldwin becomes the object of scorn and contempt to a degree which would be exceeded only by Lloyd George.[1] Thwarted in his

---

[1] For example, on 9 December 1934, he wrote that giving advice without actually making decisions was a role which perfectly suited Baldwin's character. In July 1935, he noted that Baldwin had said

29

attempt to gain the party leadership, Chamberlain turned his quest for power to other areas. It was in this context that he first became directly involved in foreign affairs. Chamberlain soon realized that his standing as a national political figure depended on his ability to demonstrate leadership in areas beyond domestic welfare policy, the arena in which his reputation was already without equal.

The period from 1930–35 was a period in which rising German military power destroyed the last vestiges of British hopes for disarmament and left Britain virtually without a policy for continental affairs. The ambivalence of British attitudes toward the League and toward her continental allies was becoming an increasingly critical problem. Power over British foreign policy, while not exactly "lying in the gutter," was nevertheless a plum waiting to be picked by a resolute leader with a defined policy. Chamberlain clearly believed he was the man for the job.

His position as chancellor of the Exchequer gave him a ready say in matters of foreign policy and, in the years 1930 through 1935, he used it on three separate occasions in an attempt to secure his personal control over policy. As we will see, Chamberlain's participation in the early stages of rearmament, his limited liability plan of March 1934, and his plan for a rapprochement with Japan in the fall of 1934 were sporadic and not altogether successful attempts to gain control of the policy-making machinery. While each met with uncertain success, together they brought Chamberlain closer to his objective.

By 1936, Chamberlain had largely succeeded in bringing foreign affairs under his control, and in so doing he became widely accepted as Baldwin's heir apparent. As early as March 1935, he believed himself to be the real power behind the man who formally occupied the post of prime minister and he was obviously dissatisfied with the role of *éminence grise*, craving the formal power of higher office. His succession to the premiership was not, however, assured until after the abdication crisis of December 1936. Even as late as October 1936, he wrote of a fear that he might not succeed Baldwin.

While the quest for power was a central feature of Chamberlain's personality, his subsequent actions cannot be understood in terms of that drive alone. For Chamberlain, the attainment of political power was certainly a goal in itself, but as such it was but one among several which he worked to achieve. Chamberlain sought to use power for the maintenance of the status quo in Europe, for the preservation of the integrity of the empire, and above all to avoid leading his country into another world war. His actions can be understood only in terms of the multiple

---

publicly that Chamberlain had criticized him for being overly candid. Chamberlain felt that Baldwin's statement had entirely missed the point; it wasn't that Baldwin was too candid, that he said things better left unsaid, but that he simply had no idea what the truth actually was.

goals he worked to attain. Before proceeding to a discussion of specific events we would do well to consider Chamberlain's more general views on politics and diplomacy.

CHAMBERLAIN'S VIEWS ON FOREIGN AFFAIRS

It would most certainly be a mistake to scrutinize Chamberlain's background, early writings, and career for the origins of abstract ideas on politics and society in the same sense that it is a futile task to seek profound theories on the nature of society and empire in the much more prolific writings of Churchill. Although their political views differed widely, Chamberlain and Churchill were much alike in that they were not the sort of men who spent a great deal of time pondering abstract philosophical questions.[2] Like the vast majority of men, statesmen included, both men acted on principles which they only vaguely understood, principles which were sometimes in rather obvious contradiction. The intensity with which they held their convictions had very little to do with reasoned calculation and a great deal to do with what is often inadequately described as temperament. Both were intensely practical men for whom the business of running a government, with all its intrigues and conflicts, was more than enough to occupy their minds.

To understand his ideas on politics and diplomacy, it is important not to search more deeply in Chamberlain's mind than he himself did. He was a man of very definite and tenaciously held opinions on virtually every aspect of human relations, which is not to say that his ideas and opinions were either internally consistent or rooted in original propositions about fundamental political questions. Chamberlain's actions were not the mechanical outcome of applying abstract principles to concrete political problems, but were the residue of highly subjective emotional conflicts. For Chamberlain, as for most people, a decision on any particular issue was what remained after the myriad of complex and conflicting emotions had done battle. The victorious forces became the "rational" explanation for actions; the defeated were banished from conscious memory but nevertheless continued to make their influence felt. The rationality of which Chamberlain was so proud was little more than a highly developed power of "selective memory." In this he was by no means unique; in fact Chamberlain's actions are comprehensible precisely because, in this important respect, he behaved as men always have. Immense leaps of fantasy or elaborate theoretical abstractions are therefore unnecessary for the credible recreation of events as Chamberlain saw them.

In part, what made Chamberlain different from other statesmen was

---

[2] This in contrast to the view held by Macleod and others who have argued that Chamberlain was an "intellectual."

his singleminded pursuit of a particular course of action once he had determined it to be correct. Lord Halifax, Chamberlain's foreign secretary, described it as follows:

> Anyone who worked with him, and I suppose I worked as closely with him as anybody, was bound to be impressed by two things. One was his complete disinterestedness and disregard of any lesser thoughts of self, and the other his unfaltering courage and tenacity, once he had made up his mind that a thing was right.

It was this unfaltering courage and tenacity more than any other characteristic, which earned Chamberlain the opprobrium of his fellow politicians. Yet, in the end, it was the failure of his policy—Hitler was not appeased—and not his method for which he was condemned.

For the most part, Chamberlain's views of world events were a reflection of what he believed was best for the British Empire, and England was the heart and mind of the empire. He believed that what was good for Britain and what was good for humanity were most often identical, but in the unlikely event of a conflict between the two, the former always took precedence. It was, to be sure, not an unusual ideological position for a Tory statesman, particularly a member of the Chamberlain family. Moreover, Chamberlain was convinced that the business of politics was not a zero-sum game in which the gains of one party are by definition the losses of another. As so many of his critics, as well as his defenders have said, Chamberlain believed that rational men sitting around a conference table could almost always come up with an acceptable compromise which would be of mutual benefit to all parties. Moreover, good businessman that he was, he could not believe that in bargaining with Hitler a mutually satisfactory compromise was impossible. Typical of his approach in foreign affairs was the following statement which he made in April 1928, ". . . there *must* be something in common between us, if only we can find it, and perhaps by our very aloofness from the rest of Europe we may have some special part to play as conciliator and mediator."

If, as Churchill undoubtedly believed, Anglo-German relations were, in every respect, a struggle to the death between a German behemoth and a British leviathan, if Germany could be relied on to use every opportunity to improve her strategic position vis-à-vis Britain, and if all that prevented it was the grip which each had on the other's throat, then the only possible policy was one of military preparedness. Herein lay a fundamental diplomatic dilemma: for two nations poised for attack, the only way to prove that peaceful change is possible is by some unilateral action, what Arnold Wolfers once called an act of "national self-abnegation." If the leviathan were to lessen its grip on the throat of the German behemoth, its own vulnerability would be increased. If one believed, as Chamberlain did, that the result of uncontrolled struggle could only be a war even more horrible than the last, then almost any risk was worth taking. Chamberlain was willing to take such risks because he believed in the possibility of reasonable, mutually acceptable solutions and also because he believed the consequences of diplomatic failure were infinitely worse. The more real the possibility of war with Germany, the more narrow became Chamberlain's perceived range of choice. Thus, by September 1938 he believed the choices were two: accommodation or war. Given his feelings about the last war and his expectations concerning a future war, Chamberlain believed that "reason" dictated only one possible action.

In a sense, Chamberlain's actions would be easier to understand had he shared the views of someone like George Lansbury. As pious Christians, Lansbury and others like him were so deeply repelled by the wholesale destruction of the war that they embraced pacifism and remained categorically opposed to war as an instrument of national policy. There is not the slightest bit of evidence to suggest that Chamberlain was sympathetic to the pacifist position. Nor, for that matter, is there evidence to indicate that Chamberlain's actions were motivated by specifically religious convictions in the manner of, for example, Gladstone in his views on the moral purpose of empire.

Chamberlain had supported British involvement in the 1914 war against Germany, and he never wavered in the belief that it should have been pursued to a victorious conclusion. Although he was horrified at the death and destruction of that war and was willing to go to almost any lengths to avoid a repetition of it, he was never able to reject war in principle. He believed that, no matter how reprehensible, war remained the final arbiter of national disputes. In an introduction to a volume of his collected speeches, Chamberlain wrote:

> To me war is not only the cruelest but the most senseless method of settling international disputes. But man of peace as I am, there is one claim which, if it were made, must as it seems to me, be resisted even, if necessary, by force. That would be a claim by any one state to dominate others by force since if such a claim were admitted I see no possibility of peace of mind or body for anyone.

This was perhaps as close as Chamberlain ever came to a fully articulated position on the question of when the resort to war was morally justified. His view on the morality of war is best described not in terms of general principles of moral conduct but by statements such as the following:

> When I think . . . of the 7 million of young men who were cut off in their prime, the 13 million who were maimed and mutilated, the misery and the

sufferings of the mothers or the fathers . . . in war there are no winners, but all are losers.

Although he believed in principle that war was a legitimate instrument of national policy, his deeply felt revulsion toward it meant that he would not lightly contemplate a policy which might lead to war. On the basis of his intimate papers and contemporary testimony, there is no reason to doubt the sincerity of such often-repeated sentiments, in spite of the fact that their articulation by a politician of the period was bound to strike a sympathetic note in popular memory and therefore redound to partisan political advantage.

Beginning of Active Participation in International Politics

The summer of 1932 marked the beginning of Chamberlain's active participation in international affairs. In June he assisted Baldwin at the Lausanne Conference, and later in the summer he led the British delegation at the Ottawa Conference. Although as chancellor of the Exchequer Chamberlain's role was central, he seems to have acted more on behalf of the Government and less on his personal initiative than would be true in the years to come.

At Lausanne, Chamberlain spoke in favor of cancellation of war debts in an effort to settle, at long last, the question of German reparations. Of this, his first exposure to the intricacies of international negotiations, Chamberlain wrote to his sisters with great satisfaction and pleasure at his success in dealing with foreigners. He noted that Baldwin was beginning to depend on him a great deal and that in fact the prime minister had come to regard him as indispensable, insisting on his being present during all of the deliberations. Chamberlain clearly relished this new role as international negotiator although he found the Germans to be profoundly ignorant.

To a no-nonsense politician like Chamberlain, the incessant posturing and jockeying for position characteristic of international negotiations was an unnecessary waste of time. He was shocked by the methods of the French whom he accused of duplicity; publicly declaring their friendship and loyalty while privately sending forth agents to sound out the intentions of their adversaries. It was, from Chamberlain's point of view, not the way good business among friends ought to be conducted.

These sentiments were to appear again and again in later years even as his experience with international negotiation and his control over policy became more complete. During this period his letters reveal a need for familial approval, a delight in his own role in decision-making (often an overestimation of his own importance), a failure to understand how international negotiation differed from domestic bargaining, and an almost xenophobic dislike of the foreigner.

Unfortunately, Lausanne did not end the German problem for British policy-makers, and with Hitler's ascension to power in January 1933, Britain's relationship with the Continent entered a new and increasingly troublesome period. This unrest, along with clear signs of Japanese belligerence in the Far East highlighted the sadly depleted state of Britain's military preparedness.

In 1919 at the close of the war, British strategic planners had believed it reasonable to assume that there would be no major war for the next ten years; therefore, the British military machine could be safely dismantled. Each year the Committee of Imperial Defence (CID) reexamined this assumption, and each year they adopted the same basic formula. In March 1932, the Government, in the wake of the Japanese attack on Shanghai, formally abandoned this so-called ten-year rule.[3] Revocation of the rule constituted official recognition of the worsening international situation but implied no specific commitment in the direction of rearmament.

In October Germany left the Disarmament Conference for the last time. The Germans had long been rearming in flagrant violation of the Versailles treaty and had made little effort to conceal that fact. These events clearly signaled to the British the existence of a potentially threatening strategic problem on the Continent as well as in the Far East.

In September 1933, Chamberlain informed the CID that the financial situation was somewhat improved and the decision was made to create a Defence Requirements Committee (DRC) whose responsibility would be to formulate specific plans for rearmament. In February of 1934, the DRC produced a major report which was to be of great significance for Britain's future security. The report stated that, while Japan posed the most immediate threat to British security, "we take Germany as the ultimate potential enemy against whom our long-range defensive policy must be directed." In the months that followed, the Cabinet began discussing ways to correct the deficiencies outlined in the report.

It was at this point that Chamberlain began to play a central role in deciding questions of rearmament. Earlier than most members of the Government and certainly before Baldwin, he realized the need for rearmament. As early as January 1934 he had said, ". . . we are giving too much attention to the details of disarmament and not enough to security." At the same time Chamberlain may well have seen a long-awaited opportunity for giving the country a lead, and that rearmament

---

[3] As chancellor of the Exchequer, Chamberlain participated in the CID deliberations on the COS proposal to revoke the ten year rule. Both in the Committee on Imperial Defence and in the Cabinet, Chamberlain reminded the Government that financial recovery was its first responsibility although he concurred in the unanimous Cabinet decision to abandon the rule.

could be the issue which would bring him into the political limelight and establish his reputation in the public eye as one qualified to speak on international issues. But his commitment to rearmament was necessarily muted by his position as chancellor of the Exchequer with the responsibility of maintaining fiscal responsibility.[4]

The MacDonald Government had been formed with the specific mandate of achieving a balanced budget and, as chancellor of the Exchequer, Chamberlain bore a special responsibility in attaining that goal. On 25 April 1933, Chamberlain spoke in Parliament.

> Look round the world to-day and you see that badly unbalanced budgets are the rule rather than the exception. Everywhere there appear Budget deficits piling up, yet they do not produce those favourable results which it is claimed would happen to us. On the contrary, I find that Budget deficits repeated year after year may be accompanied by deepening depression and by a constantly falling price level. . . . Of all countries passing through these difficult times the one that has stood the test with the greatest measure of success is the United Kingdom. . . . We owe our freedom from the fear [that things are going to get worse] to the fact that we have balanced our Budget.

Chamberlain believed that Britain's place in the world depended on a balanced budget and that economic strength was her "secret weapon." He was therefore concerned that rearmament should not proceed beyond the nation's fiscal capacity.

His subsequent role in the making of defense policy can only be understood in terms of the conflict between his role as chancellor of the Exchequer and his commitment to rearmament. To these must be added the fact, of which everyone concerned with promoting rearmament was acutely aware, that the Opposition was unequivocally opposed to armaments, and that, therefore, rearmament could proceed only in proportion to the strength of the Tory mandate or until the Opposition had a change of heart. With these factors in mind, Chamberlain entered the debate over implementation of the DRC report.

The original report proposed that £76.8 million be added over the next five years to the standard estimates, and of this nearly fifty percent was to go to the army.[5] Chamberlain proposed that the total amount to be spent on the various services be lowered, that the replacement of capital ships be postponed, that the amount spent on the army be cut in half, and that the amount spent on the Home Air Force be increased.

[4]To a considerable degree, the office helped shape the views of the holder of that office. On this point, it is interesting to compare Chamberlain's views, while chancellor of the Exchequer, with those of Churchill, who occupied that position between 1925 and 1929. Surprisingly, in the light of Churchill's later views, and in sharp contrast to the views he set forth in his memoirs, Churchill's views on international issues seem to have changed with his cabinet position or lack thereof. While at the Exchequer Churchill imposed reductions on the British defense budgets.

[5]These figures did not include £134 million per year to be spent on naval construction.

To his sisters, Chamberlain represented his efforts as a one-man attempt to reorder priorities in the face of a more or less united opposition. He noted that he could not expect to change the opinions of the services and the foreign office singlehandedly but that through his efforts he had forced them to consider the subject more carefully than they had in the past. With a note of triumph he concluded that he was now in almost complete control of the rearmament program. While this was no doubt an overstatement, on the basis of an examination of the relevant documents it is clear that Chamberlain's influence was decisive on at least two counts. In the first place, the original DRC proposals were formulated on the basis of military considerations alone; fiscal requirements were left to a later Cabinet decision. As chancellor of the Exchequer, it was all but inevitable that Chamberlain's contribution to the final decision would be in the direction of limiting over-all expenditures. In this respect, Chamberlain's modifications were certainly significant. Secondly, on the question of the distribution of funds among the various service branches, it is clear that Chamberlain decisively affected the discussions toward a change from the traditional idea of a balance among the services to a strategic doctrine emphasizing the air force as the primary arm of British defense policy.[6]

In these actions Chamberlain was certainly motivated, in the first instance, by the need for fiscal restraint, but there were other reasons for his actions. In the Ministerial Disarmament Committee, for example, Chamberlain wanted cuts in army expenditures so as to avoid giving the impression that the Government was preparing another continental army similar to that of the last war. Chamberlain's opposition to a 1914-style continental army and the avoidance of any possibility of repeating the slaughter of the Great War are themes which run throughout his political actions. The modification of the DRC proposals was but the first blow in an ultimately successful campaign against the idea of a continental army along 1914 lines.

Yet Chamberlain's understanding of the strategic value of a newly strengthened air force was at best ambiguous. On the one hand, he claimed to champion the air force out of a commitment to the doctrine of deterrence. A diary entry of 1 July 1934, for example, says that Britain would be better able to deter German aggression if it had an air force capable of bombing the Ruhr from Belgium. And in May 1935, he wrote that he had made a special effort to revise the program for rearming the air force in order that it might serve as a deterrent to German aggression. On the other hand, Chamberlain, as the historian Keith Robbins has observed, "was not a convert to the offensive bombing strategy" but was interested in increasing the role of the air force primarily as a

---

[6] It is simply not true as Middlemas and Barnes suggest that Baldwin had maintained the balance among the services throughout 1934.

defensive measure against the much feared German bombing attacks. Whether or not Chamberlain understood the technical difference between deterrence and a purely defensive strategy, it seems clear that he was primarily interested in the air force as an instrument of home defense in spite of his references to the doctrine of deterrence.

Summing up his efforts to modify the DRC report, Chamberlain wrote to his sisters that he was quite satisfied with his accomplishments, that he had gained everything he had hoped for, but that he continued to be dissatisfied with the fact that the country was not reshaping its foreign policy accordingly. Chamberlain was, no doubt, referring to his often-repeated view that political commitments ought to be brought in line with the country's capability of fulfilling them. Specifically, Chamberlain was referring to his plans then under way for a limitation of Britain's European commitments and a rapprochement with Japan.

Chamberlain expressed his abhorrence at the recent assassination of the Austrian Chancellor Engelbert Dollfuss. Comparing this event to the assassination at Sarajevo which had triggered the First World War, Chamberlain noted that Austria was once again the focus of world attention and that Germany was again the great power acting behind the scenes. The events in Austria were, he believed, even more tragic since they so closely resembled those leading up to 1914.[7] In broad outlines, these sentiments were the guiding principles of Chamberlain's policy of appeasement. Germany constituted the greatest threat to British security, and Chamberlain's worst fear was that the Nazi regime would again be the cause of another world war. It was as if he saw in these events a rereading of the script of Europe's greatest tragedy.

In March 1934 Chamberlain put before the Cabinet a wide-ranging proposal designed to restructure British policy toward Europe by limiting her continental liabilities. He noted the probability of breakdown in the disarmament conference and suggested that "a general rearmament" would probably follow. As the "greatest exporting country in the world," Britain's interest lay in a "general pacification of Europe." He argued that security could not be achieved "by pacts, covenants, or declarations which leave in doubt what action would be taken in case of need to restrain an aggressor." Without the participation of the United States, economic sanctions would probably not be effective. Military sanctions would, on the other hand, "probably be the most effective deterrent to a would-be aggressor. . . ."

As Chamberlain understood it, British liabilities, namely those of Locarno and the League, were unlimited, ". . . when the *casus foederis*

---

[7]Chamberlain was not alone in his fears that political assassination in Europe might mean Sarajevo all over again. Recalling his feelings at the time of the murder of King Alexander of Yugoslavia three months later, Churchill wrote, ". . . once again from the dark recesses of the Serbian and Croat underworld a hideous murder plot sprang upon the European stage, and, as at Sarajevo in 1914 a band of assassins, ready to give their lives were at hand."

arises we are expected if necessary to give assistance up to the limit of our powers." As an alternative to the existing situation, he proposed

> . . . a partnership in a system of mutual guarantees by the principal European Powers, in which the liability of each partner would be limited. . . .
>
> The main feature of the plan is that each of the signatory Powers would undertake in certain circumstances to supply a specified force, possibly in various alternative forms but always limited in amount, to be used, not in substitution for, but in supplementation of the existing forces of the signatories.

In sum, the plan was a proposal for an international police force designed to implement collective security on a limited basis. Chamberlain believed that "either we must play our part in pacification, or we must resign ourselves to the staggering prospect of spending £85 million on rearmament." Chamberlain had been concerned from the beginning about the costs of rearmament and by August 1934, he felt that there was some cause for alarm. He wrote that he could take no great satisfaction in the budget he was preparing to submit to the Cabinet since increases in defense spending were inevitable. He resented the bureaucrats who were irresponsibly preparing to hand out funds to anyone who asked. But as long as he was in control he intended to take a firm stand in favor of fiscal responsibility which was more than he could say of his colleagues. His limited liability plan was therefore to be a means of avoiding full-scale rearmament rather than a commitment in addition to the rearmament plans then being formulated.

The proposal was referred to the Chiefs of Staff Sub-Committee of the CID. After extensive discussion, the Chiefs of Staff reported to the Cabinet that "the difficulties and disadvantages inseparable from the scheme would make its effective application in practice very doubtful and its reliability as a deterrent would be correspondingly reduced," and that "if the deterrent fails, it involves war, and in certain quite conceivable circumstances, unlimited war." From the standpoint of official British policy, this was the end of the limited liability plan. Chamberlain, however, was not easily defeated once he had set upon a particular course of action. He continued to discuss the plan among colleagues as well as foreign diplomats and when he became prime minister, it became a central goal of his policy.[8]

In autumn 1934 Chamberlain made yet another attempt to impose his views on the Cabinet. In August he had written a paper dealing with

---

[8] As early as February 1935, he discussed on his own initiative, the plan with Flandin and was very pleased to report that the French minister was favorably impressed and agreed that Britain's responsibility could be limited to her contribution to such a force. Flandin, according to Chamberlain, claimed to speak for the entire French government.

matters of defense and foreign policy which he was now preparing to spring on his unsuspecting colleagues. He described it as a major foreign policy initiative aimed at rapprochement with Japan. He wrote that, as with the limited liability plan, it was another one-man effort and he couldn't identify a single source of support. But, he felt, since no one else had any specific proposals for dealing with the Japanese, his own plan had a chance of being accepted. He was sure the time was right for a bold initiative and he was concerned lest the British miss an opportunity which might not come again. In his memorandum, Chamberlain talked of "a universal feeling of apprehension about the future, whether it be a matter of 2, 3, 4, or 10 years, that such a threat may materialize, and that the quarter from which it will come is Germany." This being so, Britain might be forced to fight a war on two fronts, a possibility which Chamberlain wanted desperately to avoid.

> Whatever may be the outcome of the present regime in Germany I do not think we need anticipate that we should have to fight her singlehanded, and although the results of any war between civilised peoples must necessarily result in appalling loss and suffering we might reasonably hope to escape serious disaster if the hostilities were confined to European nations. But if we had to enter upon such a struggle with a hostile instead of a friendly Japan in the East, if we had to contemplate the division of our forces so as to protect our Far Eastern interests while prosecuting a war in Europe, then it must be evident that not only would India, Hong Kong, and Australasia be in dire peril but that we ourselves would stand in far greater danger of destruction by a fully armed and organised Germany.

Chamberlain noted that even if everything went "according to plan" there would still remain to be considered the British attitude toward Europe. He stated, ". . . here I submit that the main point to be kept in mind is that the *fons et origo* of all our European troubles and anxieties is Germany," and that therefore Britain "should not be too stiff with France." In sum, Chamberlain concluded, "To preserve the safety of the country and of the Empire without crippling our financial resources it is essential that we should not find ourselves in a few years' time confronted simultaneously with a hostile Germany and an unfriendly Japan. We ought therefore so to direct our policy as to eliminate one of these dangers." An agreement with Japan would be easier to secure than one with Germany. The substance of Chamberlain's views were incorporated in a Foreign Office Memorandum which came before the Cabinet on 24 October. The Cabinet however, could agree on nothing other than the fact that "consideration of the proposal should be postponed until further progress had been made in the Anglo-Japanese naval discussions."

Chamberlain bitterly regretted having no part in the ensuing negotiations with Japan, but he admitted privately that there really was no reason why the chancellor of the Exchequer should have been included in the British delegation. The best he could hope for was to be able to manipulate the discussions from behind the scenes, but he was convinced that John Simon, the foreign secretary, was not doing an adequate job. In September he reported that with the Cabinet's approval, Britain's ambassador in Japan had been instructed to sound out the Japanese according to Chamberlain's plan. Chamberlain was obviously pleased at his success in manipulating the foreign secretary and in so doing, increasing his own power position.

At about this time Chamberlain wrote to his sisters concerning a recently published volume of his father's biography. Chamberlain noted that he was particularly interested in the discussion of Anglo-German affairs since it seemed so similar to what was now taking place between the two countries. He noted that while there were differences between events described in the book and his own problems with Germany it was indeed ironic that he should be attempting a similar agreement in almost the exact circumstances as his father had done. This was to become a major theme in Chamberlain's political calculations; in every policy he advocated, Chamberlain was always concerned with how that policy might, in the end, compare with that of his father.

REARMAMENT, THE LEAGUE, ANGLO-GERMAN NAVAL TREATY, HOARE-LAVAL PACT

In the first few months of 1935, according to Chamberlain's biographer, "the British government were resisting a drift of the world back to rival alliances, and in that broad concept Chamberlain agreed." There was widespread apprehension, at least among Tory leaders, that the League, as yet untested, might be inadequate to the needs of rapidly changing international conditions. Such apprehension on the part of British policy-makers was occasioned by perceived threats to the peace from two sources: Germany and Italy. German rearmament in violation of the Treaty of Versailles could no longer be ignored, and Mussolini's aggression in Abyssinia was soon to become an unfortunate test case of the League's ability to keep the peace.

At least until 1931, it was not impossible to believe that a new era in international relations had been born at Versailles and that a threat to the peace anywhere would be met by the collective opposition of all the League's members. Collective security was to be maintained by the use of sanctions, first economic then military, against any nation threatening the peace. British statesmen had taken a leading part in the creation of the new international order and, with the United States effectively out of the picture, British support was absolutely essential to the League's successful operation. Now with Germany and Italy increasingly perceived as threats to the international peace, the sincerity of Britain's commitment to the League was brought to the test.

Within Britain, the parliamentary Opposition had long claimed that Tory policy was old-style diplomacy, paying only lip service to League ideals. Labour leaders felt that the peace could be preserved if only Britain would make a genuine commitment to the League, including the support of sanctions against any state threatening the peace. It seems that only belatedly, if at all, Labour leaders recognized that collective security, by definition, implied a willingness by the member states to go to war.

The Conservative party was never as vocal in its support of the League as was the Opposition, and as long as Europe remained at peace, there was no apparent contradiction between formal support of the League and loyalty to more traditional principles of diplomacy.

It was in this context (the League vs. old-style diplomacy, disarmament, alliances, etc.) that the debate over foreign policy options took place. In 1935, Italy seemed the immediate threat to British interests although strategic planners had already identified Germany as the ultimate potential threat to British security. On 4 March the Government issued a White Paper on defense which stated that, in view of the deteriorating international situation and the failure of the Disarmament Conference, the Government "can no longer close its eyes to the fact that adequate defences are still required." For the first time since the Great War, the British Government was publicly calling for additional spending on armaments, and the White Paper enumerated the needs of each of the armed forces in general terms. It was the first public commitment by the Government to rearmament and marked the formal reversal of years of British defense policy. In view of the parliamentary debates of the previous year, the White Paper should have come as a surprise to no one, yet public reaction was intense and provoked outspoken criticism from the left.

Chamberlain, who had been one of its major architects, stood firm. He wrote to his sisters that he had had no second thoughts since it was absolutely essential that Britain increase her defense spending and that sooner or later a public announcement was inevitable. Satisfied with the results of the White Paper, Chamberlain turned to the problem of what should be Britain's next move. On this, he reported having serious problems with the then Foreign Secretary, John Simon. The latter had not, in Chamberlain's view, done enough to support the Paper in the Commons and Chamberlain privately accused him of being a spineless coward who lacked the courage to stand by his convictions.

In March, Simon and Eden met with Hitler to explore the possibility of a negotiated settlement of Anglo-German differences. Chamberlain was disappointed with the results. Simon, he said, returned empty-handed having achieved absolutely nothing. Chamberlain believed that he himself could have accomplished more, but, this being for the moment impossible, he would have to be content with behind-the-scenes manipulation.

Looking ahead to the Stresa Conference, he wrote that in his view it would be necessary to send both Baldwin and Eden to insure that Simon did not misrepresent the British position to the Italians as well as to the French. Chamberlain hoped that Stresa might be an opportunity for reintroducing his limited liability plan since it had met with such a favorable reception at home. But, he believed, the foreign office officials were opposed to the plan and in any case Simon was not, in Chamberlain's view, a man with sufficient clout for the job. Baldwin would be of little help since he lacked the necessary mental capacity and fortitude.

Since relations between prime minister and foreign secretary were strained, Chamberlain believed that he himself was the most qualified person for the job, but he also realized that this would be out of the question. Clearly, what Chamberlain wanted even more than a successful outcome of the conference was personal control over foreign policy.

This seems to have been a period in Chamberlain's career when he was dissatisfied with his impact on policy, dissatisfied with his personal power, and dissatisfied with and contemptuous of those outside the ruling group of the Tory party. As usual, Lloyd George was the target of his most bitter invective, and he regretted that his schedule of public events gave him so little opportunity to vent the full measure of his hostility toward the former prime minister. Chamberlain also noted that while Churchill had been making many public appearances, he needed to rely on great quantities of alcohol to achieve his old level of rhetorical eloquence and even when he was able to do so, no one took him seriously.

Along with his hostility toward potential rivals, Chamberlain's letters registered his own impatience with the prime minister. He was not content to be the power behind the throne and would have greatly preferred to issue orders rather than simply make suggestions.[9] Such sentiments must, however, be seen against the background of Baldwin's near-total ineffectiveness as a political leader. Even Churchill admitted that, during this period, Chamberlain was "the packhorse of the Government."

While there was no one standing between him and the premiership, he was intensely suspicious of any possible challenge to his leadership.

[9]This seems a rather curious statement for Chamberlain to have made considering the fact that MacDonald was still prime minister and Baldwin as leader of the party would become prime minister in the event of a change of Government.

When Baldwin offered Simon the deputy leadership of the Commons, Chamberlain believed that Simon was trying to make a comeback and that eventually he would try to challenge Chamberlain's own position. However, Chamberlain wrote that Simon was deluding himself if he believed he could ever seriously challenge Chamberlain's leadership since he, Simon, lacked the character to be a leader and had no powerful political friends, not even in the Tory party itself. Chamberlain, it seems, distrusted and held in contempt anyone who might represent a threat to his power. Such an attitude of distrust toward political enemies was exceeded only by his contempt for those outside the British imperial embrace. On the occasion of the Silver Jubilee, for example, he wrote that as he looked out at the assembled ambassadors he could not help thinking how impressed and envious they must have been. Such an approach pervaded his view of the outside world and inevitably affected his policy positions.

Feiling says that Chamberlain reacted to events in an "average British way," believing that "if agreed disarmament were impossible, agreed armament was better than nothing; that anything was better than rival alliances, and that the time for forcing *diktats* on Germany had passed." Chamberlain had opposed the British Disarmament Convention of November 1933, and, in 1935, believed that disarmament had been "a complete, a costly, a dangerous failure." Hitler, he believed, was attempting to cow all of Europe into submission, and he urged Eden to convince Hitler that there were only two possibilities; either a new series of Locarno-type arrangements or the old alliance system and that while Britain advocated the first option, if Hitler continued as he had in the past, Britain would be forced to opt for the second alternative. Such statements stand in sharp contrast to the policies he would pursue as prime minister and in even sharper contrast to the motives and policies attributed to him by future historians.

In June 1935, the Anglo-German Naval Treaty was signed. Chamberlain took no part in the negotiations and was not a leader in the treaty discussions within the Government. He did however support the Government's position in favor of this, the first major British agreement with Hitler.[10] The treaty allowed Germany to build capital ships up to thirty-five percent of British strength, or, alternatively stated, it limited

---

[10]The treaty allowed Germany to build, immediately, submarines equal to forty-five percent of British strength and eventually it allowed Germany to build up to parity with the British. The submarine issue was in Hoare's view "the most vulnerable provision" but the Naval Staff believed that "Britain had mastered the . . . danger."

Students of British policy disagree as to whether or not to call the treaty an act of appeasement. Gilbert says that the treaty was "appeasement's finest hour." Middlemas claims that the negotiations should not be termed appeasement. Since Gilbert is attempting to show that appeasement had its roots in Versailles, and Middlemas that Chamberlain was the future saboteur of a more acceptable British policy, it appears that the only possible conclusion is that how one defines the term depends on whom one wants to vilify.

German fleet strength to thirty-five percent of the British. Chamberlain wrote to his sisters that he thought that Britain was correct in signing the treaty since the agreement gave Britain complete power over the German navy and indeed he thought that it was almost too good to be true. Needless to say, this is not how the Germans saw matters, nor was it a judgment with which future historians have agreed. Obviously, Chamberlain had an exaggerated view of Britain's capacity to influence continental affairs.

In Parliament, Eden defended the treaty stating that it would allow Britain twice the margin over Germany she had had in 1914. Samuel Hoare, the new foreign secretary, also defended the treaty in terms of an analogy with the last war. Hoare later offered the following explanation of the Government's reasons for seeking the agreement:

> Here again we saw a chance that might not recur of eliminating one of the causes that chiefly led to the embitterment before the Great War—the race of German naval armaments. Incidentally, out of that discussion arose the very important statement of the German Government that henceforth, so far as they were concerned, they would eliminate one of the causes that made the war so terrible, namely, the unrestricted use of submarines against merchant ships.

One historian, Keith Robbins, has stated that a factor in favor of the agreement was a belief that the Anglo-German dreadnought race had been one of the causes of the last war and that "an Anglo-German Naval Agreement would be a sign that both powers were determined that history should not repeat itself."

So it was that from the early days of Britain's attempt to find an adequate policy toward Hitler, issues and policy options were raised, not with a view to what they might achieve against Hitler, but rather what they might have done to prevent the last war. In the second half of 1935, however, it was Italy not Germany which seemed the most immediate threat to the peace and stability of Europe. Mussolini's adventurism in Abyssinia brought sharply into focus the issue of whether or not the League of Nations would be able to play an effective role in maintaining the peace. This, along with the domestic debate over rearmament and the upcoming general election, was the focus of political contention in the period. Chamberlain had begun to see himself as the pivot on which all of these issues turned. A more detached observer would probably grant him a less omnipotent role, but he was, nevertheless, a man whose views could not easily be ignored.

In June, Eden was sent on a secret mission to Rome seeking a negotiated settlement of the Abyssinian dispute. Chamberlain expressed faith in Eden's abilities and thought there was some hope for success. The British plan was not, however, well received in Rome. Chamberlain wrote that if Mussolini continued on his present course he would destroy the League and that the small powers of Europe would then have no alternative but to make whatever terms they could with Berlin. Chamberlain also noted that he saw no way to resolve the issue and that he had, for the moment, no new ideas to suggest. Nevertheless, he thought that Britain should sound out the French to see if they would cooperate in telling Mussolini that they were prepared to intervene militarily to stop the aggression. If this were to happen, Chamberlain believed that the Duce would have to back down and that a way could then be found to allow him to save face. But Chamberlain felt that the French would not participate in such a plan and this being the case, there was nothing Britain could do to stop Mussolini. At the same time however, he opposed the lifting of the League-imposed embargo on Italy hoping that France would agree to institute sanctions the moment Mussolini started a war. He doubted, however, that there would be much possibility of success if Germany and the United States refused to cooperate. The best hope for peace, Chamberlain believed, was in a restructured League and a Britain sufficiently rearmed so as to prevent Mussolini from acting counter to the British national interest.

This then was the beginning of a policy which Chamberlain was to pursue consistently up to the outbreak of war in 1939. He was, in principle, willing to use every available means of coercion up to the point where such measures might lead to war. In practice, more and more policy options were seen as entailing the risk of war and were rejected accordingly. The degree to which a particular policy involved the risk of war was always the yardstick which Chamberlain used to determine whether or not that policy should be adopted. As his personal control over and responsibility for policy increased, the area of coercive action unlikely to result in war became progressively reduced.

Chamberlain had never believed that the League was primarily an institution for the collective condemnation of an aggressor. As we have seen, he was scornful of those who saw the League as a nascent international government, and he believed that there was no alternative to the existing balance of power system. He therefore saw the League as little more than an instrument of great-power collaboration. Germany was Britain's most likely enemy. American participation in action against Germany would be useful but it could not be depended upon. Neutralization of Italy in a potential action against Germany was the most that could be expected. Therefore to Chamberlain, "League" action meant, in practice, little more than the coordination of a common policy with France.

In July Chamberlain noted in his diary that if Britain and France agreed to take any action necessary to halt Mussolini's aggression, they could do so and without much difficulty. But if the French refused to cooperate, Britain had no individual treaty commitments to France and should not single-handedly attempt the maintenance of European peace. If the League proved itself ineffective in halting the war in Abyssinia then it would be impossible to maintain the illusion that the League served any useful purpose whatsoever.

Writing in October, Chamberlain was a bit more optimistic stating that the League might yet prove useful in halting Mussolini's aggression. If this should prove to be the case Chamberlain thought it would be a great advance for civilization but he did not see this as a likely possibility. In the measures he was prepared to take and the willingness with which he contemplated the use of force for attainment of policy goals, it should be noted that Chamberlain was considerably more vigorous, if not militant, than the majority of his Cabinet colleagues.

In November, the Government decided to support oil sanctions but to attempt to postpone their imposition until an effort had been made to solve the dispute by peaceful means. Chamberlain was willing to take a considerably stronger position. In his diary of 29 November, he wrote that if necessary Britain should take the lead in opposing Mussolini rather than allow the invasion to go unopposed. He believed that Mussolini had vastly overextended himself and that any naval power could easily stop the reinforcement of the Italian army in Africa. On the other hand, he was convinced that Mussolini would not attack Britain directly but noted that he would feel much more secure once the process of strengthening Britain's defenses was complete.

Nothing bespoke old-style diplomacy more than the disastrous Hoare-Laval pact of December 1935, an arrangement whereby France and Britain would have supported Italian acquisition of two-thirds of Abyssinia in return for a cessation of hostilities. Members of the Government were as dismayed as anyone when it became known that the British foreign secretary had concluded the agreement, but the only way for the Government to disassociate itself from the agreement was by Hoare's resignation. Chamberlain felt that making a scapegoat of the foreign secretary was absurd and he was greatly distressed at the public repercussions of the episode. Chamberlain correctly understood the importance of the episode in discrediting Baldwin's leadership. He believed that Britain's international standing had suffered a serious blow which undermined the credibility of the Government.

In the aftermath of this unfortunate episode, Chamberlain wrote to his sister that she could at least take consolation in the fact that had he himself been prime minister the blame would have fallen on his shoulders instead of Baldwin's. But he was equally convinced that if he were leading the Government such a fiasco would never have happened. Indeed, when Chamberlain became prime minister, his personal control of foreign policy insured that that policy would never be beyond his control and that indeed, the Hoare-Laval affair would never have happened in a Chamberlain Government. Chamberlain's view that Simon had been incompetent in running the foreign office, and Hoare's public embarrassment in that office, strengthened Chamberlain's resolve to take personal control over foreign policy when the opportunity arose.

It was, however, in the domestic sphere that Chamberlain was most critical of Baldwin's leadership. As the 1935 General Election approached, Chamberlain increasingly felt the need for a popular mandate on the rearmament issue. That public identification with the rearmament cause might well work to his advantage was a possibility of which Chamberlain was certainly not unaware.

He disagreed privately with Baldwin over the choice of issues on which to fight the election. Chamberlain wanted to educate the electorate and fight the election on a platform of rearmament. In his diary on 2 August 1935 Chamberlain noted that Baldwin wanted to focus the election campaign on the issue of unemployment. While he believed that the Government would have a respectable case to take to the people in that area he was convinced that the Tories could never win on domestic issues. By emphasizing international issues, Chamberlain believed that the electorate could be sufficiently frightened to divert attention from problems at home. Obviously this would give the opposition an opportunity to accuse the Government of warmongering and of having secret plans for rearmament.

But, Chamberlain noted the Government did in fact have such plans which could not as yet be revealed to the public in their entirety. However, to attempt to conceal these plans until after the election could be disastrous and the Tories could be rightly accused of deliberate deception. Therefore in Chamberlain's view the best strategy was the bold course of appealing directly to the public on the rearmament issue by emphasizing the international menace which would put a damper on domestic issues of economic redistribution. Judging by the reaction of his Labour critics, Chamberlain had not overestimated the opposition to rearmament. Arthur Greenwood said of Chamberlain's position, ". . . it was the merest scaremongering, disgraceful in a statesman in Mr. Chamberlain's responsible position, to suggest that more millions of money needed to be spent on armaments." Herbert Morrison condemned Chamberlain who, he said, "was ready and anxious to spend millions of pounds on machines of destruction."

In part, Chamberlain wanted rearmament because of his perception of the international environment and in part because he saw it as an issue which could be manipulated to his own and the party's advantage. In September he wrote that public debate in recent months had vindicated his original idea to fight the election on the issue of rearmament. The fact that Baldwin's position and that of the party were in favor of "plugging the gaps" in the country's defenses and were not unequivocally supporting rearmament did not prevent Chamberlain from vigorously pressing his point of view. He wrote that he had recently made a speech in Glasgow on the rearmament issue and that the speech was entirely on his own authority since Baldwin refused to sanction such pronouncements. Chamberlain was irritated by Baldwin's failure to take an active part in the election. Baldwin, he wrote, had provided absolutely no leadership in the election yet he was perfectly willing to take all the credit for the Tory victory.

At the same time, however, he was acutely disturbed by the economic costs of rearmament. In a letter of 8 December 1935, he wrote that while the public would be stunned when they learned just how much had actually been spent over and above the original estimates, this shock was necessary to prepare the British people for the even greater increases in defense spending still to come. It was a terrible time to be chancellor of the Exchequer but he knew of no one else who could hold the line between fiscal responsibility on the one hand and an increasing need for defense spending on the other. He said that he was now absolutely indifferent to criticism because he was convinced that he was making the only correct choices. After the party had won the election and Chamberlain had secured his position as Baldwin's successor, he became increasingly concerned with the economic burdens imposed by rearmament and less and less impressed with the notion that increased security had been purchased. In February 1936, for example, he noted that there was something truly absurd about spending so much public revenue on armaments merely to convince the Nazis to behave peacefully. Once his own political future was secure, Chamberlain increasingly began to emphasize the negative costs of armaments rather than the positive security to be gained from rearming. In the months to come he consistently stressed the need for diplomatic accommodation over the need for rearmament.

Chamberlain's policy was nevertheless one of cold realism in a time when many chose the expedient and politically efficacious options of either refusing publicly to face the reality of German rearmament or hiding behind the pious platitudes of collective security and the League. As chancellor of the Exchequer, Chamberlain's position was far from an attitude of myopic concern with parsimony. He understood, as few others did, the degree to which Britain's international commitments were greater than her capacity of meeting them. Increasingly, Chamberlain saw limiting liabilities rather than increasing assets as the most realistic method of preventing another war.

ᔓ 3 ᔓ

Chamberlain in Control: 1936–37

AT the beginning of 1936, the formation of a Chamberlain Government was still over a year away. Yet, well before the actual event, control over the machinery of state shifted gradually but perceptibly from Baldwin to Chamberlain. Exactly when this transition took place is difficult to determine. Chamberlain liked to believe that he had assumed all but the formal aspects of power at least by the beginning of 1936 and probably much earlier.[1] This was no doubt an exaggeration. It is, however, certain that from 1935 on, there was a steady accretion in Chamberlain's personal power so that by the time of Munich, in September of 1938, his control was as absolute as that of any prime minister in British history.

Even given Chamberlain's great administrative ability and almost pathological appetite for power, there were always crucial decisions and policy areas beyond his control. Anglo-German relations and rearmament were the primary focus of his concern, and in these areas his power position was virtually unassailable. There were also issues, such as British policy toward Spain and domestic welfare policy in general, which, because of Chamberlain's preoccupation with other matters, were decided at a lower level of Government. There was, in sum, a limit to how deeply even the most determined and capable leader could reach in the complex machinery of government.

In 1936, the existence of serious diplomatic problems was widely acknowledged but even among the most astute political observers, there were few who were willing to face head on the twin conundrums of

---

[1] Herbert Samuel, for example, said in July 1935:

As for the Government, it was run by Neville Chamberlain. What he says goes. When he puts his foot down and says that something must be done, that decision settles it. Baldwin has plenty of good ideas and instincts but he will not fight for them.

deterring German aggression and avoiding another war. Many recognized that there was indeed a new form of political organization in Germany, a form of government fundamentally alien to the ideals of liberal democracy and threatening to British national security. Yet as long as the effects of Nazism were confined to German domestic politics, the potential threat to Britain could be ignored. By 1935 this was no longer possible. A few, such as Oswald Mosley and the British Union of Fascists, saw fascism as the wave of the future and sought to become part of it. The vast majority, however, did not. Yet the policies which most leaders proposed as a means of dealing with the German threat were riddled with contradictions: self-righteous statements on behalf of the League and military sanctions and, at the same time, opposition to any and all rearmament programs was but one example. Those whose policies were internally consistent, such as Churchill at one extreme and Lansbury at the other, offered solutions which were clearly unacceptable to the majority of the British people. Pacifism was never a creed with general public appeal, and massive rearmament brought forth images of the situation leading up to the 1914 war. Not until 1940 did the British unequivocally decide in favor of Churchill. It was, in sum, a period in British political history singularly devoid of heroes, a time when all policy options seemed more than usually laden with negative consequences.

Under Baldwin's leadership, the country drifted without a policy, or, more accurately, the Government pursued, intermittently, conflicting and ambiguous strategies. Publicly, they were committed to the League, while privately they were returning to a traditional policy of armaments. Priority within the rearmament effort had been given to modernizing the air force, but the strategic purpose of that force, whether as a defensive measure against a German air attack or whether an offensive force designed to frighten Germany into nonaggression, or perhaps both, had never been fully articulated. It was a policy comparable to the pious Christian who extols the glories of heaven and condemns the evils of sin, a position of considerable rhetorical merit but one unlikely to produce results. Pious platitudes were, of course, singularly useless weapons in dealing with Hitler. On the other hand, Tory leaders, although possibly less naïve, appeared to offer no serious alternative to Labour's platitudinous piety. In this context, Chamberlain appeared as one of the few leaders who understood something of the British problem and was willing to take the bold and vitally necessary steps toward its resolution.

REOCCUPATION OF THE RHINELAND

On 7 March 1936, German armies moved into the Rhineland in what future generations would regard as the first step in Hitler's march to

European and possible global domination. Whatever else these actions may or may not have been, they were certainly contrary to the Versailles treaty and constituted an infraction against which France would have been legally justified in taking punitive action. From the British perspective, Hitler's actions brought into question the Locarno treaty under which Britain had sought to guarantee France's eastern border. Those within France who supported the taking of military action did so on the condition that Britain would stand by France. But British support was not forthcoming and without it the French were unwilling to act. Leadership within the Entente had passed to the other side of the channel.

Many explanations have been given for British inaction. A. J. P. Taylor, for example, describes the interwar period as one in which the British were "haunted by the fear that the situation of 1914 might be repeated—that they might be dragged into war for the sake of Czechoslovakia or Poland as, in 1914, they supposed they had been dragged into war for the sake of Russia." As long as the Rhineland remained demilitarized, France could still threaten Germany. Therefore, says Taylor, the remilitarization of the Rhineland was "an improvement and a success for British policy."[2] Whatever the merits of Taylor's position, one would be hard put to find evidence that it is a view shared by many at the time.

Other historians have argued that Britain failed to take punitive action because of a widespread feeling of guilt over the perceived inequities in the Versailles treaty. Lord Lothian's statement that the Germans were only going "into their own back yard," was widely quoted at the time and has been widely referred to in histories of the period as evidence of British sympathy with German aims.[3] In any event, Hitler had the advantage of a *fait accompli,* and to remove the German troops would, it was believed, require the use of force, an option which was never seriously considered.

Even before the German action took place, Chamberlain, in a letter of 4 March 1936, noted that continental affairs were quite grim but that he had an intuitive sense that the British could get by without military involvement although he doubted whether the French had anything very useful to contribute. The solution to the immediate threat, in Chamberlain's view, lay in persuading the French, not the Germans, to compromise. This would not be easy since, as he noted, the French

[2]It is interesting to note that at the time there were those who drew quite different analogies from British experience in the last war with respect to the Rhineland issue. For example, an article in the *New Statesman* of 21 March 1936 stated:

The British public, sure that the present crisis will pass without war, remains imperturable as it remained . . . in 1908 and again in 1912 and as it remained in the crisis of July 1914, which did end in war. . . . We cannot too explicitly state our view that without a profound modification in the Nazi regime—and there are moderate as well as revolutionary forces in the Nazi regime—there can be no peace in Europe, but only a terrified waiting for war.

[3]Churchill, for example, asserted that this was a "representative British view."

people were decidedly opposed to compromise and he doubted that Flandin could persuade them differently. Chamberlain believed that he had a unique role to play in bringing about a successful resolution of the crisis and he believed he had a decisive advantage over his opponents since he knew precisely what he wanted to achieve and how he would do it. This, Chamberlain believed, was terribly important since most of his rivals were much less secure in their convictions. In general terms at least, there can be no doubt that Chamberlain did in fact know precisely where he wanted to go. His ultimate goal was the avoidance of another war, and it could be achieved only by coming to terms with Germany. Before this goal all knees had to bend, all interests be subverted, and all energies expended.

In the immediate aftermath of the German action, British and French representatives met to coordinate their response. Churchill, in league with the French Foreign Secretary, Flandin, wanted to work for the immediate imposition of sanctions against Germany. Chamberlain was vehemently opposed. In his diary, Chamberlain noted that he had talked with Flandin and told him in no uncertain terms that the British people were definitely against the imposition of sanctions in any form. The French minister had held to the view that if Britain and France maintained a united front Germany would yield without war. But Chamberlain had said that there could be no certainty that a crazed dictator would respond rationally.[4] The prime minister was even less willing than Chamberlain to undertake a policy of sanctions. Baldwin reportedly told Flandin, "If there is even one chance in a hundred that war would follow from your police operation I have not the right to commit England."[5] In Parliament, Hugh Dalton declared that "public opinion . . . and certainly the Labour party would not support the taking of military sanctions or even economic sanctions against Germany. . . ."

In the end the British view prevailed, and it was decided that the Locarno Powers would do nothing stronger than send a joint questionnaire to Hitler asking him what he regarded as "genuine treaties." Chamberlain was anxious to take credit for this action stating that it was his ideas and his initiative which had caused the French to see the wisdom of the British view. Chamberlain was surprised at how easily he had won. He wrote to his sisters that he had anticipated much more resistance from the Cabinet and while there had indeed been some difficulties, everyone was, in the end, pleased with the outcome which had actually decreased British commitments to France. Although the

---

[4] Here was a favorite technique which Chamberlain would use again and again. There is little evidence that he ever seriously considered public attitudes in making any of his foreign policy initiatives. Yet he would often make reference to "public opinion" to support positions he had taken for quite different reasons.

[5] From his memoirs, it is apparent that Eden also believed that sanctions would not accomplish a German withdrawal.

immediate crisis had passed, Chamberlain had already begun thinking of larger issues. He believed that if only the Europeans could put this business of the Rhineland behind them it would be possible to make a fresh start. Real progress could be expected since a solid basis for compromise already existed; all that was required was a renewed feeling of goodwill.

Although relations with Germany were, and always would be, Chamberlain's central concern, other issues were increasingly clouding the international horizon. In spite of feeble actions by the League, Italian armies were in the process of destroying the remnants of Abyssinian sovereignty. In April Chamberlain admitted that the Abyssinian situation was very disturbing, and he believed that if Mussolini's armies were to succeed in killing the emperor all resistance would collapse. Under these circumstances British public opinion would be outraged, but since the Italians would be in possession of the country the League would once again have proved itself capable of nothing more than having increased acrimonious sentiment on all sides and having accomplished nothing except encouraging the Abyssinians to futile resistance. Chamberlain concluded that he could see no way of ending the conflict which would not completely destroy the credibility of the League. If this happened Britain would need an entirely new policy toward the continent.

It was becoming painfully obvious, to Chamberlain at least, that the collective security system as envisaged in the Covenant was inadequate to deal with the Italian threat. Nevertheless, the Government was publicly committed to a League solution. By the summer of 1936, Chamberlain was acutely aware of the inadequacy of such an approach. He reported his concern lest the Italian success encourage the French to call for a lifting of sanctions against Italy in an effort to put the Abyssinian matter behind them and to return to the Stresa Front. Chamberlain felt that that course of events would be intolerable and that it was not yet time to admit that the League had been discredited. But at the same time he privately believed it had been discredited and that the time had come to examine the alternatives in an effort to find a new strategy for maintaining the peace. Chamberlain viewed the Italian conquest of Abyssinia, not as the ruthless destruction of a sovereign member of the League, but as an annoying distraction from the paramount goal of pacifying Germany. In a note added to a letter of 2 May 1936, he wrote that he was pleased to learn that the emperor had abdicated since this would clarify the situation and permit a revision of the League Covenant. The Abyssinian conquest raised no particular moral problem for Chamberlain, certainly none so great as to interfere with the overriding goal of great power accommodation.

Chamberlain's attitude toward Africa and the non-European world in general was laden with nineteenth-century imperial assumptions under which nonwhite territories were but real estate to be bartered and sold as national interest dictated. In another context, he wrote that if he believed a stable European peace could be achieved by transferring ownership of Tanganyika to Germany he would not for a moment hesitate to do so since it would be worth more to Germany than to Britain. This sort of moral duality in which the principles of civilized behavior applied to certain peoples and others were treated as beyond the pale was portentous of the position he would take with regard to Czechoslovakia in 1938.[6]

Nevertheless, Abyssinia was, for better or worse, a sovereign member of the League. Italian aggression against her was beyond dispute; the efficacy of the League had been put to the test and had been found wanting. The Government publicly maintained its position in favor of a League solution even as it became clear that the League was powerless. Chamberlain fully understood the difficulty of the British position and sought to bring the country to a realization that it was time to abandon the fiction of collective security.

It will be remembered that, from the time of his limited liability plan of March 1934, Chamberlain had consistently advocated a reexamination of the collective security system.[7] In April 1936 he requested that a special cabinet committee be organized to consider the future of the League. But, as Chamberlain noted to his sisters, no one in the Government was as anxious as he to see the issue resolved. By the summer of that year, Chamberlain's impatience could no longer be contained and he decided to take his case to the public.

Accordingly, on 17 June 1936, he made what was certainly his most dramatic incursion into foreign affairs as chancellor of the Exchequer. In a speech before the 1900 Club, he gave full rein to his dissatisfaction with the League, charging that the Italian action in Abyssinia was one in which

> . . . aggression was patent and flagrant, and there was hardly any country to which it appeared that a policy of sanctions could be exercised with a greater chance of success than upon Italy. . . . That policy has been tried out and it has failed to save the victim of aggression. I am not blaming any one for the failure. I merely record it now because I think it is time we reviewed the history of those events and sought to draw what lessons and conclusions we can from those events.

He said that a proposal by the president of the League of Nations Union for intensification of sanctions against Italy was "the very mid-summer of madness," and felt that it was time to "limit the functions of the

[6] Similar views can be found in Chamberlain's attitude toward Jewish refugees. See p. 172 *supra*.
[7] See pp. 38–39 *supra*.

League" so that "they may accord with real powers." He pointed out the contradictions inherent in the present policy with regard to the League.

> Is it not apparent that the policy of sanctions involves, I do not say war, but a risk of war? Is it not apparent that that risk must increase in proportion to the effectiveness of the sanctions and also by reason of the incompleteness of the League? Is it not also apparent from what has happened that in the presence of such a risk nations cannot be relied upon to proceed to the last extremity of war unless their vital interests are threatened?
>
> That being so, does it not suggest that it might be wise to explore the possibilities of localizing the danger spots of the world and trying to find a more practical method of securing peace by means of regional arrangements which could be approved by the League, but which should be guaranteed only by those nations whose interests were vitally connected with those danger zones?
>
> . . . whatever may be the policy by which we seek to secure peace for ourselves and others, whether it be a policy of isolation or of alliances or of collective security, in one form or another, it seems quite impossible for us either to protect our own interests or to play an effective part in making an effective contribution to a system of collective security unless we are adequately armed.

In retrospect, Chamberlain's criticisms seem well taken if not obvious, but at the time they appeared, as Eden said, "explosive," arousing "a storm in the House of Commons." Lloyd George used the occasion to attack Chamberlain in the House saying, "Tonight we have seen a cowardly surrender and there [pointing to the Government benches] are the cowards." Baldwin formally disassociated the Government from Chamberlain's views.[8]

In his diary Chamberlain explained that he had made the speech without asking permission from anyone and that his intention was to provide the decisive leadership in foreign affairs which was so sadly lacking. The speech, coming as it did at a time when the Government was committed to maintaining sanctions against Italy, was something of an embarrassment, although Eden, the then secretary of state for League affairs, later admitted, "There was no dispute that sanctions would have to be called off soon. The question was where and when." In fact, on the very day of Chamberlain's speech, Eden himself had proposed the removal of sanctions in a meeting of the Cabinet. The effect of Chamberlain's action was therefore to force the issue and to

---

[8] In his Guildhall Speech of April 1937, Baldwin talked of the futility of sanctions without the force to back them up and in a letter to Chamberlain of 23 July 1937, he wrote that he had greatly admired Chamberlain's speech. Clearly, what Baldwin objected to was not Chamberlain's position but the fact that Chamberlain was saying publicly what Baldwin himself regarded as true but felt unable to say publicly.

expose the fiction of Government policy based on the League. On 18 June, Eden publicly announced that sanctions against Italy had been lifted.

The Opposition was furious, stating that neither the League nor sanctions had failed, but only Eden's courage. To his sister Chamberlain wrote that his speech had been a carefully planned indiscretion of which his father would have approved. He said that he had made the speech because if those responsible would not provide the necessary leadership then someone else had to do so. It was an occasion which he could not let pass without taking action. Writing to his stepmother, he said that the speech had certainly created a public furor but that the *Times* was completely off base in writing that the speech was an improvisation of the moment. Far from it. Chamberlain said that he had known precisely what he was going to say and was fully aware of the consequences.

In this and other instances Chamberlain displayed a curiously ambivalent attitude toward the press. On the one hand he religiously scrutinized the papers to determine how his actions were reported and doted on favorable comments, while on the other he held the press in scarcely concealed contempt. To his sisters, he accused the *Times* of attempting to minimize the significance of his speech at a time when the entire country could talk of nothing else. Not only had they relegated the story to a back page under a misleading title but they had even suggested that "much mischief" had been done. Yet, Chamberlain noted, the *Times* had itself expressed similar views—such hypocrisy was really beneath contempt! This was an attitude which would become increasingly pronounced in the months to come. He began to regard virtually any criticism of his policies as either incompetent or unjust and resented it bitterly.

DOMESTIC POLITICAL MANEUVERING

In the summer of 1936, Chamberlain was beginning to articulate his own policy for dealing with Germany, a policy aimed at limiting British commitments on the Continent while attempting to satisfy, to the greatest extent possible, Hitler's demands. He was becoming increasingly sensitive to any and all criticism of that policy, a policy he believed himself uniquely destined to pursue. Whereas in the past, opposition to his rearmament proposals had come chiefly from the left, now a new challenge from the right wing of the Tory party led by Winston Churchill was beginning to make itself felt.

The demand for military preparedness and a strong stand against Germany appeared to Chamberlain even more threatening since his own brother Austen appeared to be joining forces with the Churchill faction.

In July, he wrote of his alarm that Austen was moving entirely too close to Churchill and his followers. His brother had proposed a closed meeting to discuss defense questions and Chamberlain feared that Austen might even be persuaded to voice publicly his disagreements with the Government. As a result, Austen was losing his standing in the House where he was suspected of anti-Baldwinism.[9] Nevertheless, Neville placed his brother's proposal before the Cabinet on 6 July 1936 noting, ". . . for the first time since the late Marquess of Salisbury's Government the House of Commons was divided on foreign policy." Austen, he told the Cabinet, wanted a secret session "with a view to bringing the various parties together and securing a united front." Neville regarded this as "a dangerous experiment" which "might easily create panic in the nation. The prime minister agreed that a secret session was out of the question. It might easily throw the country into a panic, and there was no precedent for it except during war." In the Cabinet, Austen Chamberlain's proposal led to a general discussion of foreign affairs in which fears of the Great War happening again were expressed. Eden said that the various nations were in such a ferment that some episode might precipitate danger.

> Some mistrust was expressed of the plan of getting the Locarno Powers other than Germany to meet with a view to inviting Germany to a new conference on the grounds that Germany was certain to regard it as a *bloc* of the four Powers with a view to agreement not only in the West but also in the East of Europe. This would be regarded as the re-creation of the policy of encirclement of Germany.

Noting the inadequacy of British defenses, the Cabinet ruled out the possibility of aid to Eastern Europe and turned to the idea of regional pacts for limiting British liabilities in Europe, a policy which Chamberlain had long advocated. Thus it was to be again and again; the very idea of a united policy against Hitler brought to mind the policies which had led to the last war. To knowingly bring about another world war was unthinkable, and therefore coming to terms with Germany seemed the only rational course.

Triumphantly Chamberlain reported to his sisters that he had had a private conversation with his brother and that the latter had, as a result, come to his senses and realized that a conference on rearmament could not possibly result in a united front. Chamberlain noted that at least Austen was prepared to be reasonable which was more than he could say of Churchill who simply would not listen to opposing points of view. Chamberlain was pleased to note that he had saved Austen from

---

[9]Considering what Neville himself had said in private about the prime minister, it is difficult to believe that anyone could have been more anti-Baldwin that Chamberlain himself.

the folly of his ways and that as a result everyone was quite relieved.[10]

From his past behavior we might suspect that Neville was concerned with far more than his brother's reputation. Already he felt a personal identification with a policy of limiting British liabilities and of meeting German demands. From Chamberlain's perspective, Churchill represented a threat to that policy as well as a potential threat to Chamberlain's position as the future prime minister.[11] Therefore he took great satisfaction in besting Churchill in parliamentary debate.

Chamberlain's political position in 1936 was that of designated successor to the prime minister. There were no other politically acceptable contenders for the position, and Chamberlain was anxious to make the transition as soon as possible. His letters in this period are filled with complaints at Baldwin's alleged incompetence and irresponsibility. Baldwin, on the other hand, wrote to Chamberlain in November of 1935, "The fact is you and I are complementary: each puts into the pool his own contribution and we make a jolly effective unit!"[12] For his part, Chamberlain had nothing but criticism for the prime minister, whom he saw as increasingly unfit for office. Near the end of June, Chamberlain reported that Baldwin's depression was just like that of Ramsey MacDonald before the latter's nervous collapse. Chamberlain said that he tried to make up for Baldwin's inadequacies but it was not the same as being himself the prime minister. The next week Chamberlain reported that he had serious questions as to whether Baldwin was fit to remain in office.[13]

By October, Baldwin's condition had improved somewhat and Chamberlain snidely noted that perhaps he would not succeed Baldwin after all since Baldwin had saved his mental health by allowing Chamberlain to do all the work. Even if this should prove to be the case Chamberlain wrote that he was being very careful to avoid committing himself beforehand to any particular political position so that he might maximize his freedom as prime minister.[14] Particularly galling to him were representations, in the press and elsewhere, that Baldwin had been the power behind the rearmament effort. In another letter Chamberlain complained that Baldwin was trying to take all the credit for rearma-

[10] Austen Chamberlain died in March 1937, shortly before his brother took office as prime minister. He was one of the few people whose opinion Neville respected and who might possibly have penetrated the wall of self-assurance which was to have such tragic consequences for Neville in the years to come.

[11] It is, however, very doubtful that in 1936 Churchill was a serious threat to Chamberlain's power position since the latter was clearly a maverick with little support in his own party, having long been the nemesis of party regulars.

[12] Baldwin had good reason for disliking Chamberlain if for no other reason than that Chamberlain had tried to unseat him as leader of the party in 1931.

[13] Baldwin, in fact, suffered what was described as "a nervous breakdown" and was almost completely incapacitated.

[14] Chamberlain was probably referring to the possibility of resurrecting his idea for an Anglo-Japanese rapprochement.

ment when in fact the prime minister had provided no leadership at all. Chamberlain's analysis was that Baldwin made such statements to conceal the fact that he was now taking an even less active role in government.

In November Chamberlain wrote that one press report had asserted that Baldwin, in response to Churchill's criticism in the Commons, had displayed a complete command of the technical issues of rearmament. Chamberlain knew that this was simply not true and that in fact Baldwin had merely read from a prepared text. The only thing original had been Baldwin's "frank" explanation of why it had taken the Government so long to begin rearming. Even this "frankness" was not the whole truth. Baldwin had failed to discuss the long and difficult period in which Chamberlain had himself spearheaded the movement to evaluate Britain's defense needs and to formulate a program for correcting the deficiencies, an effort which had been carefully hidden from the public until after the Tories had safely won the election. Thus, in Chamberlain's view, Baldwin's so-called "frankness" was nothing but a gratuitous admission of weakness. It had been a bad speech which Churchill had been quick to exploit. Chamberlain felt that Churchill's charges could have been effectively rebutted but that Baldwin was not the man to do it.

On the one hand, the references to Baldwin in Chamberlain's letters to his sisters demonstrate a strong need for familial approval and an almost petulant desire to measure up, in his family's eyes, to the high standards set by his father and Austen. On the other hand, Chamberlain's impatience with Baldwin's leadership in foreign affairs was most certainly justified. To a much greater degree than Chamberlain himslf, Baldwin represented the old prewar political style, inappropriate for dealing with Hitler and the sophisticated technologies of modern warfare. While Chamberlain was certainly not possessed of a prophetic consciousness nor the rhetorical eloquence to articulate an alternative vision of British policy, he did understand that bold decisions had to be taken lest Britain drift once again into the abyss of world war.

Economics and the Nazi Threat

In the summer of 1936, British politicians were preoccupied with Abyssinia, and in the months to come their attention would increasingly focus on the Spanish Civil War, an issue which would polarize British opinion and lead to a national debate on the merits of nonintervention. One result of this preoccupation was that, for many observers, attention was deflected from the ultimately more important issues of rearmament and the German problem.

Such was not the case for Chamberlain. While he recognized the importance of events in Spain and Abyssinia, nothing could divert his attention from the issues surrounding British policy toward Germany. On the issues of Spain and Abyssinia he supported what were essentially policies made by others. He contributed opinions when the occasion arose but refrained from articulating an independent position. On questions of Germany and rearmament, Chamberlain sought not only to influence but to dominate all discussion of the subject and to control every aspect of policy. Increasingly he was coming to feel that Anglo-German relations were his private domain and that he was the only person who had a viable plan for dealing with the situation.

While public discussion was becoming more and more concerned with Spain, Chamberlain's private letters revealed a steadfast preoccupation with Germany.[15] In June, he wrote that Hitler seemed to be biding his time waiting for an opportunity to advance the German position but if he delayed too long he might well discover that he had missed his chance. A week later he wrote that he was sure that Hitler was looking for an opportunity to further his aims and that he expected trouble the moment Hitler saw an opening. In July, he wrote that he was actually pleased to learn of the Austro-German agreement since he had not been fooled by Hitler's public protestations of peaceful intent, and Austro-German relations had long been a sensitive area where violence could have erupted at any moment. Now, that particular crisis had passed and the British had gained time to complete their rearmament plans. Whether or not Chamberlain's later policy was the best that could have been chosen, there can be little doubt that he consistently and correctly identified Germany as the pre-eminent threat to British interests and that he understood the paramount importance of formulating correct policy to meet that threat.

While Chamberlain may well have used rearmament as a vehicle for political advancement, he was nevertheless committed beyond question to British rearmament for its own sake. The 1936 and 1937 White Papers, of which he was a principal architect, testify to this commitment. Together they constituted a five-year program costing "not much less than £1,500 million."[16] To Chamberlain, the rearmament effort as embodied in the White Papers was a one-shot program which, when completed, would adequately provide for British security. As he under-

---

[15] It seems that Chamberlain, having no routine access to Foreign Office memoranda except as they concerned the Exchequer, got most of his information on events inside Germany from the British press. That this was the case can be deduced from the fact that, as a rule, his letters referred to a particular press account rather than to Foreign Office information. Surprisingly enough, this practice seems to have carried over into the period in which he was prime minister. It was not that he trusted press reports more than Foreign Office bureaucrats, indeed he held both in approximately equal contempt, but that to him press reports seemed to be a more firsthand source of information. Chamberlain invariably preferred his own perceptions to information gathered by others.

[16] An indication of Chamberlain's changing view of the need for rearmament and the seriousness of the German threat lies in the fact that in 1934 he had seen the rearmament effort as requiring only £120 million extra. In 1937, he supported a program of £1,500 million.

stood it, rearmament was not a program to be expanded indefinitely to keep pace with Germany. In fact, the possibility of another arms race was the eventuality Chamberlain most wanted to avoid.

Once the country was rearmed, Chamberlain believed that Britain could return to the important programs of domestic welfare which had always been his central concern. Alfred Duff Cooper who would later become a major protagonist of Chamberlain's policy, recalled that he

> . . . had sympathy with Chamberlain's attitude. He had been Chancellor of the Exchequer in 1931 when the country, we were told, was on the verge of bankruptcy. He had brought about a great financial recovery. He was about to welcome the return of measures of social reform. Suddenly he saw his dream dissolving. The plenty that he had laboured so hard to collect was going to be thrown away upon rearmament, the least remunerative form of expenditure.

The 1936–37 program was nevertheless, in Chamberlain's view, a reluctantly accepted necessity, but any spending beyond that level could lead to the disastrous consequence of another uncontrollable arms race.

Chamberlain's inherited economic ideology was one of rigid fiscal orthodoxy and Victorian parsimony.[17] To a man of that background, the mounting costs of rearmament were sufficient cause for alarm, even had they not brought with them ominous memories of the pre-1914 armament race. As chancellor of the Exchequer, he was, after all, the man most responsible for keeping Government spending in check.

To Chamberlain, the need for a balanced budget meant that spending on rearmament should be kept to the minimum amount necessary for British security and that limited resources should be spent where they would provide the greatest security. Even before the publication of the 1936 White Paper, Chamberlain warned Baldwin that in his view it was essential to reevaluate the current system of allocating funds among the various branches of the military and that some changes were called for. This was the beginning of a persistent attack on the notion of balanced rearmament by which approximately equal emphasis would have been placed on rearming each of the services.[18] The argument which he con-

---

[17] A telling, if somewhat trivial, example of Chamberlain's parsimony can be found in the fact that long after he became prime minister he could not bear to discard Exchequer stationery and continued to write his personal correspondence on stationery bearing the heading, "No. 11 Downing Street."

[18] Maurice Hankey, secretary of the Cabinet since 1916, had used his considerable influence to champion the army in Cabinet discussions. Chamberlain wanted to de-emphasize the role of the army. Chamberlain and Hankey were not, as one might suppose, implacable enemies. Beginning in December 1935, Liddell Hart had attacked the organization of the country's defenses. As head of the DRC, Hankey was responsible for defending the existing system. Chamberlain found Hankey's arguments ". . . so powerful and convincing that the Cabinet may feel that there is nothing more to be said on the subject." Chamberlain, however, admitted a sense of unease "about certain aspects of the situation." He recommended the establishment of a Cabinet Committee to investigate the situation, an investigation which eventually led to the establishment of the post of minister for coordination of defence. Therefore whatever else may be said of it, the conflict which later arose was not simply a conflict between Chamberlain as chancellor of the Exchequer arguing for a limitation of spending and the military arguing for any and all armaments they could get.

sistently presented to the Cabinet was one of cost effectiveness, that the greatest security per pound expended could be found in the air force. While cost effectiveness was always his official argument, Chamberlain was clearly thinking about the lessons of the Great War and the million-man continental army. He wrote privately that he could not accept the notion that a future war would be like the Great War since in the next war, British resources would be concentrated on the air force and not in massive continental armies or increased fleet strength.

Official army doctrine was that Britain should in fact be prepared to fight a future war on the Continent along the same lines as she had in 1914–18. Fighting another war on the Continent with a million-man army was, needless to say, the nightmare which Chamberlain wanted most to avoid. In such circumstances a clash of interests between Chamberlain and the army was inevitable. By the fall of 1936 the initial phases of this conflict were well under way. Chamberlain reported that he had told the Minister for the Coordination of Defence, Tom Inskip, that it was essential that a decision be reached quickly on the question of the role of the army and the territorials in the event of a new war on the continent. Chamberlain had already decided what, in his view, that role should be, and he was confident that there would be no further postponement of the issue although he felt that Inskip had to be handled with determination. It was the beginning of what was to be a long and ultimately successful attempt by Chamberlain to gain personal control over the rearmament effort.

In December 1936, as the king waged a constitutional battle over his right to marry Mrs. Simpson, Chamberlain waged a much less public battle for control of the rearmament program. The publicity surrounding the abdication crisis tended to obscure what was, in fact, an intragovernmental struggle for influence of potentially far more serious consequences for Britain's future. Unlike the unfortunate King Edward, Chamberlain emerged from the struggle triumphant and in virtual control of the nation's military.

At a meeting of the Cabinet on 9 December, the newly appointed Secretary of State for War, Duff Cooper, presented a memorandum to his colleagues asking them to "reaffirm the decision with regard to the role of the army." The decision to which the secretary referred was the following, contained in the 1936 White Paper.

> The Army has three main functions to perform. It has to maintain garrisons overseas in various parts of the Empire, to provide the military share in Home Defence, including Anti-Aircraft Defence, Coast Defence and Internal Security, and lastly, in time of emergency or war, to provide a properly equipped force ready to proceed overseas wherever it may be wanted.

It should be noted, that although the White Paper granted third priority to a British expeditionary force, it nevertheless affirmed that such a force was a necessary part of British defenses and that it should comprise one mobile and four regular divisions. While priority was to be given to equipping the regular army, the White Paper did provide for the equipment of a twelve-division territorial army to serve as a reinforcement for the field force. In his memorandum, Duff Cooper was asking the Cabinet to reaffirm the decisions taken in the White Paper, which he took to mean "the equipment of the Territorial Army as and when opportunity occurs." He argued that a future war "cannot be fought on the principle of limited liability." This was a direct challenge to Chamberlain's long-standing view that Britain should work toward the limitation of her continental commitments. The secretary made the following argument in favor of the equipment of the territorial army.

> What is wanted is peace equipment and such mobilization equipment and reserves as will enable formations to take the field at the earliest date that the training of personnel will allow. We must aim at reducing any delay after the outbreak of war to this minimum. We cannot rely on having time as we had in the last war to build up and equip an army. Our regular forces are considerably smaller and at present far less adequately equipped, if modern developments are taken into account, than they were in 1914.

The initial outcome of the Duff Cooper memorandum was that Chamberlain asked for and was granted a postponement of the question until the next Cabinet meeting.

A week later, on 16 December, Duff Cooper again raised the question, noting that "the lack of a decision on the Territorial Army was holding up the equipment not only of the Territorial Army but all of the Regular Army" and that it was also "causing uneasiness in the Territorial Army." Chamberlain countered with his own memorandum on the role of the army in which he argued that to grant Duff Cooper's request for equipping the twelve divisions of the territorial army would in effect be providing seventeen divisions for use on the continent (i.e., the agreed five-division field force plus twelve divisions of the territorial army). This, Chamberlain said, would go beyond a "reaffirmation of the previous decision," (i.e., that set forth in the White Paper). Chamberlain took the offensive against Duff Cooper.

> The Secretary of State does not explain in detail the type of emergency which is likely to require a Field Force of seventeen divisions available as soon as possible after the outbreak of war. I should imagine, however, from his parallel with the last war that he has in mind war in Western Europe in which large continental Armies are engaged. In essence it seems to me that

what we have to decide upon is the size and character of the field force which we must plan to be available on the outbreak of such a war, and I submit that this decision is one of major importance which should only be answered after a survey by the competent authorities of all possible alternatives.

In so arguing, Chamberlain was widening the forum of debate from a simple consideration of whether or not to equip the territorial army to the much larger issue of the role the army was expected to play in a future war. Reminding the Cabinet of the traditional importance of the navy and the deterrent value of the air force, he argued that the army could not be considered in isolation from the other services. Pitting the service branches one against the other was, it should be noted, a technique he would utilize with great success in the months to come.

Chamberlain believed that there had been a "continuous upward strain on our industrial and other resources," which meant that "any substantial degree of re-equipment of the Territorial Force would only result in the breakdown of the whole scheme." Turning to the political issues involved, Chamberlain admitted that "the existence of a substantial British Army, strong enough for immediate and effective intervention in continental disputes, in addition to our naval and air forces would in some respects strengthen our influence on the continent. . . . but there are definite limits to the contribution we can make in such an eventuality. . . . "[19] He urged the Cabinet not to "lose sight of the fact that the political temper of people in this country is strongly opposed to Continental adventures."

> Although when the time comes they may, as in 1914, be persuaded that intervention by us is inevitable, they will be strongly suspicious of any preparation made in peace time with a view to large-scale military operations on the continent, and they will regard such preparations as likely to result in our being entangled in disputes which do not concern us.

Here again, we see Chamberlain's characteristic use of "public opinion" to turn a debate to his advantage: Chamberlain often attributed to the public views with which he sympathized though he had no real evidence to support such a claim. He had no objective evidence as to what public opinion would or would not support in a situation like 1914, but he knew very well that he himself could not support a repetition of the Great War.[20] Attributing such feelings to the larger public

[19] It should be noted that Chamberlain did not rule out altogether the possibility of a British expeditionary force. He only said that there were "definite limits" to the British contribution. This is directly contrary to Middlemas's assertion that Chamberlain stated during the Cabinet meeting, ". . . there would be no continental role for the army because of substitution by the other two Services."

[20] The perceptions derived from the peace ballot, the East Fulham by-election, etc., have often been seen as indications of "pacifist sentiment." But it would be incorrect to argue from this that "public opinion" would not have supported military involvement in any circumstances.

was a convenient device, which Chamberlain may not have been consciously aware of using, but which was nonetheless highly effective.

To understand the changes Chamberlain was attempting to make, it is important to note his views on the division of responsibility within the Government. The post of minister for coordination of defence, which Chamberlain had worked to institute, was a new position created to deal with the perceived problems of rearming in peacetime.[21] There were differing conceptions of the duties and resonsibilities of that position. Chamberlain objected to Churchill's view that the minister for coordination of defence should alone be the nation's chief strategist. He felt that the minister's duties should be to insure that strategic issues were adequately discussed and that issues of contention among the services were fairly settled. In Chamberlain's view the single most important issue was that of defining the role of the army and territorials in a future continental land war and the proper allocation of manpower among the services. In the Cabinet meeting he reiterated this position saying that the minister had, in addition to responsibilities in the area of supply, "the function to oversee strategy."

If Chamberlain believed this to be true, he was, by his own reckoning, interfering in a policy area well beyond his authority either as chancellor of the Exchequer or as premier designate. In the Cabinet, Chamberlain expressed doubt "as to whether we were right in approaching any war from the point of view of the last war."

> To think that we could send an Expeditionary Force at the outset of a war might involve a rude awakening. He [i.e., Chamberlain] had not said that he was unwilling to equip the Territorial Army. . . . He doubted whether we were right in equipping the Territorial Force for the trenches. He thought the question had not been considered impartially. It was always assumed that we must make a contribution to a land war. As one of his colleagues said, the French might not be satisfied, but it was not for France to declare to us the distribution of our Forces. He did not want to say that no army should go to the Continent, but he had tried to make a prima facie case to show that the idea of sending 5 Regular Divisions to France at the outset of War and 18 Divisions later required reexamination.

[21]Chamberlain had supported the creation of the post of minister for coordination of defence, but he did not think that Inskip was the right man for the job. Nevertheless, he had felt that Inskip was a strong personality unlikely to create dissension in either the military or civilian bureaucracies. At the time of its creation, considerable importance had been attached to the post, and Chamberlain had himself been considered for the position. To those who supported rearmament, the appointment of Inskip to the position came as a disappointment. Churchill explained it by saying that "Baldwin had to find a man of inferior ability to himself and this Herculean task must require time for accomplishment." In the lobbies of Parliament it was said that there had been no appointment like it since Caligula made his horse consul. In Inskip's defense, it should probably be noted that he may not necessarily have been the incompetent he is commonly made out to be. Nevertheless, it is interesting to ask why Chamberlain regarded the appointment of a man such as Inskip to the post with such equanimity. When Chamberlain described someone as a strong personality it usually meant that that person could be relied on not to challenge Chamberlain's own position. It therefore seems reasonable to conclude that Chamberlain accepted Inskip and retained him until 1939 because he knew that Inskip could be controlled and would not challenge Chamberlain's own views. In this he was not mistaken.

Baldwin said that "every member of the Cabinet sympathised with the Chancellor of the Exchequer in his very difficult task." It was agreed that the matter would be postponed until after the new year by which time the chiefs of staff were to have submitted their own assessment of the role of the army in a future war.[22]

By the middle of January, Duff Cooper reported that a decision as to the role of the army had still not been reached. On 20 January 1937, Chamberlain warned:

> a point might well be reached when rearmament was finished, trade was falling and when, especially if the element of good will in our export trade had been sacrificed, a very difficult economic and financial situation would arise, more particularly as the permanent cost of maintaining our armaments would have greatly increased.

On 3 February Chamberlain directed his colleagues to the problems which had already begun to appear in the rearmament effort:

> He wished the Cabinet to realize that . . . even the present Programmes were placing a heavy strain on our resources. Any additional strain might put our present Programmes in jeopardy.

Inskip was now ready to come to terms with the chancellor of the Exchequer and proposed as a compromise the providing of equipment for the territorial army "sufficient for training purposes," an amount which he said would "provide sufficient material for the equipment of about two Divisions." Even this would not satisfy Chamberlain, who, while favoring in principle Inskip's proposal, said that "before making a decision he must know the cost of the proposed plan." Chamberlain admitted that

> . . . national safety came before finance, but the bill for armaments was running up very heavily. He attached importance also to the time factor. There was perhaps, some alleviation in the international situation, and the dangers of overloading the programmes beyond the material capacity of the country had to be considered.

Inskip countered by saying that the time factor was irrelevant as "it had become a matter of proceeding as fast as circumstances permitted." In the end Chamberlain acquiesced and the Cabinet agreed to accept Inskip's proposal.

While the acceptance of the Inskip compromise may be regarded as a

---

[22] The chiefs of staff's report reiterated the necessity of a continental role for the army and reaffirmed the conclusions of the 1936 White Paper.

tactical defeat for Chamberlain, the net result was not. The desirability of a five-division field force was reaffirmed, and with this Chamberlain agreed. He had, however, succeeded in limiting the degree to which that force could be reinforced, in the initial phases of a war, from twelve divisions to two. It was no mean achievement. It was, therefore, with considerable satisfaction that he wrote to his sisters that at long last the issue of the role of the army had been resolved and he believed that he had achieved everything he had asked for. According to Chamberlain, the regular army was to be fully supplied with the latest equipment and would be ready to move at any time. The territorials would be equally well equipped but only with sufficient weapons for training purposes. In practice this would mean that only two divisions of the territorial army would be fully ready to reinforce the regular army in four months from the outbreak of hostilities. The new role of the army contained absolutely no commitment as to the circumstances under which it would be used and that as a result, the war office had given up any notion of building an army on the scale of 1914.

In addition, Chamberlain reported that he had made the highly useful discovery that the service chiefs of the air and navy could be successfully mobilized in support of his position. This was possible insofar as the chiefs could be pitted against each other with the result that the Chamberlain line prevailed.[23]

Little is known of the apparent bitterness with which this struggle was waged. It is however certain that relations between Chamberlain and Duff Cooper were permanently poisoned as a result. Duff Cooper recalled that he had, in the fall of 1936, prepared a paper on methods of recruitment for the army and that he was bitterly disappointed when Chamberlain informed him that "no paper could be circulated to the Cabinet until it had received the approval of the Treasury." Duff Cooper noted that this and similar incidents which followed created "unhappy relations between Neville Chamberlain and myself." On his part, Chamberlain had, at a very early stage, formed a negative opinion of the secretary of war.[24] In June 1936, he had written, that Duff Cooper was proving to be highly ineffective in the war office and that he had

---

[23] Middlemas and Barnes correctly conclude that Chamberlain's statement about the War Office was premature. Liddell Hart, for example, maintained that as late as August 1937, the General Staff had persuaded Deverell, the CIGS, that any reorganization of the army was undesirable. This, together with the arguments in the following chapter, leads to the conclusion that Chamberlain was, in this instance, mistaking wish for reality.

[24] In Chamberlain's relations with his colleagues, as we have seen, there were two types of people: those he believed he could work with and those such as Lloyd George who were beyond the pale. At an early date Duff Cooper became part of this latter group and thereafter Chamberlain consistently worked to undermine his authority. Exactly when this occurred is difficult to say but it is at least possible that Chamberlain's estrangement from Duff Cooper can be traced to Chamberlain's attempted coup against Baldwin in 1931. Hore-Belisha said that Duff Cooper's victory in the Westminister by-election of that year had "saved Baldwin's career." Chamberlain bitterly resented anyone who frustrated his own ambitions, and by saving Baldwin, Duff Cooper had done just that.

provoked considerable negative sentiment in the higher reaches of government. The net result of their differences was that Chamberlain decided that Duff Cooper's name should be placed on a list of candidates to be purged at the earliest convenient date.[25]

CHAMBERLAIN AS DE FACTO PRIME MINISTER

In the final months before taking office as prime minister, Chamberlain's attitude could best be described as one of extreme impatience. He was impatient with a country unable to recognize the need for rearmament and unwilling to meet its costs, with a Government unwilling to strike a balance between burgeoning rearmament spending and the requisites of fiscal responsibility, and, most of all, impatient with a prime minister, who, he believed was incapable of leading. In foreign affairs, Chamberlain believed that even a successfully completed rearmament program would not enable Britain to play the role for which she had been cast. Therefore diplomacy had to fill the gap, and Chamberlain believed himself to be one of the only men in government who recognized this fact, and the only person who could successfully steer the ship of state through increasingly trouble waters.

His attitude toward the abdication crisis was one instance of this impatience. The constitutional question involved in Edward VIII's decision to marry Mrs. Simpson, a divorced American, was a crisis which absorbed the British public in ways which present day observers might find difficult to understand. On the one hand there was the group, of whom Churchill was the leading exponent, who defended the sovereign's right to marry as he saw fit. On the other were those who felt that the proposed marriage, morganatic or otherwise, was unthinkable. Chamberlain belonged to the extreme fringe of this latter group. To a man of rigid Victorian sensibilities the proposed marriage was a challenge to the basic tenets of the social order by which he lived. Therefore the only acceptable solution was abdication. Chamberlain presented the Cabinet with a memorandum outlining his proposals for dealing with the situation. J.C.C. Davidson, a leading Tory politician, described the memorandum as follows.

> . . . he [i.e., Chamberlain] wanted the Cabinet to send for the king and reprimand him as if he were a naughty schoolboy. If this memorandum had ever seen the light of day it would have destroyed public confidence in the Government. . . . I was terrified that if we had another constitutional crisis after S.B. went, Chamberlain would have handled it in the same blundering insensitive manner.

[25] This was, in part achieved in May of 1937 when Duff Cooper was replaced at the War Office by Leslie Hore-Belisha.

The thought of a king of England marrying a woman such as Mrs. Simpson was simply out of the question, and Chamberlain reacted with a callous insensitivity which was, even for him, uncharacteristic.[26]

Chamberlain secretly resented the credit given to Baldwin for his allegedly skillful handing of the crisis. Nevertheless, Edward's abdication cleared the way for the prime minister's own retirement, an event long contemplated by the incumbent and eagerly awaited by his successor. The date for the formal transfer of power was set for the end of May, following the coronation of the new king. Until that time Baldwin was little more than a caretaker prime minister.[27]

Chamberlain had long realized that he was going to become prime minister, yet not until the beginning of 1937 was he certain that the exigencies of health or political fortune would not conspire to deprive him of the goal he had dearly hoped to achieve. While the reasons for his actions remain obscure, Baldwin no doubt waited until the last possible moment to tell Chamberlain of his intention to resign and to fix the date.[28] As late as 16 January, Chamberlain wrote that Baldwin had said nothing about resigning although he had raised the matter with other colleagues, and Chamberlain understood that Baldwin had said he would give up his office shortly after the coronation. In the meantime Chamberlain was hard at work preparing his own policy positions. Although some of these issues were by no means pleasant to consider, Chamberlain wrote that he had no intention of being caught unprepared. While the problems before him were indeed formidable, his letters fail to reveal any indication that Chamberlain ever doubted that he was equal to the challenge. To the extent that private papers reveal the man, Chamberlain apparently faced the problems of the day with complete self-assurance and equanimity.

In the months before the formal transfer of power, he saw the question of financing the rearmament effort as a difficult problem which needed resolution before he could move on to other things. At the end of April, he gave the Cabinet a preview of what they could expect from their new prime minister. "He warned the Cabinet that we were approaching the time when he would have to propose a fixed limit to which the services would have to conform." It was a preview of the

---

[26] In a letter to his sister, of 27 November 1938, Chamberlain described a chance meeting with the Duchess in a language which barely concealed his contempt. He said that while the Duke's new wife was fashionably dressed and eager to please he simply could not abide such a saccharine display of sentimentality. Therefore he felt compelled to leave after only a few minutes since she was obviously not his kind of woman.

[27] Middlemas and Barnes state that "whereas Baldwin would intervene to help Chamberlain, he did not question the major decisions nor the implications of Chamberlain's warnings in February and April, of rising costs of rearmament."

[28] As we have noted, one reason for this might have been a certain well-hidden resentment of Chamberlain for his aggressive pursuit of power.

system of rationing which he would introduce later in the year, a system under which the services would be given a fixed total to spend on rearmament and left to fight out its distribution among themselves. As we shall see, Chamberlain's idea of a rationed budget was to become an innovation of profound significance for the rearmament effort.

While he was attempting to impress on the Government the need for economy in rearmament, Chamberlain was also working publicly to increase revenue to pay for the increasingly costly program. On 10 February 1937, Chamberlain reminded the Cabinet, ". . . it was not possible to finance the whole of our Defence Requirements Programmes from revenue." Therefore he proposed that a bill be presented to Parliament enabling the Government "to borrow to such amount as appeared reasonable." Chamberlain noted that presenting the bill to the Commons

> . . . would come as a surprise to the public and perhaps as a shock to financial circles. This he thought would do no harm. It was time that the country realized that they could not get armaments without paying. It might also be a good thing for Europe to see how determined we were to recondition our armaments.

Accordingly, Chamberlain introduced legislation to enable the Government to borrow up to £400 million for the five-year period of the rearmament program. At a time when the necessity for a balanced budget was practically unquestioned and in which the possibilities of deficit finance were not yet widely understood, Chamberlain's actions in bringing the question of finance into the public forum can only be regarded as a bold action which served to inject a badly needed note of realism into public discussion.

Even the proposed loan, however, was inadequate to eliminate a projected £15 million deficit. In order to balance the budget, Chamberlain proposed to increase the rate of income taxation together with a graduated tax on business profits which he termed the National Defence Contribution.[29] Chamberlain's proposed tax on the rate of profit expansion created a political furor. Stock exchange values fell sharply, the city and business organizations were up in arms, and many Conservative leaders were appalled at what appeared to them a socialist measure. In the face of mounting opposition, Chamberlain was forced to withdraw the proposal in June 1937. Privately, he said that the NDC was the most courageous thing he had ever attempted since by proposing it he had jeopardized his chances for becoming prime minister just when it was about to become a reality. While it is difficult to believe that he had actually put his career on the line when, in fact, his succession was a

---

[29] Shay raises the possibility that the idea of the National Defence Contribution may have arisen in Chamberlain's discussions with Montagu Norman, then governor of the Bank of England.

virtual certainty, the NDC was nevertheless a characteristically bold solution to a difficult problem and one which was politically inexpedient.

It is nevertheless hard to understand why Chamberlain had proposed what was almost certainly to be an extremely unpopular course of action. From the existing evidence, it seems clear that Chamberlain had failed "to appreciate the depth of the business community's antipathy to government intervention in the affairs of the private sector." He wrote that he was absolutely certain that the NDC was a judicious policy and that sooner or later its wisdom would be vindicated. Not only did Chamberlain view NDC as a mechanism for balancing the budget, he also saw it as a step toward meeting the criticisms of the policies which had led to war in 1914. He noted that government contracts with the large munition suppliers were of an entirely different nature than they had been in 1914–18. Chamberlain almost certainly had in mind the conventional criticisms, constantly being made by Labour, that huge and excessive profits had been made from the manufacture and sale of munitions and that this in itself had been one reason for the severity of that war. In fact, this concern that one of the factors which had made the Great War so terrible had been war profiteering by munitions makers, led in 1938 to the setting up of a commission to investigate the question of business profits in time of war.

As always in moments of important decisions, Chamberlain's thoughts turned to his father and to his own part in maintaining the Chamberlain legacy. He wrote that he did not believe in omens nor did he particularly care if he ever became prime minister but when he realized that he was about to take over the leadership of the country, his thoughts often turned to Austen and his father and he was led to ponder the possibility that a wicked twist of fate lay in store for him as well. It was a prophetic statement, almost as if he dimly perceived the dark shadows which would later be cast over his Government. Always, he compared his accomplishments and his political role to those of his father and brother. He supposed that it was part of Austen's greatness that in spite of the unavoidable analogies made by the public between him and his father that he was able to make his own unique place in history. Now, Neville Chamberlain realized that he would be measured against both of these men. But, he felt that when the time came to make these assessments, he would be beyond caring. The elder Chamberlain had won his reputation in the Empire, Austen's had been made at Locarno, and Neville believed his place in history would be secured as the prime minister who achieved the appeasement of Europe.

❧ 4 ❧

The Fall of Avalanches

ON 28 May 1937, Chamberlain kissed hands[1] and in so doing, the reality of his control over the Government was at long last officially confirmed. Three days later he was unanimously elected head of the Tory party, an action which signified the party's full confidence in their new prime minister. Given the degree of dissent over foreign policy goals which was already making itself felt, it is perhaps surprising to note that the formation of a Chamberlain Government was widely, if not universally, regarded as a positive sign. If for no other reason, the left could applaud the fact that they now had a single focus for their criticisms, whereas before, under Baldwin, it had never been exactly clear who was responsible for any given policy. On the right, Chamberlain was seen as a man of action who would be able to reverse the policy of drift which they feared would lead to another war.

THE FORMATION OF THE CHAMBERLAIN GOVERNMENT

No group was more unequivocal in applauding the new Government than the Tory politicians who would later claim to have "seen all along" the impossibility of appeasing Hitler. At the head of the line of those waiting to heap praise on the new prime minister was none other than Winston Churchill. In a speech seconding Chamberlain's nomination for the leadership of the party, Churchill said:

> A new helmsman must be found to take the wheel, after 14 eventful years. Happily, as all the speakers had said there was no doubt or question who that man should be. There was no rivalry; there were no competing claims;

[1]Pundits of the history of political protocol will note that considerable confusion resulted over the proprieties to be observed in the symbolic ascension to the premiership. In a letter to his sister, Chamberlain registered his confusion as to whether or not the kissing of hands was to be taken literally. He failed to say how he had resolved the issue!

Mr. Chamberlain stood forth alone as the one man to whom at this juncture this high and grave function should be confided.

Churchill noted Chamberlain's achievements at the Exchequer in having rescued the nation's finances "at a moment when Socialist folly and incompetence had reduced this wealthy powerful country almost to the appearance of bankruptcy. . . ." With regard to Chamberlain's participation in the rearmament effort, Churchill noted:

> Any Chancellor of the Exchequer naturally found as his normal business that he should resist and criticize and canvass expenditure, particularly expenditures on what was called non-productive channels. But when the late Government were at length convinced of the urgent need to rearm against the danger in which we stood and still stand, no one was more active than Mr. Chamberlain. Indeed no one was so active in pressing forward the policy of rearmament and in providing the immense supplies of money which had been rendered available largely through his own foresight and prescience.

Significantly, Churchill omitted any mention of this speech in his highly acclaimed memoirs.[2]

Nor was Churchill alone in his welcoming of the new Government. Of Chamberlain's known desire to take an active role in foreign affairs, Eden, a generation later in an interview with the BBC, stated:

> I certainly hoped rather than otherwise that Chamberlain would take an interest in foreign policy, because S.B. from my point of view took rather too little. So I wasn't at all disheartened in fact I was encouraged when he took an interest.[3]

Eden was joined by many of those in Government most intimately involved in foreign affairs in applauding Chamberlain's accession to the premiership. Maurice Hankey "welcomed the change, for he had become increasingly sympathetic towards Chamberlain's policy of trying

[2] No doubt there is a great deal of truth in the charge that Churchill made these statements with a view toward earning himself a place in the new Government. The Churchill-Chamberlain relationship was not however what, in retrospect, one might suppose it to have been. From their letters it is clear that the two regarded each other with mutual respect. On his part, Chamberlain found Churchill's outspoken criticism of his policies an annoyance, but he never detested Churchill in the way, for example, that he regarded Lloyd George. Churchill refrained from openly criticizing Chamberlain's Government until after Eden's resignation in February of 1938. Later, in 1940, after the fall of the Chamberlain Government, Churchill remained remarkably loyal to the former prime minister. The reasons for this unlikely friendship are not difficult to find. Both men were brokers in the business of political power, a world in which respect and admiration were accorded to the successful, and higher principle counted for very little. It was, in sum a relationship of mutual respect in which each regarded the other as a worthy opponent. Nothing could be further from the truth than the view, which Churchill himself did little to discourage, that the two were always in implacable opposition.

[3] Eden's statement is considerably more revealing than that given in his memoirs where he said simply; "I looked forward to working with a Prime Minister who would give his Foreign Secretary energetic backing . . ."

to achieve some relaxation of tension. . . ." Leslie Hore-Belisha, the then minister of transport and future secretary of state for war, also apparently looked forward to the new Government.[4] It is therefore quite clear that many of the Tory leaders who were later to be identified with an anti-appeasement position were eagerly awaiting the formation of a Chamberlain Government. Certainly a major reason for their support of Chamberlain lay in the widespread dissatisfaction with Stanley Baldwin and the conviction that Chamberlain had to be an improvement. Yet it is equally clear that no one, certainly not the Tory leadership, had a clear sense that attempting to appease Germany would end as disastrously as it in fact did.

On their part, the Opposition realized that they had a worthy opponent. Attlee said, "We know well the ability of the new Prime Minister and the sharpness of his weapons in debate." Sinclair declared, "We on these benches see in him an adversary whom we shall not make the foolish mistake of underrating." Yet from Chamberlain's perspective, the Tory mandate was unassailable and therefore he could regard the views of the Opposition with indifference and no small measure of contempt. In fact, until the fall of Chamberlain's Government in 1940, and particularly with regard to foreign policy, one would be hard put to find a single instance of Chamberlain's having seriously considered Opposition views in making any important decision.

In responding to his election as head of the Tory party, Chamberlain made what, for him, was a rare display of public emotion.

> I know you will forgive a personal note if I say that ever since Friday last my thoughts have reverted continually to my father and my brother. Both of them had qualifications far greater than I have for the highest Ministerial office. Both of them might have attained it if it had not been that, by the chances of political fortune, they had to choose between their natural ambitions and national interests which seemed to them to be paramount. I look upon my position to-day as the continuation—perhaps I may say the consummation—of their life work, and it has therefore been a matter of the keenest satisfaction to me that my election should have been proposed by two men [Derby and Churchill] for both of whom I have long entertained the highest respect and admiration and of whom I would like particularly to remember to-day that each of them began his political career with strong interest and approval of my father, and each of them subsequently became the personal friend of my brother until the date of his death.

To his sisters, Chamberlain wrote of his feeling that he was assuming an office which rightfully should have gone to either Austen or his father,

---

[4]Referring to an interview with Hore-Belisha, Crozier noted, "I got the impression as a whole that Hore-Belisha was looking forward to Neville's Premiership and that a comparatively good time might be coming under such a Premier for Ministers with comparatively liberal and radical ideas of policy."

an office which had been denied them only because of chance and the fact that both had put duty ahead of career. He added that the premiership had come to him without the slightest effort on his own behalf since he had always sought what was best for the country over personal ambition and had made no important political enemies. Chamberlain said that his accession was a tribute which would have given his father and Austen unlimited gratification and satisfaction. Recalling the long and bitter battle by which Chamberlain had risen from the obscurity of Andros and his defeat as minister of national service, his comment about having done nothing to advance his own cause appears incredible. Certainly, Chamberlain hated the kind of unctuous groveling for power he saw around him, but he himself was hardly a passive recipient of the call to high office and political power.

Chamberlain's duplicity was well illustrated in his treatment of a longtime friend, Leo Amery, who he said had paid him a visit to announce quite baldly which of the high offices he would be willing to assume if asked. Chamberlain wrote that he had absolutely no idea how people could behave in such a self-aggrandizing manner. Amery was deeply offended by a letter to him in which Chamberlain had written that he was sorry if Amery was upset at not having been asked to join the Government but that he really had to accept the fact that there would never be enough political plums to go around. Amery wrote back that he was indeed deeply offended, although not for the reason Chamberlain had indicated. Amery protested that he had not come to Chamberlain hat in hand seeking office and that to grovel at Chamberlain's feet was beneath his dignity. This incident was all too typical of the high-handed manner in which Chamberlain dealt with his colleagues.[5]

Chamberlain understood the infinitely complex structure of political power to a degree that few of his contemporaries could equal. He knew full well which faction within the Government could be safely ignored and which groups had to be included in his calculations. It was a familiar script and he knew all the lines by heart. Therefore the politics of Cabinet-making presented no very difficult dilemma and he was soon able to report that the transition had taken place without incident and that the press had correctly given him full credit for the most rapid and efficient transfer of power in modern British history.

Aside from the problem arising from Walter Runciman's disappointment with being offered no higher post than the sinecure of Privy Seal,[6]

[5]It should, however, be noted that the incident did not lead to a break in relations between the two men and Amery continued to write Chamberlain letters in which, among other things, he was one of the few people who urged Chamberlain to take action on behalf of European Jewry.

[6]Runciman was then president of the Board of Trade. Chamberlain suspected that Runciman's irritation was really nothing more than Mrs. Runciman's ambitions for her husband and her envy of the Simons. John Simon had been given the Exchequer and as a result would occupy the official residence at No. 11 Downing Street.

the only real problem Chamberlain saw in forming his Government was with the Defence Ministries. He wanted to leave Hoare at the Admiralty, but he felt that his insatiable appetite for power precluded that option and Hoare was made home secretary instead. Chamberlain felt that Duff Cooper had been a failure at the War Office, and that he should be replaced, because in the years to come, important decisions would be made in that department, decisions which would require diligence and great resolve. To date, Duff Cooper had shown himself to be indolent and incapable of handling the really important issues. On the question of the role of the army he had been both excessively rigid and politically inept.[7] Whatever validity there may have been in Chamberlain's stated view of Duff Cooper as incompetent, there is little doubt that the latter expected to be purged and that he was astonished at being offered the Admiralty.

By Chamberlain's own reckoning the change did not make sense. If Duff Cooper was indeed incompetent why was he given the important post as head of the Admiralty? Given the fact that it was Duff Cooper who had pushed for re-equipment of the territorial army and that Chamberlain was implacably opposed to the idea of a continental army, it seems reasonable to conclude that Duff Cooper was removed from the War Office not because of incompetence but because the future role of the army had not been fully decided. Chamberlain knew he could not control Duff Cooper nor exclude him altogether from high office.

The new Minister of War, Leslie Hore-Belisha, was a man who, by his own admission, knew nothing at all about the army. Nevertheless, he was a strong figure whom Chamberlain installed in office specifically because he knew that Hore-Belisha would institute the reforms he, Chamberlain, wanted. Thus was the new Government formed.

In no sense did the composition of the new Government mark a dramatic departure from the old. It primarily was a reshuffle of the same old cards. But those changes which were made were specifically designed to move men whom Chamberlain knew he could control to the center of political power.[8] Men like Samuel Hoare, the new home secretary, and John Simon, the chancellor of the Exchequer, were battle-worn veterans of years of political warfare. Each had learned his lessons well, and each was something of a sycophant. It was a Government in which, as the historian Keith Middlemas, has said, "It became more dangerous to be a heretic within the group like Eden than an infidel like Churchill outside." The new Cabinet was one in which the infidels were never even considered for appointment, and those heretics who were included would eventually be purged.

---

[7] For a discussion of the differences that had arisen between the two men, see pp. 64–66 *supra*.

[8] Swinton, for example, reported that Chamberlain once said that it "amused" him to "find a new policy for each of my colleagues in turn."

Chamberlain surrounded himself with a small cadre of like-minded men, whose personal loyalty to the new prime minister was beyond question. Men like John Simon, Samuel Hoare, and Horace Wilson (the chief industrial adviser to the Government) were alike in that the world they knew most intimately was one in which power was the major currency and personal ambition the single most important motivating force. In his diary, Chamberlain stated that his intention for this inner group was that they would be a kind of Inner Cabinet on policy questions. Had they not been in complete agreement as to the form and substance of British policy, this inner group might have served as a mechanism for the articulation of policy alternatives. As it was, their major function was as an instrument of control, a means by which Chamberlain exerted his personal hold over the Government. Foreign policy in particular was Chamberlain's policy, and the Cabinet was for the most part his obedient servant.

Individually, the members of the Chamberlain Cabinet may not have been distinguished by their independence of mind, but neither were they men of obvious incompetence. In no sense were they men of vision with architectonic plans for solving the nation's problems. For the most part, they were old men who had reached the peak of their careers and knew it. It was to be a Cabinet of administrators who would serve as an extension of the prime minister's power. "Chamberlain made it quickly clear that he intended to be master of his Cabinet," Lord Birkenhead observed, and "there appeared in [him] when crossed, a streak of ruthlessness . . . and an autocratic tendency which led him to exercise an iron control over his Cabinet."

ITALIAN INITIATIVES

With the exception of his ill-fated national defense contribution, Chamberlain viewed his first months as prime minister with calm satisfaction. Of the Imperial Conference of June 1937, he reported that he was convinced that he had been largely responsible for the rising sense of international confidence. On the domestic political scene, he felt things to be well under control, that the by-elections had gone very well indeed, that morale had been restored in the party, and that anticipated problems in the Commons seemed to vanish into thin air. His junior colleagues were doing quite well and the senior Cabinet ministers were showing a new resolve which had been widely acclaimed. He savored his newfound stature and clearly relished the prestige and power of high office. Of the official country residence at Chequers he said that he was sure that he and his wife would be better tenants than the Baldwins who had not taken much interest in the place. Even his wife was fulfilling the high expectations for which he had married and he wrote that her beauty and social grace were being favorably compared with that of Mrs. Baldwin.

Although the domestic political scene presented little cause for concern, Chamberlain was deeply alarmed by events on the continent. His first parliamentary speech as prime minister reflected this growing concern with the precarious international situation. He compared the current international scene with a mountain pass before an impending avalanche.

> I have read that in high mountains there are sometimes conditions to be found when an incautious move or even a loud exclamation may start an avalanche. This is just the condition in which we are finding ourselves today. I believe, although the snow may be perilously poised, it has not yet begun to move, and if we can all exercise caution, patience and self-restraint, we may yet be able to save the peace of Europe.

The meaning he attached to his metaphor was made clear by his comments on Spain:

> In this Spanish situation there is one peculiar feature which gives it a specially dangerous aspect. That is that to many people looking on from outside, it presents itself as a struggle between two rival systems each of which commands an enthusiastic, even a passionate body of support among its adherents in their respective countries, with the result that supporters of these two rival systems cannot help regarding the issue of the struggle in Spain as a defeat or a victory, as the case may be, for the side to which they are attached. I am not expressing an opinion as to whether that view of the struggle is correct or not, but I say that the fact that it is held constitutes a perpetual danger to the peace of Europe, because, if some country or Government representing one of these two ideas attempts to intervene beyond a certain point, then some other country taking the opposite view may find it difficult, if not impossible to refrain from joining in, and a conflict may be started of which no man can see the end.

Chamberlain believed that an armed conflict anywhere in Europe could not easily be localized and that such conflicts threatened to explode into another European war. German protestations concerning the cruiser *Leipzig* "ought not to be the subject of hostile criticism" since, in the Great War, British naval officers had made similar mistakes. Analogies with the past, in sum, pervaded and informed every aspect of the new prime minister's view of continental affairs.

To a Birmingham audience Chamberlain surveyed the international scene, noting the appearance of "new systems of government" which "differ fundamentally from one another," but insisting that all nations were alike in "the longing which . . . is at the heart of every one of them—namely, to live at peace with its neighbors and to devote its energies and resources to the advancement of the happiness and prosperity of its people." He said that the fundamental lesson he had learned in his long career in politics was that "there is always some common measure of agreement if only we will look for it." His mission as prime minister was to find that "common measure of agreement" and to do it quickly before it was too late. Privately he expressed annoyance with the Germans and Italians for their provocative statements and irresponsible newspaper reporting. Still, he found reason to believe that neither the Italians nor the Germans wanted war and that therefore the British had tempered their actions to avoid any rupture in diplomatic relations. Chamberlain said that if Britain could make her peace with Germany, Mussolini could be safely ignored.

Although Germany was Chamberlain's primary concern, it was with Italy that he saw his first opportunity to make a contribution toward European appeasement. On 21 July, Count Grandi, the Italian ambassador in London, informed Eden that he had a message from Mussolini which he wished to deliver personally to the prime minister. Chamberlain recorded his conviction that Mussolini had no expansionist intentions in the Mediterranean and that the initiative showed his peaceful goals. Yet Chamberlain suspected that there might be more to the Duce's action than met the eye. Both Vansittart and Eden expressed suspicion over Mussolini's motives and warned Chamberlain accordingly.

The meeting between Chamberlain and Grandi took place on 27 July. Mussolini, as it turned out, wanted *de jure* recognition of the Abyssinian conquest and, as Chamberlain reported the meeting to Eden, the Italians were "frightened out of their wits" by the British naval build-up in the Mediterranean. Although no record of their conversations was made, Chamberlain apparently did what he could to reassure Grandi that Britain had no aggressive intentions toward Italy and went on to suggest the unusual step of writing a personal note to Mussolini. Grandi felt that this would be useful, and Chamberlain promptly sat down and wrote the letter in which he talked of his own happy holidays in Italy, expressed his regrets at never having met Mussolini personally, and noted that Austen had talked of Mussolini "with the highest regard" saying he was "a good man to do business with." Chamberlain wrote:

> Since I became Prime Minister I have been distressed to find that the relations between Italy and Great Britain are still far from the old feeling of mutual confidence and affection which lasted for many years. In spite of the bitterness which arose out of the Abyssinian affair I believe it is possible for these old feelings to be restored, if we can only clear away some of the misunderstandings and unfounded suspicions which cloud our trust in one another.

Chamberlain concluded by expressing his readiness "at any time to enter upon conversations with a view to clarifying the whole situation and removing all causes of suspicion and misunderstanding."

The seemingly spontaneous nature of Chamberlain's actions masked the fact that the letter was part of a carefully designed plan to circumvent Eden and the Foreign Office experts. Privately, Chamberlain wrote that the letter merely appeared to be an idea of the moment when in fact he had known all along that he would write it. He thought that Grandi would be greatly impressed that a British prime minister could write such a letter without first seeking the advice of colleagues. In fact, Chamberlain reported, the letter had had the desired effect and he had heard that Grandi was thrilled and had said that the two year period of animosity between their two countries was now at an end. Chamberlain thought that his two-pronged approach of conciliation and rearmament would be successful if only the Foreign Office would cooperate. He saw signs that the bureaucrats were envious and that while this was to be expected, he had no intention of alienating his foreign secretary.[9]

Indeed, the Foreign Office had every reason to be annoyed, not just because of a question of credit for foreign policy achievements, but because their entire position based on a much more cautious attitude toward opening talks with Italy had been undermined. Later, in February of 1938, Chamberlain admitted that he had not shown his letter to Eden because he felt that Eden would object.[10]

In August, Chamberlain reported that Halifax, who was taking Eden's place while the latter was away on holiday, was completely in accord with Chamberlain's views and that Halifax had told him the Foreign Office was now willing to cooperate. This was good news, but Chamberlain wrote that he was certain that if left to themselves the Foreign Office functionaries would miss the opportunity to improve relations with Italy. It is certainly possible that even by this early date, Chamberlain had realized that Halifax would make a much more loyal servant at the Foreign Office than the more independently minded Eden. Clearly, Chamberlain believed that his conversations with Grandi and letter to Mussolini had produced a most salutary effect. He said that as he reviewed recent events he was certain that there had been an easing of political tension in Europe as a result of the Grandi meeting and that Grandi himself was willing to give Chamberlain all the credit for this

[9] In fact, the original letter contains an interesting parapraxis. Chamberlain ended with a comment that he would try not to put Eden in the "foreground" again when he obviously intended the opposite. Thus Chamberlain betrayed his real wishes for the foreign secretary.

[10] Eden said that he had made no difficulty at the time, "thinking that there was no deliberate intent to by-pass me as Foreign Secretary, but that it was merely a slip by a Prime Minister new to international affairs." In this he admitted he was mistaken. Almost forty years later Eden would remember this incident as the beginning of his rift with Chamberlain.

development. It gave one a fantastic sense of power, Chamberlain remarked, that at the Exchequer he had hardly been able to accomplish anything and now he had only to give the word and he could alter the entire course of European history. It was, one must admit, a slightly grandiose view of the power of the British prime minister.

While Parliament was in recess and Eden away from London, Chamberlain worked behind the scenes to clear the way for formal *de jure* recognition of Italian sovereignty over Abyssinia. He had decided, according to a letter to his sister, that Britain should grant such recognition immediately if they expected to reap any political returns from the Italians. Chamberlain wrote that according to Lord Perth, Britain's ambassador in Rome, the letter to Mussolini had created a powerful effect on the Italians. Chamberlain was convinced that if appropriate measures were now taken by Britain, Anglo-Italian affairs could be put on an entirely new basis and that if this happened, Britain would have taken the first important step toward the appeasement of Europe.

The Role of the Army

To accomplish his foreign policy goals, Chamberlain first needed to consolidate his control over those domestic political issues which governed Britain's capability to play a role in the international arena. It was therefore necessary that he first gain control over the rearmament effort and, secondly, achieve a resolution of the long-standing question of the army's role in a future continental war.

The groundwork for achieving the first of these goals was laid during Chamberlain's tenure at the Exchequer. To insure that the principle of fiscal stability should govern the rate and degree of rearmament, Chamberlain had devised the principle of a rationed budget. It was a radically new procedure whereby each of the services would be given a fixed total for rearmament expenditure and would be forbidden to exceed that amount. The proposal was submitted on Chamberlain's behalf to the Cabinet by Sir John Simon, the new chancellor of the Exchequer. Chamberlain explained to the Cabinet the intent of Simon's proposal.

> He had in mind . . . that it would be necessary to arrive first at a global total of the expenditure contemplated by all the Defence Services, including Air Raid Precautions. The next stage would be to obtain from the Treasury some idea as to the amount that could be spent. The comparison between the two figures, he had thought, might then be made by the Defence Policy and Requirements Committee. Probably a discrepancy would arise as to how the available money was to be subdivided between the various departments. . . . Then each Government Department concerned would have to say for itself which items within its own estimates could be reduced.

Meekly, the Cabinet accepted this new procedure with only a whimper of protest. While it was not formally adopted until February of 1938, the acceptance of the principle of rationing meant that a fixed limit would be imposed on military spending by the Treasury. Since Chamberlain's control over Simon was beyond question, the prime minister had, in a single blow, established his personal control over the rate of rearmament.

The issue of achieving a final definition of the role of the army was much more difficult. Chamberlain reported that he was particularly pleased at the performance of Hore-Belisha, whom he had sent to the War Office, on the express grounds that he wished to see "drastic changes" made.[11] By the beginning of August 1937, he was able to report to his sisters that Hore-Belisha was accomplishing exactly what he had intended and that he had already gone a long way toward shaking things up in the War Ministry. But, Chamberlain reported, the War Office was in a far worse state than he had previously believed and he was sure that a major battle lay ahead before the ministry could be rebuilt on a more solid basis. The stubborn persistence of the army leadership in sticking to archaic ideas was burdensome but Chamberlain said that he was confident that Hore-Belisha would succeed in his program of reform. With a flair for public relations, the ebullient Hore-Belisha had in fact succeeded in making reforms in an army wedded to tradition and firmly opposed to doctrines of modern strategy.[12]

Chamberlain's support for the new secretary of war was not simply a desire to minimize the army's role in any future war, but was in part based on sympathy with the new strategic doctrines propounded by Captain Liddell Hart. On 29 October, Chamberlain wrote Hore-Belisha recommending that the latter read the chapter on the "Role of the British Army" in Liddell Hart's new book, *Europe in Arms*.[13] Chamberlain was deeply impreseed by Liddell Hart's analysis and wrote to the latter congratulating him on the book, "I am quite sure we shall never again send to the Continent an Army on the scale of that which we put into the field in the Great War." Two days later Hore-Belisha reported that he had read the indicated chapter and that he was greatly taken with

[11] R. J. Minney, the editor of Hore-Belisha's papers, says that Hore-Belisha owed his appointment as minister of transport in 1934 to Chamberlain's commendation. When Chamberlain promoted Hore-Belisha to the War Office, Chamberlain had made it clear that he expected to work closely with his new minister and take an active part in the decisions of the Ministry.

[12] In the early months of his tenure at the War Office, Hore-Belisha succeeded in instituting measures to professionalize the army, in upgrading living conditions thereby improving recruitment, in upgrading the territorial army to a status of equality with the regular army, and in promoting Gort, a proponent of modernization to replace Deedes as military secretary.

[13] Liddell Hart's analysis was a specific attempt to assimilate the lessons of the last war. He concluded: "The haphazard way in which Britain's part in the continental land struggle, with its exhausting demands, was determined in August 1914, should be a warning to this generation. Today, owing to technical and tactical conditions, the dispatch of a field army to the Continent does not seem to offer any promise of effect adequate to the risks involved."

Liddell Hart's strategic ideas. Believing as he did that a repetition of the Great War with a million-man British army on the continent was the contingency he most wanted to avoid, Chamberlain found in Liddell Hart, with his ideas on mechanized war, an unlikely but nevertheless useful ally. It was a community of interests based on the belief, shared by both men, that the 1914-scale continental army must not be reconstituted.[14]

In November of 1937, this new alliance bore fruit in what was to be the culmination of the as yet unresolved debate over the role of the army in a future war. On 12 October, Chamberlain wrote to Hore-Belisha asking him to "put down on a half sheet of note paper the main reforms which you consider necessary, but which require a personality outside the service to cope with them." Hore-Belisha and Liddell Hart at once began preparing a memorandum on the role of the army for submission to the prime minister. Liddell Hart later recalled:

> The Prime Minister had made it clear that the needs of Home and Imperial defence must receive first consideration. He had also emphasized that any proposals must be kept within the financial limits of the current programme, and in aiming to increase efficiency should seek ways of saving money wherever possible. . . . I had therefore to work within these limits.

Significantly, both Liddell Hart and Hore-Belisha accepted Chamberlain's priorities as given and sought to formulate their own recommendations on that basis.

The result of the Hore-Belisha/Liddell Hart consultations was a memo submitted to Chamberlain on 1 November which called for:

> 1. The elimination of the 1914–18 mentality, which consists in regarding the whole role for which the army is prepared as a repetition of the task in the last war.
> 2. The elimination of the attitude towards any new development such as mechanisation and Anti-Aircraft Defence, as taking away money needed for the new 1914–18 Army.

The secretary concluded by listing his grievances with what he regarded as the archaic and reactionary character of the existing army structure.[15]

Chamberlain was apparently delighted with Hore-Belisha's proposals saying, "Now we can get on." On his part, Hore-Belisha believed that he had Chamberlain's complete backing and support to proceed with further reforms. The principal obstacle to such reforms was Deverell, the Chief of the Imperial General Staff, and a man who many

---

[14] Liddell Hart and his associates probably did not realize the degree to which Chamberlain wanted to pare down the expeditionary force to virtual nonexistence.

[15] It should be noted that Hore-Belisha had served from 1915–17 as an officer in the British army in France. Like Chamberlain, his views were permeated with analogies from the Great War.

believed to be of limited and outmoded views. On 24 November, Hore-Belisha spoke to Chamberlain about the necessity of replacing the CIGS with a man better suited to the new conception of the army's role. Chamberlain noted, ". . . that means I have to choose between the secretary of state and the CIGS. There isn't much doubt which I prefer." It was therefore with the prime minister's full support and encouragement that Hore-Belisha requested and received Deverell's resignation. After the event, Hore-Belisha wrote to Chamberlain, "Now that the cold plunge is over, may I thank you deeply for the support and succor you gave me when I am sure most other men would have quailed."[16]

Chamberlain was no less pleased than Hore-Belisha. The cataclysm at the War Office, he wrote, has created far fewer repercussions than anticipated. He noted that while there would certainly be a lot of mumblings of discontent among the officers, he doubted whether anything would come of it since if the military made public their discontent, Chamberlain was fully prepared to answer in kind. There existed between the prime minister and his secretary of war, a complete agreement on the crucial question of the army's role in a future continental war. In his diary, Hore-Belisha stated, "My view . . . is that our Army should be organised to defend this country and the Empire, that to organise it with a military prepossession in favour of a Continental commitment is wrong." If anything, Hore-Belisha envisaged an even more limited role for the army than did Chamberlain. Together, the two moved to resolve the long-standing debate over the army's role.

On 3 December, the Committee of Imperial Defence presented to the Cabinet a memo entitled "British Relative Strength in the World as of January 1938." The report noted with alarm that with defense commitments extending "from Western Europe through the Mediterranean into the Far East" and given the state of British defense preparations, the country was dangerously overcommitted.

> We cannot foresee the time when our defence forces will be strong enough to safeguard our territory trade and vital interest against Germany, Italy, and Japan simultaneously. We cannot therefore exaggerate the importance from the point of view of Imperial defence of any political or international action that can be taken to reduce the numbers of our potential enemies.

Chamberlain used the occasion to give to the Cabinet one of his periodic lectures on the direction he proposed to give to British foreign policy. Surveying the list of Britain's potential allies, Chamberlain concluded that the possibilities were "not very encouraging." Therefore, Chamberlain told the Cabinet that the current efforts were aimed at

[16] Deverell was replaced by Major-General Lord Gort, a man whom Hore-Belisha believed was "eager for the reform and modernization of the army."

preventing a simultaneous war with Germany, Italy, and Japan. Chamberlain recalled his own efforts at achieving a rapproachement with Japan but felt that, for the moment, Italy offered the greatest possibility for improving relations.

As was his long-standing practice, Chamberlain worked behind the scenes to lay the groundwork for policy initiatives. To his sisters, he revealed that he was engaged in a number of private conversations with Cabinet members in which he presented the strategic dilemmas before the Government. When he had demonstrated to his colleagues that their own ideas were unsatisfactory, the ministers would have no choice but to accept Chamberlain's own point of view. He reported that he would soon bring them all together for deliberations and he was already certain of the result. It is not difficult to reconstruct the intent of these quiet talks; Chamberlain was saying in effect that Britain could not afford to rearm fully in each of the services, that something had to go, and that that something had to be the continental army. It was a carefully orchestrated maneuver, and Inskip was to be the instrument of its execution.

On 22 December, Inskip submitted to the Cabinet a memo entitled "Defence Expenditure in Future Years," a memo which was to become the vehicle by which Chamberlain finally succeeded in imposing on the Government his views on the role of the army. Inskip informed the Cabinet of the alarming costs of rearmament, noted that under current programs of expenditure cost estimates were rapidly being overspent, and recommended that the role of the army be changed. He proposed a new scale of defense priorities under which the first priority would be the defense of Britain; the second, defense of her trade routes; the third, defense of overseas territories and dominions; and last, ". . . our fourth objective, which can only be provided after the other objectives have been met, should be cooperation in the defence of the territories of any allies we may have in war."

This of course was exactly the role for the army which Chamberlain had always wanted. Somewhat surprisingly, Hore-Belisha, whose department was most intimately affected by the Inskip proposal, agreed with the need for a more limited role for the army. The secretary

> acknowledged that the Cabinet had never accepted the whole of the War Office programme for developing a large field force for service in Europe. A Continental expedition was for him last in the list of priorities. The international situation was not, he said, analogous with 1914. He had been impressed with the French Maginot Line which required only 100,000 men to hold it. If Britain was to scrap the idea of an Expeditionary Force, he said, that would encourage France to extend the Maginot Line to the sea.

Chamberlain himself delivered the *coup de grâce* which silenced any nascent opposition to the army's new role when he stressed:

. . . the importance of the maintenance of our economic stability as an essential element in our defensive strength. . . . In [Chamberlain's] view, this was a matter of first importance. It might be that in the next war our enemy would aim at a "knock out" blow, but the evidence before him did not show that that was likely to succeed. If that view is correct, the factor of our staying power must be present in the minds of other Governments as well as of ourselves.

In the light of the arguments presented by Inskip, Hore-Belisha, and the prime minister, the adoption of the new role for the army was a foregone conclusion. All that remained was to determine what troops and resources, if any, would be left over after the first three priorities had been met.

In February 1938, Chamberlain told the CID that the most Britain "could possibly send in any circumstances would be two divisions and that even in regard to that no definite decision could be taken in advance." Chamberlain said that he felt "it was clearly necessary to tell the French of the changed role of the Army." But he wondered "if we could stop there." Simon said that he thought the analogy of 1914 was somewhat misleading, "since in the pre-war staff conversations we had definitely told the French that we would supply an expeditionary force of a certain size."[17] Simon's comment touched off a general discussion over whether, by telling the French of Britain's intention to send even this minimal field force, the Government would be increasing the danger of recreating the situation which had led to the Great War. Chamberlain said, in conclusion "that there was general agreement that, so far as the Army was concerned, all that we would tell the French was that they must not *count* upon any force whatsoever, and that the maximum we could send would be two divisions." The following month, the two-division field force was officially accepted.

THE HALIFAX VISIT

In autumn 1937, Chamberlain saw international politics as a vast menacing web with Germany at its center. Trouble might break out at any time and in any place, and if such conflicts were not localized, the result would inevitably be another world war. Making foreign policy in such circumstances was a deadly game with the highest possible stakes. The appeasement of Europe was the general, if ill-defined, goal, and one had to make initiatives wherever and whenever the opportunity arose. It was not always possible to deal with the problem directly at its

[17] Only Halifax and Eden registered apprehension over this drastic change in British military strategy. Eden felt "some apprehension" over the new strategy but in the end agreed that Inskip's arguments were irresistible. Halifax felt that the best policy would be to keep all options open.

German core and, for the moment, Italy seemed to offer the greatest promise.

Yet coming to terms with Germany had always been Chamberlain's highest priority. Soon after he took office he made an overture in the form of an invitation for Neurath, the German foreign secretary, to visit England. Nothing came of this initiative but Chamberlain, not easily thwarted, was determined to seize the first opportunity for opening contacts with the Germans. In October 1937, an invitation was issued for Halifax, in his capacity as master of the Middleton hounds, to visit Germany for an international hunting and sporting exhibition. In this, Chamberlain believed he saw the long-awaited opportunity to move forward with plans for an Anglo-German détente.[18]

Halifax said that he would accept the invitation only if the foreign secretary approved.[19] Chamberlain learned that when Halifax had consulted Eden and Vansittart the former had been quite pleased and eager that Halifax should accept while the latter had been distinctly apprehensive, believing that Halifax would be asked a lot of difficult and unpleasant questions. Chamberlain was horrified when he learned of the existence of dissension in the Foreign Office over the proposed visit. He wrote to his sister that this was yet another chance about to be missed and that he simply would not allow it to happen. Accordingly, he had called Eden and Halifax together and settled the matter. Halifax would go and that was that. Chamberlain noted that he was now biding his time waiting for the chance to settle his differences with the Foreign Office. Chamberlain told his sisters that he was formulating wide-ranging plans for global appeasement, for controlling the arms race which if unchecked would bring about a world wide holocaust. It might just be possible to frustrate Hitler's aggressive designs.

As Chamberlain saw it, the approach to Germany was an exceedingly delicate business in which the actions and statements of Eden and the Foreign Office had been not at all helpful. In particular, he feared that there was something in the Foreign Office mentality which would not allow those bureaucrats to focus on the really important issues in foreign policy, that they were always distracted by minor details and tempted to make emotional and ill-considered pronouncements.

Particularly galling to Chamberlain was Eden's propensity to give bellicose and threatening warnings to the fascist states, which Chamberlain felt tended to lump Germany and Italy together when Britain's major goal was to keep them apart. Chamberlain was referring to a speech Eden had made at the opening of Parliament. As Chamberlain

[18] That Chamberlain was proceeding on a predetermined plan of his own design was recognized by Samuel Hoare, who said that the "visit was part of Chamberlain's governing plan from which he could not be deflected either by criticism or ridicule."

[19] In his memoirs, Halifax suggests that Eden was more enthusiastic over the visit than he himself was.

was ill with gout, Eden used the occasion to articulate his own view of British policy toward the dictators. Chamberlain was annoyed at what he saw as Eden's deviationist tendencies. He said that Eden's speech was an enormous personal victory but that from Chamberlain's point of view, Eden had made a number of unfortunate references. Unknown to Eden, Chamberlain met privately with Grandi to let him know that in spite of Eden's statement his own attitude was as it always had been.

Eden did not share the prime minister's optimism over the potential offered by the Halifax visit, and felt that if Halifax were asked to go to Berchtesgaden instead of meeting Hitler in Berlin, it might give the impression that Britain was "in pursuit" of Hitler. Nevertheless, the foreign secretary gave his reluctant approval to the proposed visit. Chamberlain eagerly anticipated the visit hoping that Hitler would use Halifax to make official contact with the British. Privately, he noted that he found it difficult to accept the fact that Hitler might pass up such an occasion and that the visit would be a sure sign as to whether Hitler was serious about getting on better terms with Britain.

Eden returned to London from the Brussels Conference and met with Chamberlain on 14 November. In the course of what turned out to be a rather stormy interview, the two men discussed a variety of issues including rearmament, and for the first time aired their differences. Eden recalled that "at the end of some exchanges which became rather sharp, the Prime Minister adjured me to go home and take an aspirin." Eden, chastened by his first confrontation with Chamberlain, wrote a letter of apology saying, "I'm sorry you thought me 'feverish' on the subject of rearmament." Later, Chamberlain wrote to his sister that it was unfortunate that Eden had been away at the Brussels meeting since he had had to struggle for everything he had achieved. He was not sure about Vansittart, never knowing what he thought or what he was saying and to whom. Happily, news of the proposed visit had leaked to the press making it impossible to back out. At that point the major issue of contention had been Halifax's instructions. Chamberlain felt that at least he could be grateful for the fact that he and Halifax were of one mind on these matters and that as a result, he could be certain that Halifax would not commit any indiscretions in his meeting with Hitler.[20] But, Chamberlain wrote, all of this really didn't matter since he was certain that the country was behind him. This was the first expression of an idea which must, by that point have been on Chamberlain's mind; namely, that Halifax made a more loyal executor of the prime minister's will than did Eden.

Halifax, whatever may have been his merits as a statesman and spokesman for the old ruling class, was certainly not at this time *au*

[20]Eden, on the other hand, had specifically ordered Halifax to listen and confined himself to a "warning comment on Austria."

courant on events in Germany and was more than willing to follow Chamberlain's lead. This was clearly indicated in a letter which he wrote to Eden before leaving for Germany. Halifax said that Chamberlain "was very strong that I ought to manage to see Hitler even if it meant going to Berchtergarten [*sic*]—or whatever the place is." Furthermore, on arriving in Berchtesgaden, Halifax actually mistook Hitler for a footman. On his return from the meeting with Hitler, Halifax reported:

> I must say I sometimes feel surprised that they are not more bitter than they are, and I think it must surely go some way to explain why they are so determined, cost them what it may, to place themselves in a position in which other people have to treat them with respect, and I cannot help thinking that this explains in part their willingness to surrender individual liberty for the sake of power.

These were not the words of someone with a profound understanding of the Nazi revolution. Nevertheless, it is hardly surprising that Chamberlain found Halifax a more congenial and pliable servant than Eden.

While Halifax was in Germany, Chamberlain remained at home anxiously awaiting news of the meeting with Hitler. He reported to his sisters that to the best of his knowledge the meeting had been felicitous since it had been disclosed that Neurath had been extended an invitation to visit Britain. Chamberlain had instructed Halifax to issue such an invitation if the initial meeting had gone well. Even before receiving Halifax's report, Chamberlain was convinced that his policy was bearing fruit, and he wrote that there was a relaxation in international tension as a result of the new Anglo-German detente. Chamberlain's perception of "detente" in Anglo-German relations was based on nothing so much as his devout wish that it should be so. It was an arrogance coupled with contempt for the Foreign Office. He ended his letter by saying that he was eager to see Halifax but could do so only after Halifax had paid the obligatory visit to the Foreign Office.

It was virtually unnecessary for Chamberlain to hear Halifax's report, so certain was he of the positive results of the visit. The detente which he saw between Germany and Britain was also, he believed, happening with Italy. To his sisters he reported a conversation with Princess Marie Louise, who reported that Grandi had told her that the British prime minister had brought about a new feeling of goodwill in Italy and that all Europe believed that only Neville Chamberlain could resolve the present international crisis. Rothermere, Chamberlain said, had instructed his newspapers to lend their full support to the only person who could save the peace. Such comments were grist for Chamberlain's mill and he collected them assiduously. These reports were all very useful, he wrote, since they helped convince the public to follow his directions.

Chamberlain felt that the Halifax visit had been an enormous accomplishment since it had helped create the climate in which it would be possible to begin discussing the more practical questions which needed to be resolved in a final settlement of German grievances.[21] Chamberlain was referring to the fact that the Germans had indicated a willingness to discuss a possible colonial settlement. At least from that moment onward, Chamberlain was convinced that a settlement of outstanding colonial claims might serve as a prelude to the discussion of the more important issues of European appeasement. He believed that the Germans wanted Togoland, the Cameroons, and possibly South-West Africa, although they would not demand Tanganyika as well if they could be given an alternative area. With regard to matters closer to home, he noted that he was certain Hitler wanted to control all of Eastern Europe and to maintain a very close relationship with Austria although Chamberlain doubted that this meant an outright annexation of Austria. Really, Hitler only wanted for the Sudeten Germans what the British had wanted for the Uitlanders in the Transvaal.[22] Chamberlain even saw prospects for disarmament and Germany's return to the League. These issues, he thought, constituted an adequate basis for further negotiations although there were certainly a large number of problems yet to be resolved. Chamberlain wrote that, in sum, he saw no reason why he couldn't simply tell Hitler that Britain would not use force to prevent him from accomplishing his goals in Eastern Europe in return for a guarantee that Germany would not use force to achieve them. Here, almost a year before the event, was the justification Chamberlain would use for Munich. He said that he had a very clear notion of how to proceed with Germany although ultimate success would take time and Britain could expect certain inevitable frustrations. He believed that the barriers to success were not insurmountable if only the press and the Commons would play along and allow the delicate negotiations to proceed quietly and at their own pace.

Even before the results of the Halifax visit were known, Chamberlain had decided that the next step must be consultation with France. At the end of November, a meeting with the French ministers duly took place. He discouraged any ideas the French might have had of a British inter-

---

[21] Eden drew very different conclusions when he noted that the Halifax meeting was "without positive results." Hoare, said that "the visit failed to produce any good result." It is difficult to find any account of the meeting which does not substantially support Eden's view. Halifax had even spoken of "possible alterations in the European order which might be destined to come about with the passage of time."

[22] The Uitlanders, or "outlanders" were a group of settlers who had migrated into the Transvaal in search of gold. As such they constituted a minority under the control of the Boer government. It was the British championship of the rights of the outlanders which was the ostensible cause of the Boer War of 1899. Joseph Chamberlain had been chief of the Colonial Office in the Salisbury Government. In this capacity he had often been accused of jingoism which many saw as a major contributing factor to the outbreak of the Boer War. That war was moreover, widely seen as the prelude to the Great War with Germany in 1914. Chamberlain's comparison between the Sudeten Germans in the 1930s and the outlanders in the 1890s was thus for him a natural analogy replete with personal and family meaning.

est in the fate of Czechoslovakia. After the meeting, Chamberlain expressed pleasure with his handling of the French and claimed that he had gained their goodwill through his cautious and methodical handling of the discussions. Chamberlain wanted nothing from the French but their acquiescence in his policy. As long as they showed no sign of taking an independent line, Chamberlain was content to leave matters as they were.

Having assured himself that the French would offer no resistance, he began preparing the way, at home, for new initiatives. He assured the Cabinet that the Halifax visit had shown German willingness to discuss a colonial settlement as a first step toward appeasement. To the House of Commons, he read a communiqué which he privately said pointed the way to an entirely new colonial policy. An examination of this communiqué reveals that Chamberlain had overstated the case.[23] There was nothing to indicate a dramatic departure. Chamberlain wrote privately that his proposal had not been well received in the House and that there were clear indications that he would be allowed to proceed only with the greatest caution. Nevertheless, Chamberlain concluded that the worst obstacles were now behind him and he was well on his way to accomplishing his goals. He believed, or pretended to believe, that he had been given a mandate from Parliament as well as the French to proceed with discussions with Germany.[24] That this was not the case need hardly be stated.

PURGING THE DISSIDENTS

In the autumn of 1937, as important domestic decisions concerning rearmament and the role of the army were being taken, and as initial approaches to Germany were being made, Chamberlain was also eagerly awaiting an opportunity to further the Anglo-Italian detente which he believed had grown out of his initial meetings with Grandi.

He had interrupted his holiday that summer to return to London for the purpose of discussing possible ways of furthering the Italian conversations. He wrote privately that there was, as could be expected, considerable apprehension about the Italian dictator and a reluctance to

---

[23] The relevant part of the communiqué said:

A preliminary examination was made of the colonial question in all its aspects. It was recognised that this question was not one that could be considered in isolation, and moreover would involve a number of other countries. It was agreed that the subject would require much more extended study.

[24] Thus, from Chamberlain's perspective at least, there is little truth in Schwoerer's contention that Chamberlain "made no real effort to deal with the opposition to colonial appeasement or to discuss with other countries the proposal he insisted upon presenting to Hitler." Chamberlain was probably not mistaken in his assumption that domestic politics or French attitudes would present no insuperable obstacles to a colonial settlement if the Germans were willing to play up.

grant formal diplomatic recognition of his claims in Abyssinia. On the other hand, Chamberlain believed that his letter to Mussolini had greatly moved the Italian people and that if he were to be allowed to continue his efforts, considerable progress could be made toward normalizing relations with Italy. If Anglo-Italian relations could be reestablished on an amicable basis, it would be a great step toward the appeasement of Europe. Chamberlain was keeping close tabs on Eden to insure that the Government moved forward the opening of full-scale talks with Italy. In this project he was glad to be able to give Eden a lot of assistance. Although he was displeased by the Foreign Office where there was very little creativity or vision, there was as yet little sign that Chamberlain was aware of a growing rift between himself and the foreign secretary. Eden, he felt, was quite willing to take his advice without complaint but it was really quite tedious constantly having to reeducate the Foreign Office officials and even having to rewrite their communications. Chamberlain wrote that he was very concerned that his work toward restoring Anglo-Italian relations could easily be overturned.

In September, British and French diplomats agreed on naval patrols in the Mediterranean in an effort to end the torpedoing of merchant ships trading with Spain. The Nyon Conference, as it was called, is generally regarded as an Anglo-French diplomatic triumph. Chamberlain claimed it as a great personal victory but he was afraid that the British may have sacrificed improved relations with Italy to achieve it. He realized that Eden had never been convinced of Mussolini's goodwill and that the Italians were certainly not doing their share. As a consequence nothing much could be done at the present time. Chamberlain feared that Eden would represent the conference as a victory over Mussolini and tried to convince the foreign secretary to cancel a scheduled speech to a party rally at the Welsh town of Llandudno. Chamberlain was anxious to open talks with Mussolini as soon as possible, but given the bellicose nature of pronouncements from Rome and given the opposition which existed in the Foreign Office to the opening of such talks, Chamberlain was, for the moment, unable to act. This is how matters stood in the closing months of 1937.

If he was forestalled from acting in the diplomatic sphere, there was nevertheless much he could do to silence his political opposition at home and to consolidate his hold over the Government. Of those who opposed Chamberlain's policy, no one was more articulate and outspoken in his criticism of Nazi Germany than Robert Vansittart, the permanent head of the Foreign Office, a man noted for his virulent criticism of the Nazi regime. In a letter to his sister on 5 December, Chamberlain alluded to his plans for him saying that he had put into effect a secret plan to sabotage Vansittart and that he anticipated the plan would bear fruit before Christmas. To summarily dismiss a man of Vansittart's stature would have been politically unwise, therefore Chamberlain conceived of a plan to "promote" him to a newly created position with unclear and, as it turned out, minimal authority. The following week he was able to boast of his success: after all the time Baldwin had spent trying to get rid of Vansittart, it gave him great pleasure to report that he had done it in only a few days. Of course the public knew nothing of what had happened, but all the same Vansittart was out of action and he had really had no choice in the matter. Eden later wrote that he had himself long desired to replace Vansittart and, in his memoirs, claimed credit for initiating the change.[25] To the public at large it was made to appear as if Vansittart were being elevated to a stature similar to that of Horace Wilson, the chief industrial adviser. Neither Eden nor Vansittart himself apparently realized the degree to which the latter had been elevated into obscurity.[26]

Chamberlain was becoming more and more impatient with a political system in which dissent could be freely expressed. He noted that there was a certain flaw in the political process of democratic countries which demanded that the Government reveal its every intention while the fascist states were under no such restrictions. Dissent from the Opposition was to be expected, but criticism from within his own Government was intolerable. Such was the position of Duff Cooper, whom Chamberlain accused of committing "blazing indiscretions" in his speeches on Spain.[27] This kind of dissent was absolutely intolerable. Chamberlain said that he had written Duff Cooper a letter the likes of which he had probably never seen before, and added that were he in Duff Cooper's place he would offer his resignation in the hopes that it would not be

[25] However, Eden admits that Chamberlain was "insistent" on the change and adds, somewhat defensively, ". . . this of itself would not have been enough if I had not felt that there were other advantages."

[26] It was not until February of the following year, shortly before his resignation, that Eden began to realize what had happened:

It was on February 7th that Vansittart came to see me to report a conversation in which a member of the Cabinet had said that Sir Robert had been "kicked upstairs." This colleague had gone on to say that, from now on, foreign affairs would be run by the Prime Minister, with the help of a small committee, of which the spokesman naturally would be a member, and that if I myself did not fall in with their wishes, I should follow Vansittart pretty soon. One of Sir Robert's friends who was present had written the conversation down and brought it to him. I thought the Prime Minister should know of this, so I told him. He greeted the story with astonishment. I was not reassured.

Eden's source was well informed as to Chamberlain's intentions.

[27] It was an interesting choice of phrase since Chamberlain had used the exact same phrase to describe his own "midsummer of madness" speech in the summer of 1936. It was a telling indication of the degree to which the standards of conduct which Chamberlain applied to himself were becoming divorced from those he applied to others.

It seems likely that Chamberlain was using the occasion to deliver a warning to the secretary against opposing him in the Cabinet discussions on the role of the army which were then in progress. In any event the warning was not lost on Duff Cooper, who meekly responded that he was greatly distressed by his indiscretion and that the like would never happen again.

accepted. Clearly, Chamberlain would not have been disappointed had there been changes at the Admiralty!

ROOSEVELT'S INITIATIVE, EDEN'S RESIGNATION

Progressively and systematically Chamberlain was removing or silencing any colleagues who dared oppose him. As the sources of effective dissent diminished in number, Chamberlain became more and more convinced that he, and he alone, could lead Britain (and the world) through the turbulent diplomatic waters which threatened to engulf the country in yet another world war. His initial overtures, first to Italy and then to Germany had, he believed, produced salutary results; now the task was to keep both sets of negotiations on track.

In this atmosphere of delicately plotted initiatives toward the fascist powers, Chamberlain received on 12 January 1938, a secret message from President Roosevelt delivered through Lindsay, the British ambassador in Washington. Roosevelt asked the British to support an international peace initiative which would be made public on the seventeenth pending British approval. Roosevelt's seemingly innocuous proposal greatly upset Chamberlain who saw it as a political bombshell. Behind Chamberlain's alarm lay a long history of frustration with the Americans whom Chamberlain saw as unreliable and unwilling to cooperate in his plans for European appeasement.

Ever since his days at the Exchequer, and the failure of his attempt to gain American support for an initiative in the Far East,[28] Chamberlain's attitude toward the Americans had been one of scarcely disguised contempt, while at the same time recognizing that a more active American role in the Far East could be useful in relieving pressure on the British in that area.[29] Shortly after becoming prime minister he had discussed the possibility of a personal visit to the United States but declined to go because, as he said, the time was not yet right for such a meeting. In August 1937, he again mentioned the invitation from Roosevelt, but added that it would be a long time before the Yanks would be useful partners in world affairs. Chamberlain said that he had done what he could to encourage them to play their part in the Far East but the American leaders were too intimidated by their own people to be able to play a constructive role. A similar attitude of distrust and contempt can be found in his response to Roosevelt's famous quarantine speech. Cham-

---

[28] See pp. 39–40 *supra*.

[29] For example, in September 1936, referring to a proposed devaluation scheme, Chamberlain had said that Morgenthau had made a complete fool of himself and that he had tried to telephone Chamberlain but that Chamberlain would have nothing to do with such American ineptitude.

The following month he wrote that he was so disgusted with Morgenthau over the recent agreement on monetary affairs that he would not deign to shake the American's hand.

berlain wrote that he had ambivalent feelings about the speech. On the one hand it might be a sign that the Americans were at last willing to assume their responsibilities. But on the other what did Roosevelt really mean by the term "quarantine"? It was not a particularly felicitous term since diseased persons do not usually run around armed to the teeth. As could be expected, the Opposition saw Roosevelt's speech as a sign that the Americans were ready to cooperate in a policy of economic sanctions against Japan. In fact, his critics were about to make the case that it was only the cynical Tory Government which prevented the valiant and high-minded Americans from saving the "Chinks" from Japanese bombs. Citing intelligence reports from Washington, Chamberlain said he was convinced that the Americans were not prepared to undertake any action that was not totally without risk. Britain, he said, could not risk a war with Japan at the present time and he feared that after much high-blown rhetoric the Americans would ultimately back out and leave Britain holding the bag. If the Americans had only followed his lead when he had proposed a joint *démarche,* this whole mess could have been avoided. As it was they were simply jumping in blindly without bothering to consult with anyone. Still Roosevelt's speech was not, in Chamberlain's view, without positive effect since if the fascist powers learned that they could not completely discount the Americans it might cause them to reconsider. It was for that reason only that Chamberlain said he had been willing to play along with Roosevelt, pretending that the American leader's speech was more important than it actually was. But Chamberlain said he was playing his hand close to his chest and making no promises.

Clearly, he was irritated with the Americans for threatening to usurp Britain's and therefore Chamberlain's own leadership position. He wrote to his sisters that a message had been sent to Roosevelt attempting to spell out the consequences of a policy of economic sanctions against Japan. The Yanks had replied that they had never even dreamed of imposing sanctions and that the term "quarantine" was only an idea in the first place. If only the Americans would keep out of it and follow his lead, Chamberlain allowed, the Japs would be forced to compromise.

In the closing months of 1937, Chamberlain continued to hope for American involvement in the Far East. Although he felt one could never depend on the Americans for anything more than rhetoric, he still had some fleeting hope they might take useful action. In January, he noted that he hoped that the Japs would smash a few American heads, but, those "little devils" were too shrewd to make such a mistake and Britain would therefore be forced to act alone hoping the Americans would follow.

Against this background of extreme, and not altogether unwarranted, distrust of the Americans, Chamberlain's response to the latest Roosevelt initiative was not surprising. It was immediate, curt, and negative. He made no effort to consult either Eden or the Foreign Office although he had ample opportunity to do so. His later claim, that because the foreign secretary was then out of the country there was no time to consult him, was patently untrue.[30] On 14 January Chamberlain delivered a reply in which he told Roosevelt of his own efforts toward opening talks with the dictators, expressed concern lest Roosevelt's initiative interfere with these efforts, and asked the president to hold his hand for the moment.

Whatever may have been the considerations which prompted the American president to make such a proposal, it is clear that Roosevelt's offer was something considerably less than what Churchill later called the "proffered hand stretched out across the Atlantic." Chamberlain had solid reasons for concluding that the offer was not an indication of American willingness to take part in European affairs.[31] Yet, regardless of one's views of American reliability, the United States was simply not a power whose actions could be dismissed with such cavalier disdain. In this case at least, Chamberlain's prejudices were in rather clear conflict with the British national interest. His undiplomatic and blunt response was, moreover, an obvious affront to Eden, who had repeatedly and publicly called for closer Anglo-American cooperation.[32]

Why then did Chamberlain deliberately choose to circumvent Eden and the Foreign Office by sending a reply to Roosevelt which he knew full well would not, to say the least, have met with their approval? Evidence in Chamberlain's letters at the time sheds some light on his motives. On 16 January, he stated that in the current state of affairs things were so delicate that he dare not commit his views to paper. On the twenty-third, he talked of strenuous and anxious endeavors to defuse a time bomb which had just crossed the Atlantic. Of his response to Roosevelt he said that he had been successful in preventing an explosion but he was wary of the future. The following week he again noted the need for secrecy and said that the bomb had not yet gone off and

[30] Roosevelt had set a deadline of 17 January for the British response. The message was received on the evening of 11 January and given to Chamberlain on the twelfth. Chamberlain's reply was dated 14 January. By the evening of the fifteenth, Eden had returned to London. On the morning of the sixteenth, he met with Chamberlain at Chequers. There would therefore have been sufficient time to consult Eden before responding had Chamberlain desired to do so.

[31] Hoare cites such incidents as the World Economic Conference in 1933, the Nye Commission, and the Neutrality Acts as Evidence to this effect. Langer and Gleason argue, ". . . there was never any question of approving or supporting [British] specific policy and certainly no thought of assuming any political or military commitment in connection with it."

[32] There is, however, little in the documentary evidence to suggest that Roosevelt was particularly affronted by Chamberlain's actions. In fact, Roosevelt in his response said, "In view of the opinions and considerations advanced by the Prime Minister, I readily agree to defer making the proposal . . . in order that His Majesty's Government may see what progress they can make in beginning the direct negotiations they are contemplating." Eden, on the other hand, quotes Sumner Welles as saying that Chamberlain's response came as "a douche of cold water." Eden himself said: "The growing tendency for confidential Anglo-American discussions on a deteriorating world scene which I had been doing my best to encourage, was clumsily nipped.

that he hoped he could deal with it in such a way that no real damage would be done but that it had nevertheless caused him considerable anxiety. And again on 6 February, he said that the bomb had still not exploded thanks to his own decisive action which had averted a potentially disastrous situation. Now, it seemed that relations among Italy, the United States, and Japan were back on course and would remain so unless the Germans did something to wreck their gradual improvement. At first glance, Chamberlain's attitude of acute alarm seems puzzling given the seemingly innocuous nature of Roosevelt's message. The idea of an international peace conference seems hardly to have been a time bomb.

One possible explanation is that Chamberlain saw the opportunity to rid himself of an increasingly burdensome foreign secretary and realized that the Roosevelt initiative would force a showdown with Eden.[33] Chamberlain must certainly have realized the potential for an explosive rupture in his relations with Eden. And, it is certainly possible that, at least unconsciously, Chamberlain was pushing Eden toward resignation. Yet there is ample evidence for at least one other explanation. At the time of the initiative, Chamberlain had spoken of "poor Anthony," who had been forced to cut short his vacation in France to return home, and expressed his satisfaction that there would now be time for a leisurely discussion with Eden since there were so many things to be discussed. While Chamberlain's insensitivity to Eden's position was indeed staggering, these were hardly the words of a man anticipating a confrontation. In fact, Chamberlain had good reason not to expect trouble from his foreign secretary, who only a few days earlier had written him saying that he realized that there would always be people who would try to magnify the policy differences between prime minister and foreign secretary but that such idle comments could never destroy the close cooperation which had always existed between them. Certainly, Eden's letter did nothing to counter Chamberlain's impression that his foreign secretary was a pliant tool to be used as he saw fit. Chamberlain, with some justification, probably interpreted Eden's letter as a mandate to proceed in foreign affairs along the lines he himself preferred.

Another explanation of Chamberlain's alarm over the Roosevelt initiative might be that Chamberlain believed he saw history repeating itself. Might not Anglo-American collaboration seem to Hitler like the lining up of an opposing power bloc, an attempt at encirclement, just as in the last war? In his diary, Chamberlain wrote that he thought Roosevelt's plan was absurd and likely to incur the scorn of both Ger-

[33]One piece of evidence in support of this view is that Chamberlain had used a similar metaphor to refer to his successful effort to rid himself of Vansittart: "The mines are already laid and will be exploded some time before Christmas." Possibly his use of the term "bomb shell" signaled another such maneuver.

many and Italy. Besides, there was the very real danger that Hitler might see it as another attempt by the democratic bloc to subvert the fascist bloc. Everything possible must, he believed, be done to prevent the division of the civilized world into two mutually antagonistic blocs because this would inevitably lead to war. Chamberlain placed great importance on his own plans for opening talks with Italy, and he no doubt genuinely believed that the Roosevelt initiative threatened future progress in this area. Equally important, however, was Chamberlain's resentment of anything which did not fit in with the mission he felt himself uniquely qualified to perform.

Eden had incurred the prime minister's disfavor by sending his own telegram to Lindsay in an effort to "modify this calamitious sequence of events." A stormy interview followed between Eden and Chamberlain, resulting in a recognition, at least on Eden's part, that fundamental differences existed between himself and the prime minister. So strongly did Eden object to Chamberlain's actions that he talked of resignation. After further discussion in the Foreign Policy Committee of the Cabinet, a compromise was reached between their two positions.[34] On his part, Chamberlain seems to have been strangely unaware of the seriousness of his differences with Eden. As late as 13 February, he deprecated press reports of a serious split between the two, saying that it was all completely untrue and that in fact he and Eden had never been more completely in accord than they were at the present time.[35] Even after Eden's resignation Chamberlain claimed he had not known until the eighteenth, two days before the fact, that there would be an open break between them.

One can only conclude that to Chamberlain the idea that his foreign secretary could hold views different from his own and have the courage, if not the audacity, to act on them was simply inconceivable. Ever since his "midsummer of madness" speech in the summer of 1936, Chamberlain had circumvented Eden's authority, and he quite probably saw no reason why he could not continue to do so. In a highly revealing comment, Swinton recalled:

> . . . looking back over these years I am the more surprised that Anthony never took a firmer line much earlier. Chamberlain knew what he was about in his first exercise in running foreign policy from the Treasury, in his midsummer of madness speech. . . . A man beaten once in politics at this level can be beaten again. Chamberlain knew from that moment that he had the measure of Eden. What could be done once could be repeated with confidence.

[34] Eden said ". . . if the whole business had not been secret, I should have resigned there and then."
[35] The record of Cabinet discussions of the Roosevelt initiative tends to support Chamberlain's assertion of his "complete agreement" with Eden. They reveal no sign of disagreement or at least disagreement of such magnitude as to warrant resignation.

Either Eden had given Chamberlain no clear indication of the depth of their differences or Chamberlain chose to ignore them. There is, as we have seen, evidence for both positions. In either case, the effect was the same; Chamberlain believed that despite certain differences, Eden could be pressed into line.

The question of opening conversations with Italy, the issue which finally led to Eden's resignation, had long been discussed by Eden and Chamberlain and also within the Foreign Office. In these discussions much turned, or seemed to turn, on the question of Britain's granting *de jure* recognition of Italy's conquest of Abyssinia. In general, Chamberlain had expressed willingness to grant recognition as part of a general settlement of Anglo-Italian differences. Yet, in a letter to Halifax, Chamberlain had said, "I do not want to rush any fences or begin any serious conversations until we have thought out as clearly as possible what we are prepared to give and what we want in return," but he felt the end of August or the beginning of September "should be time enough to start the negotiations." He believed "that the possibility of success turned on de jure recognition," and that "we should therefore be prepared to give it now (or say now that we will give it), provided we can get something for it. It is very necessary to remember," he said,

> . . . these Dictators are men of moods. Catch them in the right mood and they will give you anything you ask for. But if the mood changes they may shut up like an oyster. The moral of which is that we must make Mussolini feel that things are moving all the time.

At one point, Chamberlain raised the question of whether or not any agreement made with Mussolini could be trusted, but he dismissed it quickly saying, ". . . there is nothing in this argument."

Eden, on the other hand, generally tended to take a more cautious view of the recognition question.[36] However, the differences between Eden and Chamberlain over the question of recognition were not as substantial as those which existed over the question of timing, or the issue of whether talks should be opened at all. Because Roosevelt, in

[36] The real differences between the two on this point are easily exaggerated. The Foreign Office (in what was referred to as Plan A) wished to use recognition as a bargaining counter to gain concrete concessions in the Mediterranean. Eden objected to this, preferring his own (Plan B) under which Britain would "grant de jure recognition on its merits, while accompanying our measures which would be calculated to improve our tactical position vis a vis Italy, while at the same time opening the way to Anglo Italian conversations." Chamberlain found neither Plan A nor Plan B acceptable, preferring to give recognition as part of a general settlement of all outstanding differences. In this as in other areas, Eden evidently accepted Chamberlain's view and at the end of January told the French that "Great Britain . . . could only grant de jure recognition of the conquest of Abyssinia as part of a general settlement, . . ." Chamberlain's plan was to proceed simultaneously with both Germany and Italy toward a general settlement. Eden felt that ". . . there seems to be a certain difference between Italian and German positions in that an agreement with the latter might have a chance of a reasonable life, especially if Hitler's own position were engaged, whereas Mussolini is, I fear, the complete gangster and his pledged word means nothing."

responding to Chamberlain's letter, had indicated American disap-
proval of granting *de jure* recognition, and because precisely at that time
Chamberlain indicated his intention of proceeding with talks, the
Chamberlain-Eden differences were forced into the open.

The Italians were well aware of these differences and skillfully did
everything possible to strengthen Chamberlain's hand against Eden.
Privately, they communicated to Chamberlain an eagerness to begin
conversations at once. One of the ways this was achieved was through
Chamberlain's sister-in-law, Ivy Chamberlain, who was then in Rome.
Lady Chamberlain, apparently on her own initiative, showed Count
Ciano, the Italian foreign minister, a letter she had received from Neville
indicating the latter's eagerness to open talks. The highly irregular nature
of this interchange can hardly be understated. Here was the sister-in-
law of a British prime minister openly wearing the fascist badge and
discussing the most important diplomatic issues without either the
knowledge or the consent of the British Foreign Office but with the full
support of her brother-in-law, the prime minister. Ciano's positive
response was communicated through Lady Chamberlain to Neville, who
again responded with a letter which Lady Chamberlain and Count Ciano
took directly to the Duce himself. The letter indicated Chamberlain's
willingness to grant *de jure* recognition of the Abyssinian conquest and
an eagerness to open full-scale Anglo-Italian conversations by the end
of the month. Mussolini's reactions were "definitely favourable" and
the Duce dictated a letter to Ivy to be delivered to Chamberlain. Such
unprecedented meddling by the prime minister forced Eden to write to
Chamberlain in protest, ". . . without wishing to be unduly punctil-
ious," he wrote, "I am sure you will understand that this kind of unof-
ficial diplomacy does place me in a most difficult position."
Chamberlain, for once realizing he had gone too far, wrote Eden a letter
of apology but was careful to add, "I don't really think however that
she has done any harm."[37]

It is unnecessary to describe the final sequence of events leading up
to Eden's resignation. The die had long been cast. The relationship
between Chamberlain, a model of Victorian propriety, and Eden, Britain's Beau Brummell, had always been one of paternalism rather than
collaboration. Grievances piled one upon the other so that, despite a
mutual desire to preserve the external trappings of harmony and institutional respectability, an open break was impossible to avoid. Their

---

[37] Although Eden claimed he had no knowledge of their existence, Chamberlain was apparently
using, through Horace Wilson, Sir Joseph Ball as a secret intermediary between himself and the Italian
Embassy. In his memoirs, Eden presented material from Ciano's diary and elsewhere in describing
the nature of these contacts. Eden claimed that Ciano had given an account which greatly exaggerated
their importance. The substantive importance of the message conveyed by Ball is less significant than
the existence itself of this secret link, which was yet another indication of the lengths to which Chamberlain would go to achieve his ends.

differences were brought before the Cabinet where it soon became abundantly clear that, almost to a man, the Government stood solidly behind the prime minister. Attempts were made to paper over the differences, but it was clear to Eden that the prime minister wished him to go and he did.[38]

The evidence concerning Eden's resignation is confused and in part inconclusive. It is possible, as some historians have argued, that Chamberlain meant to replace Eden from the start. However, the evidence from Chamberlain's private papers indicates that Chamberlain was surprised and even shocked on learning that Eden felt their differences to be so serious as to warrant his resignation. It would appear that Chamberlain's protestations of shock and dismay were genuine. Certainly he was aware of differences, even fundamental differences, between himself and his foreign secretary, but past experience led him to believe that Eden could quite easily be pushed into line. Nothing in Eden's prior behavior indicated to Chamberlain that he was anything but a pliant executor of Chamberlain's will.

Chamberlain had progressively undercut Eden's authority from the very beginning, until, in the end, Eden had no ground on which to stand. In terms of major issues of British foreign policy, Eden had virtually no independent authority left. Certainly he had never shared Chamberlain's enthusiasm for negotiated agreements with the dictators but, in the end he had always bowed to the prime minister's will. Even if Chamberlain with his attention focused narrowly on his particular policy was unaware of the depth of Eden's opposition, the latter did less than he could have to educate the prime minister or to drive home his opposition in a language which Chamberlain would have understood. In sum, Eden's mythical reputation, retrospectively acquired as a symbol of resistance to appeasement, is, at least in part, ill-deserved.[39]

While much could be added to this account of the initial months of the Chamberlain Government and the prime minister's steadily increasing control over that Government, enough has been said to indicate the measure of the man and the goals he sought to achieve. As if by predetermined plan, Chamberlain had succeeded in eliminating one by one the obstacles which stood between him and the realization of his paramount goal of the appeasement of Europe. Within months after

[38] David Carlton, in his recent biography of Eden, quotes a letter from Malcolm MacDonald. The latter had been asked by Chamberlain to intercede with Eden at the last moment to prevent him from resigning. In MacDonald's view the decisive reason for Eden's decision to resign was his poor health and mental exhaustion.

Confusion over the meaning of Eden's resignation has arisen, in part, because in the Cabinet Chamberlain said, ". . . there was not a fundamental difference of policy," between them, and Eden said he ". . . did not think that the differences between the Prime Minister and himself were fundamental, but were differences in outlook and method."

[39] Maurice Hankey, for one, believed that Chamberlain had been "incredibly patient—much too patient . . ." in his handling of Eden.

taking office, Chamberlain had gained control over both the scope and the scale of rearmament. He had eliminated those within the Government who would oppose him, and he had made the initial overtures toward Germany and Italy on which so much depended. Now, with Eden safely out of the way, the road was open for further contacts. If only Germany or Italy would give some positive sign of their willingness to negotiate, everything could be achieved.

ℵ5ℵ

The Anschluss and Beyond

Eden's resignation was an enormous relief to Chamberlain as if he had been freed of an unwanted encumbrance. Eden had become a nagging annoyance and a constant reminder of things Chamberlain preferred not to think about. Now that the last authoritative nucleus of opposition had been eliminated, Chamberlain saw before him an opportunity to move toward the appeasement of Europe, an opportunity which might not occur again. It was during this period that Chamberlain began to move resolutely into a fantasy world of his own creation, a world in which the slightest sign of German interest became a positive response to a British initiative. Anglo-German relations were rapidly entering an arena in which hubris faced villainy on equal terms. Nothing else mattered.

With an almost audible sigh of relief, Chamberlain noted that he felt relieved of a powerful burden and that he was heartened by the fact that the Cabinet, the House of Commons and finally, the entire nation had supported his position. While he had suffered the scorn of a growing number of political enemies, he had also received the loyal support of his personal allies. The enemies, he felt, were not to be taken seriously and his colleagues were clearly prepared to close ranks in support of their leader. Chamberlain wrote to his sisters that he harbored no doubts whatsoever since the time was ripe if a second world war was to be avoided. Chamberlain was expressing a fundamental conviction on which much of his subsequent policy was predicated: history must not be allowed to repeat itself, another Great War must be averted at all costs.

For the moment, so great was his power that the history of British foreign policy and the history of Chamberlain's views on that policy were one. Yet even as his control over the machinery of government approached an absolute limit, seeds of opposition were taking root. As if by a predetermined dialectical process, an alternative policy based on a grand alliance against fascism was beginning to flourish. Yet not until 1940 with the fall of Chamberlain's Government did the new policy finally supplant the old. In the meantime, Chamberlain's power was supreme, and he used it with a vengeance in pursuit of pre-established goals.

An Overture to Germany

Chamberlain believed that the Halifax visit had shown Germany's interest in a settlement of colonial questions. Moreover, he believed that ". . . the Colonial question was in German eyes the only outstanding problem remaining between the two countries." Whereas before, Germany had demanded the return of all her prewar African colonies, now the Germans indicated a willingness to accept compensation elsewhere in Africa for the loss of Tanganyika. Chamberlain believed this to be a "surprising" and hopeful sign of change in German policy.[1] If the Germans were interested in discussing colonies, Britain should not be caught unprepared; accordingly, Chamberlain began preparing a plan for the settlement of Anglo-German differences in Africa. He proposed to the Foreign Policy Committee[2] that the issue be treated not as a question of whether or not to return Germany's colonies, but rather as "the opening of an entirely new chapter in the history of African colonial development to be introduced and accepted by the general agreement of the powers interested in Africa."

> The new concept would be based on the complete equality of the Powers concerned and of their all being subjected to certain limitations in regard to the African territories to be administered by them under the scheme. Germany could be brought into the arrangement by becoming one of the African Colonial Powers in question and by being given certain territories to administer. His idea was that two lines should be drawn across Africa, the northern line running roughly to the south of the Sahara, the Anglo-Egyptian Sudan, Abyssinia and Italian Somaliland, and the southern line running roughly to the south of Portuguese East Africa. There should be general agreement among the Powers concerned that all the territories

[1] Willingness to discuss the colonial question was, it should be noted, a departure from Chamberlain's (and the Government's) view of long standing that H.M.G. was not prepared to discuss the transfer of mandated territories. In March 1937, Chamberlain said that he "would not be prepared to have discussions if the return of the Cameroons and Togoland merely represented Germany's initial demands and that these would be followed by other and evergrowing demands." His change in attitude was, no doubt, a result of the Halifax visit and what Chamberlain liked to believe was a new German willingness to negotiate.

[2] The Foreign Policy Committee was formed after the remilitarization of the Rhineland in 1936. In 1938, it was composed of Chamberlain, Halifax, Hoare, and Simon, plus Dominions Secretary Malcolm MacDonald, Minister for Coordination of Defence Inskip, Lord Chancellor Hailsham, Minister of Colonies Ormsby Gore, and Stanley, secretary of the Board of Trade, with Hankey as secretary of the Committee. The Committee met regularly until July 1937 after which it lapsed until its revival in January 1938 shortly before the Munich crisis. Chamberlain used the Committee as a forum for testing new policy initiatives before such issues were discussed in the larger Cabinet.

between the two lines should be subjected to the proposed new rules and
regulations covering the administration of the territories.

It was one among many such initiatives which Chamberlain would
eventually propose in an effort to open discussions with the Germans.
As had been the case so often in the past, Chamberlain was able to carry
the day because he was the one man with a definite plan which he
presented at the outset of deliberations and which served as the basis
for discussion. Because no one else had a clearly articulated alternative,
his views often prevailed by default.

With the acquiescence of the Foreign Policy Committee, Chamberlain
moved forward by recalling the British ambassador to Berlin and
instructing him to attempt a meeting with Hitler in order to discover if
the German dictator was interested in a broad agreement on all outstanding differences between their two countries. The Ambassador,
Nevile Henderson, was a man ideally suited to Chamberlain's purposes, a man seemingly unable to distinguish between his role as chief
collector of intelligence and his self-proclaimed mission as chief apolo-
gist for the Nazi regime. In his memoirs, Henderson recalled that he
had been told "to inform Hitler that His Majesty's Government would
be ready, in principle, to discuss all outstanding questions." The
ambassador returned to Berlin on 4 February but was unable to meet
with Hitler until 3 March because of the political turmoil arising from
the Blomberg marriage.[3] When the meeting eventually did take place,
Henderson found Hitler in a fit of hysterics from which came one clear
message beyond Hitler's usual diatribe on the evils of the British press
and demands with respect to Austria and Czechoslovakia: ". . . it was
clearly not colonies which interested Hitler" and that this matter "could
wait for 4, 6, 8 or even 10 years." Hitler was, in sum, firmly and unequivocally declining to accept the proffered hand.

This overture to Germany occurred simultaneously with those directed
toward Italy in line with Chamberlain's plan to proceed with both powers at once. Whereas the approach to Italy had been a matter of considerable Cabinet discussion, particularly at the time of Eden's resignation,
the plan for a colonial settlement with Germany was disclosed to the
full Cabinet only after Henderson had been dispatched to Germany with
instructions to proceed. Here as in other instances, Chamberlain had
used the Foreign Policy Committee to circumvent the authority of the
Cabinet. It was not until the following week, after the Hitler-Henderson
meeting, that the Cabinet learned that action had been taken. At that

---

[3] Blomberg, Hitler's minister of war, married, with Hitler and Goering as witnesses, a woman who
later turned out to be a prostitute with a police record. The German generals were indignant and in
the furor that followed both Blomberg and Fritsch were dismissed, Neurath was replaced by Ribbentrop at the Foreign Office, and, in general, forces of moderation were eliminated from the Nazi government.

time, the new Foreign Secretary, Lord Halifax, discussed the question of Britain's response to the German negative. Halifax proposed that in responding to Hitler,

> He [Halifax] would not conceal his disappointment . . . as to the Führer's response, though he would intimate that this made no difference to their desire to improve relations. . . . The last thing [the British] wanted to see was a war in Europe, but the experience of all history went to show that the pressure of facts was sometimes more powerful than the wills of men, and if once war should start in Central Europe, it was impossible to say where it might not end or who might not become involved.

Chamberlain noted that Halifax's "way of putting the matter was admirable."

From the privacy of his study, Chamberlain watched with growing concern the ominous new developments in Germany. He admitted that these events had come as an almost total surprise to the British policymakers and significantly complicated the diplomatic situation. Although he was decidedly apprehensive about the future direction of German policy, he thought that, at least in the short run, German military capability had been diminshed. His feeling of apprehension was no doubt compounded by Henderson's warning that "Hitler was contemplating some immediate action about Austria."

Therefore, when German armies began crossing the Austrian frontier on the morning of 12 March Chamberlain was not particularly surprised. In fact, he had written to his sisters stating that there had been many signs of an impending Nazi takeover of Austria but that he had wished this could be effected peacefully. As early as 19 February, Chamberlain had told the Cabinet that "it was difficult to believe" that the eventual result of German policy "would not be the absorption of Austria and probably some action in Czechoslovakia." Whether by carefully premeditated plan or by pragmatic opportunism, Hitler's armies were, despite initial blundering and ill planning, soon in occupation of the whole of Austria. What was once a sovereign member of the League was now an administrative subdivision of the German Reich. The British, having once again been presented with a *fait accompli*, were forced to reevaluate the premises on which their policy had heretofore been based.

Clearly, what concerned Chamberlain and his cadre of supporters was not the fact of Austria's destruction but the method by which it was achieved. In fact, during the brief crisis leading up to the Anschluss, the Government had given Hitler every reason to assume that the British, however much they might abhor military action, would do nothing to oppose it. After Austrian Prime Minister Schuschnigg had announced his intention to hold a plebiscite and German military action to prevent it had become a possibility, Halifax had informed Ribbentrop that "the threat of force was an intolerable method." But Chamberlain, leaving no doubt as to Britain's intentions, added that the two countries "could begin working in earnest towards a German-British understanding once we had all got past this unpleasant affair." In Berlin, Henderson made it clear that he agreed with Goering that Dr. Schuschnigg "had acted with precipitate folly." These were hardly the sort of statements which might have deterred Hitler from advancing into Austria.

Even before the German action Chamberlain had had a private meeting with Ribbentrop in which he pleaded with the Reich minister to intercede with Hitler in an effort to convince the latter to halt his invasion plans. But Chamberlain said he had placed little hope in the meeting since Ribbentrop was of such limited intelligence and was so filled with his own self-importance that he was totally incapable of understanding the British point of view. While Chamberlain may have been correct in his estimate of Ribbentrop's abilities there can be no doubt that in planning the Austrian invasion, Hitler, at least, had correctly understood the strength of British determination to avoid military involvement on the continent. In any case, the German occupation of Austria was now an accomplished fact.

In his weekly letter to his sisters, Chamberlain appeared or wished to appear unshaken by events on the continent. Those despicable Germans, he said, had delayed his departure for a weekend in the country. He very much wished they would simply disappear but, alas, that was not to be. At least he could take heart in the fact that the occupation had been accomplished without the loss of life.

The Anschluss had convinced him, he said, that collective security was useless in preventing such action and that military power was the only effective means of curbing Hitler's expansion. He believed that military force could be more effectively utilized through a system of alliances than through the cumbersome and ineffective League of Nations system. Yet, for Chamberlain, the return to the alliance system brought with it the dangerous possibility of re-creating the same alliance patterns which had led to, if not caused, the Great War.

Chamberlain believed that the entire disaster could have been avoided if Halifax instead of Eden had been foreign secretary at the time of his letter to Mussolini. Chamberlain believed that if an agreement could have been reached with the Duce, Mussolini might not so easily have assented to Hitler's actions.

The principal effect of the Anschluss on Chamberlain's view of continental affairs was that it caused him to redouble his efforts at reaching a negotiated settlement with the Axis powers. At the same time, however, he believed that the British should demonstrate their resolve by making a public announcement of an increase in the rearmament program. Chamberlain also wanted to undertake private conversations with the Italians. Everyone involved in foreign policy formulation, including Chamberlain, believed that if Hitler were planning a new aggressive move it would be toward Czechoslovakia, with a view to incorporating the Sudeten Germans into the Reich. Chamberlain himself told the Cabinet that ". . . if we can avoid another violent coup in Czechoslovakia, which ought to be feasible, it may be possible for Europe to settle down again and some day for us to start peace talks with the Germans." The incorporation of Austria into the German Reich was no doubt a setback for the prime minister's policy, although not an insurmountable one. In fact, Chamberlain was even able to interpret events so as to vindicate his own views. "What a fool Roosevelt would have looked if he had launched his precious proposal," he told the Cabinet, and "what would he have thought of us if we had encouraged him to publish it, as Anthony was so eager to do and how we too would have made ourselves the laughing stock of the world."

Reactions to the Anschluss

Chamberlain's personal interpretation of the meaning to be attached to the Anschluss was clear and unequivocal. While a show of British strength might serve a useful purpose, the better option was a redoubled effort toward reaching a negotiated Anglo-German settlement. Of this, Chamberlain was absolutely certain. Therefore, his first task was to insure that the Cabinet would not interfere.

On 12 March, Chamberlain opened the emergency meeting of the Cabinet by saying that although there was probably not very much that could be done, he had thought the Cabinet should meet. The tone of the Cabinet minutes of that meeting leaves no doubt that in foreign affairs the prime minister was calling all the shots. It was equally clear that the Cabinet had been supplanted by the Foreign Policy Committee as the forum for the making of policy.

The emergency session was merely an occasion for Chamberlain to interpret to the Cabinet the meaning of events in Central Europe. He told his colleagues that Germany's actions were "most distressing and shocking to the world" and that they "made international appeasement much more difficult."

> In spite of all, however, he [i.e., Chamberlain] felt that this thing had to come. Nothing short of an overwhelming display of force would have stopped it. Herr Hitler had been planning to take this action for some time and Dr. Schuschnigg's blunder had given him the chance. . . . So he believed that what had happened was inevitable unless the Powers had been able to say "If you make war on Austria you will have to deal with us." At any rate the question was now out of the way.

Chamberlain told the Cabinet that he believed some announcement about increasing the rate of rearmament was appropriate and that this increase should be in the air force and in anti-aircraft defenses, but he wanted the announcement to be made at a later date. For the moment, he warned the Cabinet "against giving the impression that the country was faced with the prospect of war within a few weeks." This was all that Chamberlain asked of the Cabinet. No collective Cabinet decisions were to be made and there was to be no discussion of the future direction of British policy or the alternatives available. Such matters were decided elsewhere.

The following day, on 15 March, at a meeting of the FPC, Chamberlain began to clear the way for new initiatives. He did not ask for, nor accept, advice from his colleagues. The form and substance of these new initiatives had already been worked out between the prime minister and the foreign secretary. The FPC meeting was for appearances only, so that Chamberlain could present his own policy to the full Cabinet as the product of supposedly long and exhaustive deliberations by a specialized body of the Cabinet. It was also useful in that the deliberations were a device by which Chamberlain's policy could be made more acceptable to the Commons and to public opinion in general. Chamberlain clearly recognized that the Anschluss had strengthened the hand of his political opponents within the Tory party and he therefore needed a solid core of support within the Government to proceed.

The first matter to be settled was the effect of the Anschluss on Anglo-Italian relations. Theoretically at least, the Italian offer to open conversations was still in effect. So also was Eden's previous pledge that the opening of talks should be linked to a withdrawal of Italian troops from Spain. In fact, Chamberlain had reaffirmed this pledge in the Commons on 21 February.[4] Now, privately in the FPC, he repudiated that pledge, saying that he "did not think that . . . the Government were necessarily pledged to the view that the Spanish question must be settled before the Anglo-Italian Agreement could be executed."

Nevertheless, Chamberlain told the FPC of his intention to inform Ciano "that Hitler's recent action in regard to Austria, had made it very much more difficult for the British Government to make an agreement with Italy." Moreover, Chamberlain told the Committee that the Anschluss had greatly strengthened the hand of those in Britain who opposed conversations with the dictators. In conclusion, Chamberlain said,

He did not think anything that had happened should cause the Government to alter their present policy, on the contrary, recent events had con-

---

[4] Specifically, he had said that Anglo-Italian negotiations would not begin unless "the Agreement contained a settlement of the Spanish question."

firmed him in his opinion that that policy was a right one and he only regretted that it had not been adopted earlier. He agreed, however, that recent events had greatly disturbed public opinion and that the Government's policy would have to be explained and justified to public opinion ever more carefully and thoroughly than would otherwise have been necessary.

Chamberlain thus recognized that the Anschluss made it impossible to renege on the public pledge not to conclude an agreement with Italy without first attaining a settlement of the Spanish question. The implication of Chamberlain's words was indisputable; the prime minister was quite prepared to reach an agreement with Italy on the best terms possible even without a clear sign of Italian good faith. He said, "Ciano should also be told that if Italy sincerely wished for an Anglo-Italian agreement, he must assist us to get over the bad reactions on public opinion of Hitler's actions for which he recognised of course neither Italy nor himself were in any way responsible." Taken literally, Chamberlain's statement seemed to imply that he, at least, believed that the Government had more in common with the Italians than with their own opposition.

Government policy, as articulated in the secrecy of the Foreign Policy Committee, was now rapidly diverging from policy articulated by the Tory Opposition led by Winston Churchill. In the House of Commons, meeting in the wake of the Anschluss, Churchill, in the somber and prophetic tones for which he has become justly famous, called for a "grand alliance to arrest this approaching war." While Churchill deliberately avoided making an open break with the Government, a grand alliance was hardly a policy which Chamberlain would favor. For the time being at least, Chamberlain felt secure enough to proceed along independent lines and safely ignore rising opposition from both the left and the right. In fact, the strength of Chamberlain's parliamentary mandate would remain secure until well after Munich.

In the meantime, the most significant discussion of foreign policy options was taking place outside the public forum. On 18 March, Halifax presented to the Foreign Policy Committee a memo in which he set forth the alternatives open to Britain with regard to Germany and the Sudeten question. The foreign secretary reminded the Cabinet that Britain's only existing commitment to Czechoslovakia was that of one League member to another. However, France had signed a treaty with Czechoslovakia in 1925 in which each country had pledged itself to come to the other's aid in the event of unprovoked aggression by Germany. In addition, in 1935 the Soviet Union had signed a similar treaty with Czechoslovakia, but one in which it was specified that the treaty would become operative only if France came to the assistance of Czechoslovakia as the victim of aggression. To the British and Chamberlain in particular, these treaties looked all too similar to the web of entangling alliances which had existed in 1914. Therefore, the dilemma was one of extraordinary delicacy. Any attempt by Britain to deter Germany in the Sudetenland would involve an additional British commitment to Czechoslovakia, a commitment which appeared exceedingly dangerous.

Halifax submitted that there were basically three alternatives open to Britain. The first was a grand alliance against the dictators as advocated by Churchill. The second was a renewed commitment to France which would, because of the Franco-Czech treaty, be an indirect guarantee to Czechoslovakia. The third was to do nothing in the way of increasing British commitments and to encourage the Czechs to make the best terms possible with the Germans.

Both Chamberlain and Halifax left little doubt which of these alternatives they preferred. To the FPC, Chamberlain gave his assessment of Hitler's intentions with regard to Czechoslovakia, saying that it "might be rash to forecast what Germany would do, but at the same time the seizure of Czechoslovakia would not be in accordance with Hitler's policy which was to include all Germans in the Reich but not to include other nationalities." It seemed likely "that Germany would absorb the Sudeten German territory and reduce the rest of Czechoslovakia to a condition of dependent neutrality." Hankey reminded the Committee that for economic reasons Czechoslovakia "could not exist as a separate political and economic entity." Inskip felt that the country was a highly artificial residue of the Treaty of Versailles and that he "could see no reason why we should take any steps to maintain such a unit in being."

Chamberlain's only reservation to the Halifax proposal was to suggest that it was not enough merely to approach the Czechs with the suggestion that they meet German demands. He wanted a concurrent approach to Germany which would involve that country in the negotiations. This, he said, "would have the advantage that it would secure permanency." With regard to France, both Halifax and Chamberlain noted that Britain "could not afford to see France overrun." By avoiding any further continental commitment, Britain would retain her freedom of action and avoid automatic involvement in a continental conflict. The great advantage of this strategy of action was, of course, that Britain could keep both France and Germany guessing.

With the full force of the combined Chamberlain-Halifax arguments, the outcome of the FPC deliberations was a foregone conclusion. The three options presented by the foreign secretary were the only alternatives considered. There was very little debate; no one supported the idea of a grand alliance. A few expressed their support for France, but their arguments carried little conviction. The Chamberlain-Halifax line was accepted.

As he presented his case to the Committee, no other conclusions than those Chamberlain himself had arrived at seemed possible. As he said,

> . . . the more one studied the map of central Europe the more hopeless was the idea that any effective help could be swiftly brought to Czechoslovakia in an emergency. . . . It followed therefore, that we should have to say that it was impracticable effectively to aid Czechoslovakia in time and that all we could do would be to make war on Germany, but we were in no position from the armament point of view to enter such a war and in his . . . opinion it would be most dangerous for us to do so.

To support Czechoslovakia meant war, a war for which Britain was ill-prepared. Interestingly enough, neither Chamberlain nor anyone else raised the possibility that Germany might be deterred from attacking Czechoslovakia by a renewed British commitment to that country.[5]

Chamberlain said that France's domestic political situation meant that she was "in a hopeless position" to make war on Germany. Therefore, Chamberlain said he would have thought, ". . . the policy of France would have been directed to giving us wholehearted support in an attempt to find a peaceful solution, to avoid any risk of an outbreak of war and to reestablish the confidence of Europe which had been shattered by recent events." Chamberlain said that he ". . . did not think that Germany would resent representations by us that the Sudeten problem should be settled by negotiations between Czechoslovakia and herself though she would no doubt strongly resent any suggestion that that question should be settled for her by foreigners." Chamberlain went on to say:

> If Germany could obtain her desiderata by peaceful methods there was no reason to suppose she would reject such a procedure in favour of one based on violence. It should be noted that throughout the Austrian adventure Herr Hitler had studiously refrained from saying or doing anything to provoke us and in small matters such as passport and exchange facilities for British subjects returning home from Austria consideration had been shown. All this did not look as if Germany wished to antagonise us, on the contrary, it indicated a desire to keep on good terms with us.

Thus it was that, less than a week after the Anschluss, without seeking military advice, in opposition to the Foreign Office, without consulting

---

[5]The use of a British commitment to Czechoslovakia as a deterrent to Germany was, of course, precisely the course which Churchill so eloquently articulated in the Commons on 14 March and again on 24 March. Significantly, this option was not even discussed in the FPC meeting or in the full Cabinet.

France, and in almost complete ignorance of Soviet attitudes, the Foreign Policy Committee accepted Chamberlain's policy and abandoned any attempt to resist further German aggression in Czechoslovakia.

The policy, it should be noted, was not merely a passive one of doing nothing to resist Hitler but rather a positive move in anticipation of what was believed to be the future course of German policy. Rather than wait on events, the British were committing themselves to a policy of urging the Czechs to compromise before Hitler sought a solution by force. It need scarcely be noted that internal Czechoslovakian politics had nothing whatever to do with that decision.

The following day, after the basic decisions had been taken, the Committee was given the advice of the chiefs of staff. The military chiefs concluded that nothing the allies could possibly do could prevent Germany from overrunning all of Czechoslovakia, and if this happened, Italy and Japan would probably seize the opportunity to further their own end, and the result would be world war. The chiefs of staff's report was a convenient support for the Chamberlain line and persuasive evidence which could be used to gain acceptance by the Cabinet.

In presenting the FPC decision to the full Cabinet, Halifax said that both he and the prime minister had been inclined to favor the idea of a grand alliance, but that upon hearing the report from the chiefs of staff, they had concluded, and the FPC with them, that the best course would be to try to "induce the Government of Czechoslovakia to apply themselves to producing a direct settlement with the Sudeten Deutsch" and to "persuade the French to use their influence to obtain such a settlement." Halifax said that "it was a disagreeable business which had to be done as pleasantly as possible. . . ." Chamberlain reiterated Halifax's arguments, adding, ". . . it was difficult to believe, however, that if the subject were discussed seriously between the two nations, the French would not be glad to find some method to relieve them of their engagement." Chamberlain emphasized the importance of reaching an agreement with Italy, adding, ". . . the conversations in Rome were proceeding with almost embarrassing ease and rapidity. . . ." With even less discussion than in the FPC, the Cabinet accepted the Chamberlain-Halifax line.

On 24 March, Chamberlain addressed the House of Commons on the question of British policy in the wake of the Anschluss. He began by saying, ". . . I cannot imagine that any events would change the fundamental basis of British foreign policy which is the maintenance and preservation of peace and the establishment of a sense of confidence that peace will in fact be maintained." Discussing the inadequacy of the League, Chamberlain argued against efforts to revitalize the League by instituting mechanisms for military cooperation among a small number of nations; ". . . however wholeheartedly the League may be prepared to give its sanction and approval to such projects as a matter of fact it does not differ from the old alliances of pre-war days which we thought we had abandoned in favour of something better." Therefore, Chamberlain concluded, Britain had no alternative but to seek her own security through rearmament while recognizing that her interests on the continent included the maintenance of the Covenant and her specific obligations to Belgium and France under Locarno.

Recent German actions in Austria, he said, had resulted in a "profound disturbance of international confidence." The pre-eminent concern of His Majesty's Government was the restoration of that confidence, and Chamberlain asked, rhetorically, if this might not best be secured by a direct guarantee to Czechoslovakia or an assurance to France that Britain would come to her aid in the event of French involvement in a war with Germany in fulfillment of her treaty obligations to Czechoslovakia. Chamberlain rejected both options on the grounds that "the decision as to whether or not this country should find itself involved in war would be automatically removed from the discretion of His Majesty's Government. . . ." In effect, Chamberlain was arguing that placing faith in automatic alliances had led to a great world war, and that even while recognizing vital British interests on the continent, Britain must not allow herself to return to the mistakes of 1914.

While dismissing with cavalier disdain the Soviet offer of a great power conference on Central Europe, Chamberlain concluded with the following warning:

> Where peace and war are concerned, legal obligations are not alone involved, and, if war broke out, it would be unlikely to be confined to those who have assumed such obligations. It would be quite impossible to say where it would end and what Governments might become involved. The inexorable pressure of facts might well prove more powerful than formal pronouncements, and in that event it would be well within the bounds of probability that other countries, besides those which were parties to the original dispute would almost immediately become involved.

This then was Chamberlain's balance, delicately struck, between the desire to warn Germany against further military actions and the fear lest Britain should encourage France to take too bold a stance in support of her Czechoslovakian ally. His only mention of Czechoslovakia was to say that Britain would "at all times be ready to render any help in their power" to the Czechs in order that they might "meet the reasonable wishes of the German minority."

The message that had been transmitted to the French, however, went considerably further in specifying what Britain was or was not prepared to do. The British said, what they had always assumed to be the case, that Britain would come to the aid of France "in the event of an unprovoked act of aggression on her by Germany," but that HMG "could certainly not go so far as to state what their action might be in the event of an attack upon Czechoslovakia by Germany." The British urged joint action with the French to help remove the causes of friction, or even of conflict, by using their good offices with the government of Czechoslovakia.

Chamberlain had begun by gaining acceptance for his views in the narrowest possible forum. In persuading his colleagues in the FPC, Chamberlain had gained *de facto* allies in the larger Cabinet. Having acquiesced in the FPC, a colleague could not very well oppose Chamberlain in the full Cabinet. The same principle applied to the larger government forum. Once the Cabinet had decided on a policy, the price of public opposition in the Commons was resignation. At this level, a dissident minister had to deal with the Eden dilemma; that is, for resignation to be politically credible, the minister must articulate an alternative course of action, and this, unfortunately, no one in the Government was either willing or able to do. Such was the meaning of Chamberlain's comment that his political strategy had always been first to make up his own mind as to the correct option to be pursued and then to persuade his colleagues by taking them step by step through his own decision-making process. It was a supremely effective strategy.

Chamberlain wrote that his speech in the Commons had been an enormous victory and that he could not recall that any British statesman had ever made a crucial policy statement that had been as widely acclaimed as his own.[6] While such claims were no doubt exaggerated, it does seem fairly certain that then, as at the time of Munich, the vague and ill-defined force known as public opinion was squarely behind the prime minister. While Chamberlain no doubt misread German intentions and saw reasonableness where there was none, there can be little doubt that he understood full well the dynamics of British domestic politics and the degree to which he could make policy independent of traditional constitutional constraint. In sum, he had correctly assessed the weakness of the opposition and the strength of his own position. It is therefore no great exaggeration to say that the country lay in the palm of his hand.

In the midst of this flurry of activity, Chamberlain's letters reveal the private feelings of a master politician. With an imminent fascist victory in Spain, with the persistent political instability in France (whose government Chamberlain suspected of having secret contacts with the Brit-

---

[6]It should be noted that there was by no means universal acclaim in the press for Chamberlain's speech. One critic claims that ". . . the underlying mood was one of disappointment with the vague and negative character of the Prime Minister's pronouncement." See Rock, *Appeasement on Trial*, p. 62. However, the *Times* of 25 March warmly endorsed Chamberlain's speech as did John Maynard Keynes in the *New Statesman* of 26 March. On the negative side were the editorials in the *Manchester Guardian* of 25 March and the *Economist* of 26 March.

ish left), with the conniving Russians attempting to involve the British in a European war, with all these dangers to deal with, Chamberlain felt that the Opposition's cry for a more bold and coherent policy was more than a little unfair. The idea of a grand alliance had, he wrote, occurred to him long before Churchill's speech. Indeed, Chamberlain wrote, the idea had everything in its favor except that it was simply not feasible. After reviewing the arguments concerning the indefensibility of Czechoslovakia, he concluded that he had virtually given up any idea of a formal pledge to Czechoslovakia or of a pledge to France with respect to her treaty commitments to that nation.

Even before his speech in the Commons of 24 March, Chamberlain's mind was moving ahead to even bolder measures. In a letter to his sister, Chamberlain confided that he was thinking of a new approach to Hitler to follow up on previous overtures by Halifax and Henderson. His idea was to remind Hitler that he had been warned that military action against Austria would have the most adverse effects on the British public. Therefore Hitler had no one to blame but himself for the bellicose criticism he was receiving. Moreover, Hitler's action had thus virtually precluded any further discussion of a colonial settlement.

But Chamberlain was willing to let bygones be bygones and believed that together they could work on repairing the damage. He would remind the German leader that the British public believed Hitler was about to attack Czechoslovakia and that no one would believe his protestations to the contrary. Chamberlain said that he would ask Hitler to tell him precisely what he wanted for the Sudeten Deutsch and that if Hitler's demands were well-founded, Britain would urge the Czechs to acquiesce in return for a German pledge of no further involvement. Chamberlain noted that if Hitler would play along, he might be willing to join in an Anglo-German guarantee of Czechoslovakia. While he was not sure he was willing to go quite this far, Chamberlain wrote that he believed he had at least a plan for opening negotiations, a plan to which Hitler might be receptive.

Having once committed himself to the notion of an Anglo-German guarantee of Czechoslovakia it was but a short step to the idea of a meeting between Chamberlain and Hitler in which a joint agreement could be negotiated and then forced upon the Czech people. Just as in the case of Abyssinia, the wishes of the peoples involved and the moral question of the possible destruction of a sovereign state mattered hardly at all. The important thing to Chamberlain was that these changes be accomplished peaceably. Nor was Chamberlain particularly concerned with the fate of the Czech people in the event of a German attack, or with the strategic indefensibility of a Czech state in which the Sudetenland passed to German control. What concerned him above all else was his belief that German aggression would inevitably lead to the involvement of Britain in another world war.[7] Long before he became prime minister, the course he would follow had been settled in Chamberlain's mind. The post-Anschluss deliberations did little more than insure that his view of British policy and his alone would prevail.

ANGLO-ITALIAN AGREEMENT AND THE ACQUIESCENCE OF FRANCE

The seeds of carefully planted political initiatives had developed institutional permanence and now, under Chamberlain's vigilant care, were beginning to bear fruit. That the German action in Czechoslovakia should be countered with increases in the rate of British rearmament was something which no one, including Chamberlain, denied. Each of the service chiefs accordingly put forth proposals for increases in his department. However, the rationed budget was the rock on which the hopes of the military foundered. Chamberlain methodically played the service chiefs one against the other to insure that nothing would be done to upset fiscal stability on which he believed so much depended.

With Simon dutifully waving the by now almost sacred banner of budgetary constraint, rearmament expenditures could not be allowed to exceed the ration by more than a minimum amount. Therefore the War Office was actually asked to cut its estimates by £82 million to allow for the expansion in the air force. This expansion, under the so-called Scheme K, was a direct response to the increased British fear of a German air attack. Thus the acceleration in rearmament in the aftermath of the Anschluss was in effect an increase in defensive air protection at the expense of the army and its ability to play an effective role in a land war on the continent.

At Cabinet meetings at the end of April, the matter of a British military response to the Anschluss received decisive resolution. The prime minister himself supported the idea of beginning formal staff conversations with the French, but the decision to reduce the role of the British army in a future continental war to a token field force meant, in effect, that Britain would have very little to discuss with the French in that area. As Chamberlain so succinctly put it, ". . . the French were bound to receive a shock sooner or later, surely the sooner the better."[8]

A second result of Chamberlain's carefully laid plans was the swift

[7]Hoare recorded a similar conclusion concerning Chamberlain's motives: "The overriding consideration with Chamberlain and his colleagues was that the very complicated problem of Czechoslovakia ought not to lead to a world war and must at almost any price be settled by peaceful means."

[8]To the Cabinet, Chamberlain quoted a Chiefs-of-Staff Sub-Committee report (C.O.S. 707) which stated, "We must draw attention to the fact that the French General Staff and nation, as in 1914, will expect that, once we are committed to co-operation, we shall, in fact, be committed to co-operation on a far larger scale." While Britain's initial contribution to a continental land war had been limited to a token two divisions, everyone recognized that in the course of another full scale Franco-German war, Britain would not likely be able to restrict her commitment to this minimal level. Therefore, the question of military staff talks raised frightening possibilities and Cabinet colleagues warned Chamberlain to use "the utmost caution" in his approach to the French. He needed no reminder.

conclusion of the Anglo-Italian agreement on 16 April. With Halifax instead of Eden at the Foreign Office, negotiations with the Italians had presented no problem, and an agreement was signed affirming the status quo in the eastern Mediterranean. Britain promised to work, in Geneva, for the recognition of the Abyssinian conquest once Italy had withdrawn her "volunteers" from Spain. The issues which had seemed so intractable to Eden and which had occupied reams of Foreign Office correspondence were neatly swept away.

The signing of the agreement was the occasion for an exchange of personal letters between Chamberlain and Mussolini. Describing his letter to Mussolini to his sister, Chamberlain wrote that he had categorically rejected the draft proposed by the Foreign Office. The latter, he claimed, was simply incapable of believing that Britain and Italy could have any common interests. The Foreign Office had objected because Mussolini was likely to publish any cordial letter by the British prime minister. But a public expression of British goodwill was precisely what Chamberlain claimed he intended and his version of the letter was dispatched over the objections of the Foreign Office.

For Chamberlain, the signing of the Anglo-Italian agreement was the triumphant culmination of protracted, behind the scenes, political effort. Privately, he wrote of his great satisfaction at safely surmounting yet another obstacle in the long road to appeasement. He regretted that the time was not yet right to move forward in improving relations with the Germans but he believed that once the Czechs began to deal with the Sudeten problem it would again be possible to improve British relations with Germany.

One by one the political cards had fallen into place. Aside from the great imponderable of Germany, there remained only the problem of convincing the French to accept the British view. This was achieved in a series of Anglo-French meetings in London on 28–29 April.

The agenda for these meetings had been carefully arranged so that the issue of staff talks preceded discussion of Czechoslovakia. Since the latter depended on the former, that is, whether or not France would support Czechoslovakia in the event of German aggression depended on what she might expect in the way of British aid, the agenda of the discussion prejudiced the outcome in Chamberlain's favor. Daladier accepted Chamberlain's view of the need for staff talks but felt that since "it was extremely difficult to separate the component parts in the national defence system . . . ," he wanted the increased contacts to include their respective armies as well as air forces. Chamberlain granted Daladier's point but noted "a difference between the position now and the position in 1914," namely, that Britain was now building an air force "of a very formidable character" which would in the event of another war "play a part out of all proportion to that played by the British air force in the Great War." Moreover, Chamberlain said, that in a future war, Britain could not "count upon being able to purchase munitions from the United States to the same extent as had been possible during the Great War."

Chamberlain believed that the Germans would aim at a "knock-out blow" from the air. Britain's strategy must therefore be to conserve her industrial and manpower reserves in order to survive the initial attack with sufficient men and materal to win in the long run. Therefore, he told the French, ". . . it would obviously not be possible successfully to fulfill the industrial considerations . . . and at the same time send a British army to serve abroad on the same scale as in the Great War." In an effort to squelch any remaining French hopes of British support Chamberlain concluded that the "military participation of Great Britain in a war on the Continent would not be on a sufficient scale to justify conversations between the Army Staffs. . . ." Chamberlain said that "His Majesty's Government had no desire to commit themselves to sending two British divisions to France on the outbreak of war." The most he could say was that this possibility was not excluded "if the Government of the day decided accordingly."

Only after Chamberlain had made clear his intentions with regard to staff talks was the subject of Czechoslovakia raised. The prime minister bluntly stated that "if the German Government decided to take hostile steps against the Czechoslovak State, it would be impossible, in our present military situation, to prevent those steps from achieving immediate success." Daladier countered with protestations of French willingness to fight if necessary, of Germany's malevolent intentions, and of the Czechs' ability to resist effectively. Chamberlain admitted the possibility that if Germany were confronted by the united opposition of France, Britain, and Czechoslovakia, Hitler might back down.

> This was what the Americans in their card games called bluff. It amounted to advancing a certain declaration in the hope that that declaration would prevent the events we did not wish to occur. But it was not a certainty that such action would be successful. It might be true that the chances against war were 100–1, but so long as one chance existed, we must consider carefully what our attitude must be, and how we should be prepared to act in the event of war.

Chamberlain concluded by saying that he had never excluded the possibility that Britain might be compelled to go to war if things more precious than wealth, life, or property were at stake, "but he could only agree to go to war in the very last resort and could not envisage such a possibility as something to be undertaken lightly. He had himself seen war and had seen how impossible it was for anyone engaging in any war like the last war to come out of it stronger or happier." Therefore only dire necessity would ever persuade him to wage a preventive war. Daladier replied that he too "had gone through the last war for four years as a combatant, and had served as an infantryman from the Somme to Alsace. He had seen the destruction of the richest provinces of his country. He had seen his best friends killed around him, and after such an experience one's only thought could be to do everything possible to avoid a repetition of such atrocities."

In the end, Daladier's bluff was called and the French leader was found wanting. Regardless of what the French may or may not have felt they had retained of their freedom of action, Chamberlain's mind was, on this score, perfectly clear. He said, ". . . it is left to us alone to ask the Germans what they want in Czecho-slovakia, I am not without hope that we may go through without a fresh demonstration of force." As a result of these meetings, the British and French publicly announced their intention to hold staff talks on air force matters. Simultaneously, the British assured Hitler that this did not mark a change in British policy, and a few days later Chamberlain remarked that the Germans had not reacted too badly to news of the Anglo-French meeting.

The conclusion to be drawn from that meeting was, at least in Chamberlain's view, that the French were willing meekly to follow the British lead. Within weeks of the Anschluss, first the Foreign Policy Committee, then the full Cabinet, and then the House of Commons had been converted to his position. One factor in explaining the ease with which Chamberlain was able to exercise this enormous influence was his ability and willingness to manipulate the powerful images of historical memory. With the conversion of France, the last piece had fallen into place leaving Chamberlain flushed with victory.

Vanity and an exaggerated sense of self-importance are no doubt common flaws of the political profession, and a man's private letters are, perhaps, an unfair gauge of his susceptibility to them. Chamberlain's letters, nevertheless, remain those of a man in whom these qualities were present in abundance. He felt his speech of 24 March had won universal approval in Europe and, with thinly veiled contempt he spoke of the lack of courage in such people as Oliver Stanley and De la Warr. With supreme self-assurance he boastfully noted that he had simply taken stock of the circumstances and determined for himself what was the proper thing to do. With a keen ear for gossip, he recorded the petty intrigues going on behind the scenes, but he saw himself as being above such wretched pettiness. He believed that he had the trust and the support of the British citizenry in a way that Baldwin never had. Yet even in the midst of his self-congratulatory indulgence, Chamberlain maintained some sense of his own vulnerability, that the political and diplomatic triumphs of today could turn quickly into defeat.

With such statements Chamberlain expressed a vague apprehension, a perception that he was moving too far too fast toward the end of a political limb predestined to break. Even as he savored the sweetness of political victory, gloating over each bit of praise, there was a faint premonition of impending doom. He realized the dangers of political isolation in receiving only the kind of information favorable to his own point of view. With regard to the Italian agreement, letters to the prime minister were about evenly divided, although he believed that those in favor were of a substantially higher caliber and that those against were mostly from crackpots and political enemies.

The Anschluss and the British reaction to it led many among the opposition to increasingly vitriolic attacks on the Government and on Chamberlain personally. As had so often been the case in the past, the critics were quite sure they opposed Chamberlain's policy but were much less clear on the alternative that they wished to institute. Chamberlain's letters became increasingly bitter at what he considered to be unjustified attempts to make him appear a fascist sympathizer and an enemy of the League, but at the same time he recorded a determination not to be deflected from the course he had chosen.

THE MAY CRISIS

In Britain, the political and diplomatic activity following the Anschluss was perhaps the last occasion on which a comparatively leisurely discussion of diplomatic options was possible. From that point onward, events in Germany moved with such rapidity that policy-makers on both sides of the channel could do little more than react to events as they unfolded. The time for quiet discussion of peripheral issues such as colonial restitution and disarmament had long since passed. Now the issues were literally either peace or war. Few believed that if Britain were forced into war the result would be anything less than a full-scale conflagration, at least on the scale of the last war and probably much worse.

Chamberlain's public utterances reflected this growing alarm. "We are like people living at the foot of a volcano," he said, "and we remember it blew up once before and we begin to wonder whether it is to be our fate to be smothered in ashes or see our homes destroyed and devoured by burning lava." As always, memories of the Great War were ever present in his mind like an invisible inner force moving and guiding his every action. At a National Government rally, he said:

When I think of those four terrible years and I think of the 7,000,000 of young men who were cut off in their prime, the 13,000,000 who were maimed and mutilated, the misery and suffering of the mothers and the fathers, the sons and the daughters, and the relatives and the friends of those who were killed and wounded, then I am bound to say again what I have said before, and what I say now, not only to you, but to all the world—in war, whichever side may call itself the victor, there are no winners, but all are losers.

It is those thoughts which have made me feel that it was my prime duty to strain every nerve to avoid a repetition of the Great War in Europe. And I cannot believe that anyone who thinks what another war would mean, can fail to agree with me and to desire that I should continue my efforts.

Without knowing the personal history of the man, it would be possible to explain such statements as the cynical manipulation of historical images for partisan gain. Certainly Chamberlain was capable of disguising the naked pursuit of personal power in the rhetoric of altruism and high moral purpose, and he knew full well the rhetorical value of public references to the Great War. But knowing what the Great War had meant to Chamberlain, one can only conclude that the often expressed fears of history repeating itself were, in fact, deeply held and authentically based convictions. Ironically, for a man who found it almost impossible to communicate emotion even to close friends and family, Chamberlain's public speeches, even more than his private letters, reflected the impassioned underpinnings of reasoned action.

These speeches were remarkably consistent in their major themes. Always, there was the image of a world poised on the brink of disaster: falling avalanches, teetering on the edge of the abyss, the eruption of volcanoes. While he believed that the British people deplored fascism (and communism), these new ideologies were facts of life which had to be accepted if not condoned. Those governments, like that of Britain, had to be composed of men capable of seeing the reasonableness of compromise. In international politics every effort had to be made to prevent the world from again being divided into two rival blocs. Above all else, Britain had to avoid automatic commitments which would remove the great questions of peace and war from the control of British statesmen.

In the spring of 1938, the Sudeten Germans, a minority within the multinational Czechoslovakian state, were the focus of Chamberlain's greatest fears. Historical memory of a more recent sort led him to believe that Hitler would seek to incorporate the Sudeten minority into the German Reich by force of arms just as he had done in Austria. If this happened, France might stand by her treaty commitments and possibly the Soviets as well. The world and Britain with it would then be sucked into the vortex of world war. Therefore everything depended or seemed to depend on a successful resolution of that conflict. All of Chamberlain's analysis was, however, predicated on the notion that Hitler's maximum demands were for the incorporation of all ethnic Germans into the Reich and for the economic domination of southeastern Europe. Without giving the slightest thought to the strategic implications of such an expanded Germany, Chamberlain was prepared to accede to these demands in full, as long as they were attained without the use of force.[9]

It therefore seemed reasonable to Chamberlain that the Sudeten minority would eventually become part of Germany. In May 1938, however, few people, least of all the parliamentary opposition, were prepared to accept the outright cession of the Sudetenland to Germany against the wishes of the Czech government. Exactly when Chamberlain himself became convinced that cession was the best course is difficult to determine. As late as 21 March, Chamberlain had told Geoffrey Dawson of the *Times* that he thought a neutralization of Czechoslovakia along Swiss lines "was not impossible" and had told Halifax that this was "the least bad" of the available alternatives.

Only a few weeks later, however, at a luncheon given by Lady Astor he told a group of American and Canadian journalists that he was prepared to go considerably further. As it was reported in the *New York Times*, Chamberlain had said that he favored "a separation of the German districts from the body of the Czech republic and the annexation of them to Germany."[10] These informal comments were most likely yet another of Chamberlain's "calculated indiscretions," an attempt to communicate directly to the Germans his readiness to cooperate in forcing the Czechs to cede the Sudetenland to Germany. There is no evidence to indicate that Chamberlain had given any serious thought to the strategic indefensibility of a Czechoslovakia so altered.[11] Chamberlain realized that he was treading a fine line between Hitler's demands and the growing opposition within Britain. It took the war scare of 20

[9]Simon Newman, in his *March 1939*, and others have forcefully argued that Britain was not prepared to concede Germany an economic free hand in southeastern Europe and that, in the wake of the Anschluss, the British undertook a policy of economic containment to check German trade expansion in that area. Newman's work refutes that of, for example, Gilbert & Gott, pp. 195–96, who claim that Britain had "generally and publicly conceded" German economic hegemony in that area.

The intent of the present work is not to deny the existence of a British effort at economic containment but to argue that such a policy was almost completely subordinate to the policy of appeasement. From Chamberlain's perspective, at least, we can be quite sure that if the price of general European appeasement were granting German economic hegemony in southeastern Europe, Chamberlain would gladly have paid it. Simon's thesis is dealt with in greater detail in Chapter VII.

[10]The *New York Times* 14 May 1938. Other accounts were published on 14 May in The *New York Herald-Tribune* and the *Montreal Gazette*. All of these press reports agreed that Chamberlain had in fact proposed cession as his favored solution. These reports were the subject of acrimonious accusations in the House of Commons leveled at the prime minister by Archibald Sinclair and others.

Chamberlain contemptuously refused to discuss his comments to the American newspapermen but also refused to deny their veracity.

[11]That he failed to do so appears even more curious given the fact that Chamberlain was one of the first to point out Czechoslovakia's increased vulnerability as a result of the Anschluss. If, as in fact appears to be the case, Chamberlain was already prepared to work actively for the cession of the Sudetenland to Germany, it was not a policy which he felt he could admit in the Cabinet. As late as 25 May, he told his Cabinet colleagues that he agreed with Halifax in believing a cantonal system along Swiss lines to be the best solution and that the "Sudeten Deutsch should remain in Czechoslovakia but a contented people."

May to swing the balance decisively in Chamberlain's favor and to prepare the way for the Munich settlement.[12]

Chamberlain hoped that the Anglo-Italian agreement had succeeded
at least in part in detaching Mussolini from the Axis and that Hitler had
been made aware of the new Italian policy at his meeting with Mussolini in Rome. While he had no concrete evidence to assume that this
had in fact happened, he nevertheless was able to write on 13 May that
for the time being things were slightly less troubled, and that while
difficulties with Czechoslovakia would persist until the Sudeten question was resolved, he believed that there was no cause to suspect imminent danger and quite possibly such a catastrophe could be avoided
entirely.[13]

Chamberlain's illusions were rudely shattered on 19 May when reports
of German troop movements near the Czech border began reaching
London.[14] Two days later, Ambassador Newton reported from Prague
that the Czechs had begun to call up the reserves. The May Crisis, as it
was later called, took the British and Chamberlain in particular by complete surprise.

There were no emergency meetings of the Foreign Policy Committee
or of the Cabinet; decisions were made by Chamberlain and Halifax
alone. The two decided on a message to the Germans stating that if war
broke out and France, in accordance with her treaty obligations, came
to the aid of Czechoslovakia, HMG "could not guarantee that they would
not be forced by circumstances to become involved also." Once the initial warning had been given, however, everything possible was done
to nullify its effect.[15] In Berlin, Henderson, in his all too characteristic
manner, was trying to make amends for having offended the Germans
during the crisis. Within a few days, the British resumed their efforts
to pressure Czechoslovakia into compromise. On 31 May Halifax cabled
Ambassador Phipps in Paris stressing "the importance of putting the

[12] It should also be noted that Chamberlain's control over the Cabinet was increased during this
period by the elimination of two more of his opponents. Swinton's forced resignation and Ormsby-
Gore's move to the Lords left Duff Cooper, Elliot, MacDonald, and Stanley as the only Cabinet members who would not passively accept Chamberlain's dictation in the Cabinet.

[13] One reason for Chamberlain's optimism was that Konrad Henlein the leader of the Sudeten Deutsch,
had recently visited London and convinced almost everyone, including Vansittart, of his moderation
and willingness to compromise.

[14] Whether or not there actually were German troop movements directed against Czechoslovakia,
and whether the Czech reaction was a legitimate response to a perceived threat or a maneuver to
discredit appeasement, are matters of dispute by historians. A.J.P. Taylor in *The Origins of the Second
World War*, p. 165, has asserted that "no German troops had been moved" and even suggests that the
Czech reaction may have been inspired by the British Foreign Office. Wallace, p. 378, in a much more
persuasive and fully documented argument says that German troop movements on the Czech frontier
did in fact take place and that even by Nazi criteria they were rather abnormal movements. Moreover,
he argues that the Czech leaders wanted nothing less than to discredit Chamberlain and force a showdown with Hitler.

[15] A cable was dispatched to the French warning them not to "read more into those warnings than
is justified by their terms." The British left no doubt that they would come to the aid of France in the
event she was directly attacked by Germany but warned the French not to assume that Britain would
take immediate joint military action in defense of Czechoslovakia.

greatest possible pressure upon Dr. Beneš without delay," and suggesting that "if Czechoslovakia were really unreasonable the French Government might well declare that France considered herself released from her bond."

Chamberlain was greatly disturbed by the events on the Czech border since it seemed as if Hitler's army was bent on a military solution in spite of efforts being made to seek a diplomatic one. His letters reveal that at this point Chamberlain was more than a little disheartened by rising discontent within Britain itself as well as the lack of results on the diplomatic front, but he believed that he could not think of resigning because to do so would undercut public trust in the government. He therefore determined to carry on until the crisis was resolved. Writing on 22 May, he noted that he had not yet given up but that the Germans were by temperament domineering and were fully aware of their present military superiority. Until this situation changed and Britain could deal with them on equal terms, international affairs were likely to remain unsettled.

When the crisis had passed, Chamberlain, with the rest of the country, breathed an almost audible sigh of relief. He believed, as did most people at the time, that Britain had narrowly missed involvement in a full-scale continental war. He believed that the Germans had been ready to stage a military take over and that they had been dissuaded from doing so only because of the British action, an action which had, however, caused the Germans to lose face. Chamberlain therefore concluded that the Germans were completely unreliable and dishonorable. On the other hand, Chamberlain did not completely believe that the lesson of the May Crisis was that one simply could not trust the Nazis since in the months that followed, he was willing to stake everything on the hope that Hitler would after all be a man of his word. One can only conclude that the May events taught Chamberlain nothing about Hitler and German fascism except that efforts to force Czechoslovakia to compromise must be redoubled.

❧ 6 ❧

Berchtesgaden and Godesberg

FOLLOWING the May Crisis, Chamberlain and Halifax had done everything possible to downplay press accounts which might have given the impression that it was Allied determination to act which had prevented a German invasion. Privately, Chamberlain wrote that European newspapers had given him all the credit for resolving the crisis and that this was most inopportune from his point of view. Within Britain as well as in France, he had done everything possible to put a damper on such reporting. It was Chamberlain's greatest fear that "incidents" like those which he believed had brought about the May Crisis, might explode, as at Sarajevo, into a world war. He felt that if it would be possible to steer clear of such events in the future, it might be possible for him to put forward concrete proposals toward the resolution of the Sudeten problem.

THE SUDETEN CRISIS WORSENS

As spring passed into summer without further incident, the desperation, if not the intensity, of diplomatic activity lessened perceptibly. Chamberlain was determined that his plans for a summer holiday should proceed as planned. After the emotional intensity of the May Crisis, the country seemed to relax slightly, although events in the Sudetenland were never far from making press headlines.

In June, Halifax and the Foreign Office were again beginning to show signs of independent initiative. Where these activities supported his own, Chamberlain did not interfere. Among these was a £6 million loan to Turkey which Chamberlain noted had been granted for diplomatic not business reasons. In Chamberlain's view, this was the first time Britain had used her economic clout for political ends. He said that he had supported the loan against Treasury objections on grounds that since fiscal stability had already been thrown to the winds they might as well go all the way. He imagined that this would anger the Germans, but noted that the Turkish loan was nothing compared to what he was thinking of next.

Chamberlain was most likely alluding to a plan for British economic penetration in southeastern Europe, a plan originating in the Foreign Office and presented by Lord Halifax to the Foreign Policy Committee on 1 June. The intent of the Foreign Office plan was to counter German political and economic expansion in the Balkans with a revived Danubian Federation. Chamberlain, while not openly hostile to the idea, offered the following objection.

> . . . no country liked to be dependent on a single customer, and it was quite natural for Germany, as for other countries, to endeavour to find as many buyers of her goods as possible, so as to be able to play one off against another and so secure better terms. He was doubtful whether it was right to assume that if Germany's economic life was strengthened that would necessarily be a bad thing. Might not a great improvement in Germany's economic situation result in her becoming quieter and less interested in political adventures.

Chamberlain's comments are particularly interesting as an indication of the degree to which he was prepared to see German expansionism in southeastern Europe as an acceptable and perfectly natural thing.[1]

Nothing came of this plan which would, in fact, have been a kind of economic containment policy aimed at checking further German expansion. To have put such a policy into effect would have meant a return to the divided strategies of the Baldwin years. Under Chamberlain there was to be but one British policy toward Germany and that policy was initiated, controlled, and executed by the prime minister himself.

The following week, Halifax submitted to the FPC a plan which would replace the existing security treaties with a neutralized Czechoslovakia. The FPC agreed to transmit the proposal to the French. Chamberlain was, of course, prepared to go considerably beyond the mere neutralization of Czechoslovakia, but the Halifax proposal was nevertheless, from Chamberlain's point of view, a useful step in the right direction. Here again nothing came of the initiative, and on 10 August the French formally rejected it as inappropriate.

By the middle of June, Chamberlain was able to report that the nego-

[1]Simon Newman in his important book on the subject, takes a very different view claiming that the plan was of major importance as an alternative, simultaneously pursued, to Chamberlain's policy of diplomatic accommodation. Newman claims that "Chamberlain therefore allowed the Foreign Office to formulate the means of keeping Britain's options open, and rarely objected to their policy." This is a somewhat exaggerated view of the influence of the Foreign Office, and tends to distort the fact that on matters of high policy, the prime minister's view was always decisive.

tiations between the Czechs and the Sudeten Germans were proceeding so well that he found himself able to direct his attentions toward resolving the problems in Spain. A settlement of the Spanish Civil War was important to Chamberlain principally because on it rested the possibility of putting into operation the Anglo-Italian Agreement.

By early July, Chamberlain clearly doubted that Mussolini would meet the precondition of showing some sign of disengagement from Spain which would put the agreement into effect. In his view, the Duce was acting like an impetuous brat and it was almost impossible to know how to deal with him. Chamberlain wrote that he could at least take some consolation in the fact that Halifax and not Eden was running the foreign office since, unlike Eden, Halifax kept his equanimity and was willing to follow orders. While Chamberlain maintained contact with the Italians,[2] he attempted no direct communication with Hitler until shortly before Munich.

The now quite acrimonious attacks and bitter criticisms leveled at Chamberlain by political opponents like Churchill, Lloyd George, and Sinclair did nothing to alter his unshakable conviction that the course he had chosen was the only correct one. Indeed, Chamberlain may well have interpreted such attacks as signs that what he was doing must be right. Like a tortoise, the more violent the external assault, the more resolutely did he withdraw into a shell of self-righteous rectitude and determination. As he wrote to his sister, he was entirely certain that his policy was the correct one and that as a consequence he could not be persuaded by any arguments of the Opposition. He said that he had reviewed all of the options for a military response and was convinced that none of them would work unless Britain were willing to go to war. As his ideas on settling the Czechoslovakian problem became increasingly rigid, Chamberlain began to dwell obsessively on each expression of support, each bit of praise for his policies, in an effort to bolster his own resolve.

It is possible to understand, if not justify, Chamberlain's willingness to ignore attacks on his policy coming from the Labour Party as well as from the Churchill wing of his own party, but it is much more difficult to understand the almost complete quiescence among Chamberlain's supporters in the Conservative Party. Chamberlain loyalists were almost totally unwilling to question or challenge the prime minister on any issue having to do with appeasement. This remarkable passivity is one of the most striking features of British politics in the Chamberlain era.

For his part, Chamberlain remained, throughout the summer of 1938, unshakable in his conviction that progress was being made in settling the Czechoslovakian dispute. His private letters always conveyed the

[2] On 6 August Chamberlain reported a secret meeting with a Sr. Crolla of the Italian Embassy concerning a plan for the settlement of the issue of Italian involvement in the Spanish Civil War.

feeling that things were in fact getting better. Looking back on the May Crisis, he said that the Germans had had their opportunity to dominate all of central and eastern Europe and that such an opportunity was not likely to present itself again. Neither political problems at home, nor Italian intransigence abroad could alter Chamberlain's optimism. He continued to scrutinize each bit of information coming from Germany, always hoping for something to affirm his hopes and preferring to ignore, as far as possible, those reports which did not support his prejudices. In mid-July, he noted, the Nazi press had, according to government instructions, been printing favorable accounts of the British prime minister and his policies. But Chamberlain was unsure what this could mean; perhaps it was their uneasy economic position. Nevertheless, Chamberlain wrote that he had an intuitive belief that things would, in time, work themselves out. The next week he reported that he had received a top-secret communication, delivered through private sources, that Hitler was prepared to dispatch a personal envoy to speak with the British prime minister. Chamberlain had made a wary but affirmative response.

He was not sure what this overture could portend but felt that it was the most positive signal he had yet received that the Nazis were prepared to act responsibly. He speculated that perhaps since Britain's relations with Italy were still slightly cool, this might be the time to gain a German advantage over the Italians. Chamberlain was referring to an offer made through the unlikely sources of Hoare's brother, Oliver, and Lady Snowden to send Weidemann, Hitler's aide-de-camp, to London for discussions. Weidemann met with Cadogan and Halifax on 18 July. The British apparently concluded from this meeting that Hitler did not plan to use force against Czechoslovakia in the immediate future.[3]

Chamberlain was greatly annoyed that news of the Weidemann visit had been leaked to the press. He said that the newspapers had been completely irresponsible in their willingness to reveal the substance of confidential negotiations. In any case, Chamberlain seems to have been willing to accept Weidemann's assurances at face value. He said that the Germans had presented such a reassuring account of their plans that he would still be able to leave London for a brief rest in the country.

In an effort to stimulate the Sudeten negotiations, the decision was made to send Walter Runciman as a "private" mediator between the Czechs and the Sudeten Deutsch. While Chamberlain certainly approved of the Runciman mission, there is no indication that it was one of his carefully planned initiatives. Since Chamberlain had already embraced the idea of cession, it may well have been that he placed no great hopes

---

[3] On the other hand, Weidemann in his official report of the meeting said that he had told the British, in answer to the question of whether Hitler intended to use force to settle the Sudeten question, "I am in no way authorized to say anything official about this."

on a mediated settlement but thought that the mission was at worst harmless and at best offered some possibility of success. It is quite likely that even at this early date, Chamberlain was considering far more drastic measures.

By the beginning of August, there was little sign of a negotiated settlement of the Sudeten question, and reports reaching London pointed to the increased probability of German military action against Czechoslovakia. On 28 July, Henderson cabled reports of German military preparations and a rumored date for a German invasion. The British military attaché in Berlin, Lieutenant-General Mason-Macfarlane, gave news of a partial test mobilization "to an extent and on a scale which was never approached even in pre-war days." On 4 August, Henderson wrote that although he believed Hitler had not yet irrevocably decided to seek a military solution to the Sudeten question, "the possibility that he may do so has now . . . become more real." Always opposed to the possibility of Britain's taking a firm stand, Henderson warned, ". . . that would be the greatest tragedy of all . . . though it might be acclaimed as final, in fact would merely mean postponing the evil day. We do not want another May 21st. A second such rebuff to Hitler would never be forgotten or forgiven and *Der Tag* would become as inevitable as in the years preceding 1914." Such reports did little to lessen Chamberlain's sense of impending catastrophe.

In spite of the disheartening news from the Continent, Chamberlain was determined that nothing should interfere with his plans for a summer holiday and a welcome opportunity to pursue his passion for fishing and other pleasures of country life. Yet the facade of normality, an English prime minister on holiday in the country, failed to conceal a deepening feeling of gloom that the holocaust which he had for so long worked to prevent was about to become a reality. Perhaps the worsening international situation was not unrelated to his taking to bed with what he described as a sinus condition. However, he noted that he was personally unaffected by disquieting news from Germany.

The worsening state of continental affairs soon put an end to his holiday, but Chamberlain noted that he was glad to be back in London since events were going badly with the Germans and he was relieved to be able to instruct Halifax in person rather than through the post. By the following week, he was too ill to write his weekly letter to his sister and for the first time in his career dictated the letter to a secretary. By 21 August, he was able to write of some slight improvement in his health and perhaps, not coincidentally, an improvement in the situation in Czechoslovakia. Looking back on the last few weeks, he noted that he had been very disheartened, as if his entire effort at appeasement was about to collapse, and that even though continental affairs had not gotten better he was now in a better position to cope with the situation.

He was convinced that, had he not been in London, Halifax and the foreign office would have handled things differently, but that only the future would reveal if his decisions had been correct.

Together he and Halifax had drafted a plea to Hitler to desist, in the interest of peace, from his military preparations and "not to do anything which might sterilise Lord Runciman's mission and prematurely and unnecessarily create a fresh crisis in Europe."[4] Chamberlain clearly believed that the Czech crisis had reached the critical stage but felt that if the British could just get by the next few weeks, there might yet be daylight at the end of the tunnel. He shared the view, widely circulated in government circles, that much depended on the tone of Hitler's speech to the Nuremberg party rally to be held on 12 September. He deeply regretted that so much depended on the decisions of one whose sanity was indeed questionable. To Chamberlain, Hitler was certainly a fanatic, perhaps even mentally unbalanced, but Chamberlain never understood the degree to which German fascism was much more than a simple dictatorship but rather a vast social movement actively supported by masses of German people.

PLAN Z

On 30 August, members of the Cabinet were secretly recalled to London from their summer holidays unaware that the comparative calm of July had been broken by ominous rumors of German military preparations against Czechoslovakia. Just as after the Anschluss the French attitude had ceased to be a major determinant of Chamberlain's policy, so, now, Cabinet acquiescence was taken for granted. The Cabinet was not asked to make decisions but only to endorse those already taken.

Chamberlain and Halifax shocked their colleagues with the ominous reports from Germany. As Halifax presented it, the question before the Cabinet was whether or not Britain should repeat the warning of 21 May, a warning which some believed to have deterred a German invasion of Czecholsovakia. Both the prime minister and the foreign secretary argued against a new warning. Halifax repeated the now familiar arguments that nothing the British could do militarily could save Czechoslovakia. Chamberlain added his own reasons for not repeating the warning. First among them was Britain's military weakness. "No state," he said, ". . . certainly no democratic state ought to make a threat of war unless it was both ready to carry it out and prepared to do so." That in the past British statesmen had neglected this lesson of history

---

[4]Ribbentrop was outraged that the British had appealed directly to Hitler without consulting him. He sent a chilling reply which in British eyes seemed to nullify the effect of the Weidemann visit.

had led to "unfortunate results" such as the Schleswig-Holstein case.[5] Indeed, said Chamberlain, a bluff such as that of 21 May might work, but if it didn't the result would be war for which Britain was unprepared.

British military weakness was indeed an indisputable fact, and Chamberlain's reference to it was powerful evidence in support of his case. But Chamberlain's credibility in this instance is marred, not so much by his previous opposition to rearmament spending (which could be seen as a response to the felt need for maintaining fiscal solvency), but by the fact that this was the first instance in which he had used such an argument. Before his becoming prime minister and persistently thereafter, Chamberlain had done what he could to limit rearmament spending as closely as possible to the limits of the original 1934 rearmament program. While supporting the completion of the existing programs, he had consistently opposed any additional spending. Now, for the first time, he made the case that Britain was militarily unprepared for war. Clearly, Chamberlain was using military weakness as an ex post facto justification for conclusions which he had already reached by other means.[6] It was not military weakness, one might argue, which led Chamberlain to act as he did, but his personal realization that war with Germany might not only be a likely outcome but was in fact imminent. To make the decision consciously to lead the country over the brink was something Chamberlain simply could not bring himself to do. Neither, for that matter, could his Cabinet colleagues. In the end, the Cabinet

[5]The degree to which such arguments were determined by what Chamberlain believed to be the "lessons of history" is amply illustrated in a series of letters exchanged between Chamberlain and the historian Harold Temperley beginning on 28 July 1938. On that date, Professor Temperley wrote a letter to the *Times* suggesting a similarity between Chamberlain's statements in the Commons and those made by Canning. The following day, Chamberlain wrote his own letter to the *Times* in which he denied that his parliamentary speech had been based on a knowledge of Canning and suggested that the parallels drawn by Temperley were merely an indication of the continuity of British thought. On 29 July, Temperley wrote personally to Chamberlain suggesting that the latter might like to read his study of Canning since history really did seem to be repeating itself.

Between Chamberlain's trip to Berchtesgaden and his return to meet Hitler at Godesberg, Temperley again wrote to the prime minister suggesting parallels between Canning's policy toward the continental despots and Chamberlain's own problems with Hitler and Mussolini. Temperley commented that he was thrilled to hear of Chamberlain's meeting with Hitler and suggested that Chamberlain's position was now exactly like that of Canning with respect to Portugal in that they were both cases where the country was entirely behind the prime minister's efforts.

Temperley's comments very much impressed Chamberlain, and on several occasions he made reference to Canning and the dictum that in diplomacy one should never threaten unless one was prepared to make good the threat. Canning's experience seems to have bolstered Chamberlain's resolve to pursue policies which he had decided on for other reasons. On 11 September, for example, he wrote to his sister that his position had been strengthened by reading the study of Canning whose major principle of foreign policy was that one should not threaten unless one was in a position to enforce the threat.

[6]The same can also be said of the arguments made by Chamberlain concerning Dominion views and public opinion in general. While Chamberlain sometimes mentioned these as reasons for not issuing a firm warning to Hitler, the available evidence suggests that he first made up his mind as to the proper course and then used his interpretation of public and Dominion feeling to support these views.

decided not to issue a new warning to Hitler and that the decision not to do so should remain secret.

However, what the Cabinet did not know was that the prime minister had already decided on a much more drastic course: a personal visit to Hitler. According to Horace Wilson, Chamberlain made this decision during the course of a late night conversation at No. 10 Downing Street on 28 August. In any case, he certainly had decided on it before the Cabinet meeting of 30 August. Before that time, he told no one except Henderson and later, Halifax of his plans.

On 3 September he wrote that he was desperately trying to find some means of avoiding war and that while he was unwilling to divulge its exact nature, Chamberlain said that he had a secret plan which was bold and so unorthodox that it had completely shocked the foreign secretary. However, Chamberlain noted, it was an eleventh hour plan and he hoped that putting it into effect would be unnecessary. From the standpoint of diplomatic protocol and precedent, it was indeed an unorthodox plan, but in the light of Chamberlain's career and long history of "bold initiatives," the idea of meeting Hitler face to face, in a last minute attempt to settle the Czech dispute, was but a logical extension of past behavior. In fact, as he later told the Cabinet, his original intention had been to leave for Germany before telling Hitler he was coming!

The following week, Chamberlain began laying the groundwork for what he called Plan Z, by attempting to persuade first Halifax and then the other members of the Inner Cabinet, Hoare and Simon, that the new plan should be tried. Hoare was at first skeptical and warned Chamberlain that "he was taking a great political risk by personally intervening in a way quite likely to fail." To this Chamberlain replied that he would "never forgive himself if war broke out and he had not used every expedient for averting it." Simon was of course willing to follow anyone's lead. Halifax was less easily convinced, not because he had an alternative view, but because he was caught between Chamberlain and the Foreign Office and was apparently converted by whichever side had last captured his attention.[7]

Chamberlain found the Foreign Office notion of "keeping Hitler guessing" to be singularly without merit. On 6 September, he wrote with undaunted optimism that events had made it increasingly unlikely that Hitler would attempt a military solution and he hoped that it might

[7]The differing views of Chamberlain and the Foreign Office resulted in a policy which reflected divided, even conflicting, strategies. In general, Chamberlain's view predominated. Yet, on 9 September, a warning was sent by Halifax for delivery to Ribbentrop, which stated that if France became involved in a war with Germany, ". . . it seemed to His Majesty's Government inevitable that the sequence of events must result in a general conflict from which Great Britain could not stand aside." Certainly, the warning contained nothing which the British had not always assumed to be true, yet delivering such warnings to Hitler was not Chamberlain's policy. This particular warning, delivered unofficially by Henderson, appears to reflect the influence of Vansittart on Halifax.

yet be possible to avoid the drastic measures of Plan Z. Chamberlain's letter of the following week clearly reflected a growing atmosphere of tension within the Government. It had been a fairly gripping period, he wrote, sufficient to undo the resolve of anyone less secure in his convictions.

He complained to his sister that no one had any idea how difficult things had been with fresh and upsetting information coming in rapid succession, with intruders of all sorts vying for his time offering unsolicited opinions, and with the press doing its best to sabotage all he was trying to accomplish.[8] Chamberlain was clearly beginning to realize the risk he was taking. He noted that if in the long run things went amuck and the worst in fact happened, there would be plenty of people like Churchill who would hold him accountable and say that if he had only stood up to Hitler, presenting him with an ultimatum, then war could have been avoided. Indeed Chamberlain was right and this is precisely what happened. Moreover, Chamberlain was perfectly correct in noting that if he was ultimately shown to have been mistaken it would be equally impossible to show that an alternative policy would have worked. But, Chamberlain noted, he was absolutely certain that it would be wrong for any country to allow the crucial question of war or peace to pass out of its control. One implication of this letter seems to be that Chamberlain had, in his own mind, determined to proceed with Plan Z although he had not as yet decided on the exact date.[9]

On 10 September, a meeting of the Inner Cabinet took place at No. 10 Downing Street. In addition to the "big four" (Chamberlain, Halifax, Simon, and Hoare), Cadogan, Wilson, and Vansittart were present as official advisers. Before them was an urgent message from Henderson in Nuremberg begging his colleagues not to repeat the warning of 21 May. He stated that Hitler was determined to achieve a solution of the Sudeten problem and that, in the electric atmosphere of Nuremberg, any false move by the British would "drive Hitler straight off the deep end." The message seemed convincing evidence, if any were needed, that an official warning to Hitler must not be sent. The assembled ministers quickly agreed that Chamberlain's plan should be attempted. In effect, whether they realized it or not, they were giving Chamberlain carte blanche to proceed with Plan Z as he saw fit.

The following day, Chamberlain wrote to his sister that the time to implement the plan had still not arrived but that he feared that Hitler might take some sudden action which would pre-empt his own efforts. This however was a chance he was willing to take but he was anxious

---

[8] The *Daily Mail* had printed the story that Britain had sent Hitler an ultimatum, and Chamberlain had been forced to send disclaimers to Prague, Paris, and Berlin.

[9] A note in the British Documents states: "Until the afternoon of 13 September Mr. Chamberlain had in mind that his plan might be put into effect on or about 17 September."

to do nothing which would lessen the possibility of its being put successfully into effect. Chamberlain believed that Plan Z offered much more than the possibility of settling the Sudeten crisis, that it in fact might prove the occasion for opening an entirely new era in European diplomacy. Like Ambassador Henderson, Chamberlain believed that Hitler would not present an ultimatum at Nuremberg but that his future plans were extremely uncertain.[10] Chamberlain believed that for his plan to achieve its intended purpose, everything depended on dramatic effect, that it should take the world by surprise and gain Hitler's support by the power of momentum.

Even though the Nuremberg speech proved to be less bellicose than many had anticipated, events within Czechoslovakia appeared to be taking a new and alarming course. In the Sudetenland riots broke out, Czech police fired on a crowd killing six people, and martial law was proclaimed. On 13 September, Henderson warned that "only immediate action by the Czechoslovak Government can avert recourse to force by Germany."

Chamberlain believed that the time had now come to act because, as he later wrote, there were two essential conditions: firstly, that the plan should be instituted at the precise moment things looked most hopeless, and secondly, that it should be entirely unexpected. Late in the evening of 13 September, Chamberlain sent this brief personal note to Hitler.

> In view of increasingly critical situation I propose to come over at once to see you with a view to trying to find a peaceful solution. I propose to come across by air and am ready to start tomorrow.
>
> Please indicate earliest time at which you can see me and suggest place of meeting. Should be grateful for very early reply.

Later, he explained that he had seized an opportunity which would not occur again; that he had acted quickly and on his own authority in dispatching the message and that only on the following day did he inform the Cabinet of his action.

On 14 September, the full Cabinet met and, for the first time, learned of Plan Z. The ministers were overwhelmed by the dramatic effect of what the prime minister had done. Chamberlain told them that he

> . . . hoped the idea would appeal to the Hitlerian mentality. Herr Hitler liked to see the heads of State, and it might be agreeable to his vanity that the British Prime Minister should take so unprecedented a step. But he also had in mind that you could say more to a man face to face than you could put in a letter. . . .

[10] On this and other occasions, Chamberlain's analysis as he presented it to his sister was a restatement of Henderson's dispatches. It therefore seems that Henderson's views, perhaps because they so closely approximated his own, almost always received Chamberlain's closest attention.

He believed that Hitler might demand a plebiscite in the Sudetenland; if this happened, in Chamberlain's view, ". . . it was impossible for a democracy like ourselves to say that we would go to war to prevent the holding of a plebiscite." Although he had reservations, Chamberlain thought that following a successful plebiscite, it might be possible for Britain, France, and Germany to guarantee the newly reconstituted Czech state and that this guarantee could replace the existing security treaties. Chamberlain's proposal met grumblings of discontent but no significant opposition. At 3:30 P.M. the message came that Hitler was at Chamberlain's disposal.

THE BERCHTESGADEN MEETING

On the morning of 15 September, Chamberlain's plane left Heston airport for Germany. It would be difficult to overstate the dramatic effect of Chamberlain's action on the British public; never before had a British prime minister attempted anything even remotely resembling Chamberlain's undertaking. At age sixty-nine, Chamberlain was making his first journey by plane, a seven hour flight, to the southeastern corner of Germany to meet with Adolf Hitler in an attempt to avert war over the Sudetenland. For the moment all domestic opposition paled before the enormous surge of popular support which came pouring in from every quarter; share prices on the stock exchange rose, and the newspapers seemed to be outdoing each other in their praise and support for the prime minister.

Chamberlain believed, or at least acted as if he believed, that he had been given virtually unlimited authority to negotiate a settlement of the Czechoslovakian dispute. While it is true that the Cabinet had enthusiastically and unanimously endorsed Chamberlain's actions in offering to go to Germany to confer directly with Hitler, it is by no means certain that the Cabinet was giving Chamberlain an unrestricted mandate. In fact, Chamberlain had specifically promised the Cabinet that he would "enter into no definite engagement in regard to a plebiscite." Although he stated his willingness to discuss the matter of a plebiscite, he agreed to make no specific commitment and certainly no agreement on the direct transfer of Czech territory.

However, in Chamberlain's mind, the fate of the German minority in Czechoslovakia receded to the point of insignificance before the overwhelming need to avoid another world war. To avert what he believed to be the worst of all possible catastrophes, Chamberlain was prepared to go to almost any lengths in an effort to achieve accommodation. But he was also well aware of the domestic political constraints under which he was working. He was, in effect, trying to reconcile three separate sets of interests: Hitler, who wanted the Sudeten Germans in the Reich, the Czechs who did not, and those within the British Government who believed that there were limits to the pressure to be applied to the Czechs to compromise.

The story of Chamberlain's meeting with Hitler has been told so many times before that a detailed recapitulation is unnecessary. At Berchtesgaden, Chamberlain opened the conversations with Hitler by proposing that they begin with a general discussion of their respective points of view, "leaving, perhaps, the Czechoslovak problem till tomorrow."[11] Following Chamberlain's lead, Hitler said that the Anglo-German naval treaty had been made on the assumption that there would be no war between their two countries, but now with the talk of Britain's going to war with Germany he thought it would be better to denounce the treaty. Chamberlain's account continues.

> When I reached that point in the translation by Schmidt I interrupted and said "Does the Führer mean that he might denounce the treaty before we go to war?" He replied that, unless there was an understanding on both sides that in no circumstances would we go to war with one another, in his opinion it would be impossible that the treaty could stand. . . .
>
> I did not challenge him, however, on that except to say that I wished him to understand that there was a difference between a warning and a threat. I reminded him that after 1914, it was said that if we had then told Germany that we would have come in, there would have been no war, and I thought that they should understand before hand what were the necessary implications.

At that point Hitler turned the discussion to the question of Czechoslovakia and indicated in no uncertain terms that he planned to incorporate the Sudetenland into the German Reich and, although he did not specifically reject the notion of a plebiscite, he was prepared to risk a general war to achieve it. Hitler said that if the British accepted the principle of self-determination, the talks could continue.

Hitler's demands for transfer of the Sudetenland and his rejection of Chamberlain's idea of another appeal to the two parties, needless to say, went well beyond the maximum the prime minister had been authorized to accept. The idea of a plebiscite was never raised (and hence never specifically rejected by Hitler).[12] The question under dis-

[11] It may well have been Chamberlain's intention to manipulate the agenda of the discussions in an effort to influence the outcome. It also reflected the fact that Chamberlain's interest in the discussions was first and foremost to seek a general settlement of Anglo-German differences which would lead to the appeasement of Europe. Czechoslovakia was always a minor issue which stood in the way of achieving this settlement.

[12] Specifically, Chamberlain had, in discussing the practicalities of population transfer, used the phrase ". . . without prejudice to the theoretical question of secession. . . ." The term secession does not appear in the German version of the meeting where, at the appropriate place, Chamberlain is recorded as simply saying that ". . . as a practical man, he had set himself the question how an eventual decision with regard to the inclusion of the Sudeten Germans in the Reich could be carried through in practice." Hitler, moreover, used the term "self-determination" although he clearly could have used "cession" as well.

cussion was how much Czech territory should be transferred. Chamberlain's response seemed to show a determination not to be bullied by Hitler; "If the Führer is determined to settle this matter by force without waiting for a discussion between ourselves to take place, what did he let me come here for? I have wasted my time." But in fact, Chamberlain wanted to leave no doubt in the Führer's mind where he stood personally. Later, he recalled telling Hitler privately that he didn't care in the slightest whether the Sudeten Germans were in or out of the German Reich. Whichever they preferred.[13] Chamberlain suggested the transfer of those areas with eighty percent ethnic Germans while Hitler demanded all areas where the Sudeten Germans formed a majority of the population.

The British prime minister gave every appearance of casting himself in the role of impartial mediator, not only between Germany and Czechoslovakia, but also between Hitler and the British Government. Having assumed such a role, the obvious next step was to return to London in an effort to bring the Government closer to agreement. Chamberlain accordingly left Berchtesgaden having agreed to demands which went well beyond anything the Government had envisioned. Instead of a plebiscite to determine the wishes of the Sudetenlanders, he had agreed to a transfer to Germany of those areas in which ethnic Germans constituted a majority and was returning to London merely for Government authorization. Hitler's only concession was a promise to refrain, if possible, from seeking a military solution while Chamberlain consulted his colleagues in London.

Writing to his sister a few days after his return from Germany, Chamberlain left no doubt as to what he thought he had achieved. With meticulous detail he described his first impression of Hitler. He noted that the Nazi leader had spoken softly in a hushed manner. Chamberlain said he saw no signs of insanity although at times the German dictator had become very agitated, pouring forth invective on the Czechs with such rapidity that Chamberlain had had to interrupt in order to allow for translation. Immediately, Chamberlain realized that things were much more serious than he had imagined. He believed that the German armies, awaiting only Hitler's order, were ready to strike. Chamberlain was convinced that something decisive on his part had to be done and done quickly.

Chamberlain wrote that he believed in retrospect that he had made a considerable impression on the Nazi leader. Horace Wilson had told

[13]While in a letter to his sister Chamberlain may well have exaggerated his statements for effect, his official transcript of the meeting is substantially the same. ". . . I had nothing to say against the separation of the Sudeten Germans from the rest of Czechoslovakia provided that the practical difficulties could be overcome." In the German version, Chamberlain is reported as saying, "He could state personally that he admitted the principle of separation of the Sudeten areas." In either case, the impression could hardly have been one which would encourage Hitler to moderate his demands.

him that several people close to Hitler had, after the meeting, told him that Hitler had been greatly moved and that he had been quite favorably impressed by Chamberlain's style of negotiating and his quick grasp of the essentials. Precisely what Hitler in fact thought of Chamberlain is not known, but it is clear that he did nothing as a result of the Berchtesgaden meeting to alter his plans for the invasion of Czechoslovakia. On the other hand, Chamberlain was convinced that he had won Hitler's goodwill and, in spite of a certain harshness and cruelty in Hitler's manner, that the German leader was, in the final result, a man of his word.

Chamberlain's sense of accomplishment was bolstered by the public acclaim with which he was greeted on his return to London. Letters of support and encouragement came pouring in from all quarters. Number 10 Downing Street was filled with flowers and all manner of gifts from admirers both within Britain and on the continent. He later told the house of Commons, "I have no doubt whatever . . . that my visit alone prevented an invasion." In great detail, Chamberlain reported these triumphs to his sisters; he was a man well pleased with his achievements. At the end of a long and revealing letter, Chamberlain summarized his feelings concerning the Berchtesgaden initiative, saying that Plan Z was a conception of which his father would have approved. Indeed, this was no idle comment since in broad outline the Munich initiative, like so many of Chamberlain's policy decisions, was conceived in the matrix of a well-remembered family history.

Persuading the French

Despite a tremendous outpouring of popular enthusiasm within Britain and abroad supporting what was perceived to have been the prime minister's great triumph at Berchtesgaden, Chamberlain now faced a political struggle of the first magnitude. It was not only necessary to convince members of his own Government that they should acquiesce to Hitler's latest demands, demands which went well beyond anything they had heretofore envisioned, but also to present these demands in a way that would be at least minimally acceptable to the French. Finally, not the least of Chamberlain's problems was that of convincing the Czechs that they should passively submit to the dismemberment of their country. That such a formidable task was not only possible but achieved in less than a week is both a measure of Chamberlain's personal power and a measure of the fear created by the perception of ominous war clouds lurking on the continental horizon.

In broad outlines, the story of how this formidable task was achieved has been told many times, but seldom from the perspective of Chamberlain himself. His tactics were those he had used before; gain the support of the narrowest possible group, in this case the Inner Cabinet, and then gradually enlarge the circle of the committed to include first the British Government and then those of France and Czechoslovakia. Toward that end, the Inner Cabinet met on 16 September, were informed of Hitler's Berchtesgaden demands, and dutifully accepted Chamberlain's analysis and his ideas on what was to be done. The following day, a meeting of the full Cabinet was convened. Chamberlain bluntly told his colleagues that there were two and only two options, either accept self-determination or be prepared for certain and inevitable war. Only Duff Cooper offered any opposition but, given the choice of war or self-determination, even he was not prepared to opt for war. In the face of Chamberlain's presentation of the options, it was clear that no one was prepared to advocate going to war, and therefore the principle of self-determination was tacitly adopted.

During the Cabinet discussion of 17 September, Chamberlain made no mention of the term "cession." Agreement was only on accepting the principle of self-determination. In fact Chamberlain told the ministers, ". . . it had never entered his head that he should go to Germany and say to Herr Hitler that he could have self-determination on any terms he wanted." This was a piece of deliberate deception since at Berchtesgaden Hitler had demanded and Chamberlain had acquiesced to the principle of cession.

On 18 September, Daladier and Bonnet, having been summoned to London, met with Chamberlain at No. 10 Downing Street. To the French ministers, Chamberlain summarized the results of his meeting with Hitler and concluded:

> There was only one condition on which violent action could be avoided. This was that we should be prepared to discuss certain measures of self-determination. If we could accept the view that this was the next step to be taken, the Prime Minister understood that the German Government would be willing to discuss the ways and means of putting the principle into effect in an orderly fashion.

If the principle of self-determination were not accepted, Chamberlain told the French, then it was perfectly clear that war would result. Daladier expressed the fear that if self-determination were granted as a general principle, it might eventually lead to the complete destruction of Czechoslovakia by other nations with irredentist claims on Czech territory and that Germany would use it as a pretext for further expansion. Throughout the morning and into the afternoon, discussion ranged on the question of self-determination, a general principle which the French were unwilling to force upon their Czechoslovakian allies. At this point, Chamberlain put forward, *for the first time,* the principle of outright *cession* of the Sudetenland to Germany as a way of overcoming Daladier's objection to a plebiscite and limiting the applicability of self-determination to the Sudeten case. This suggestion proved to be the key by which Daladier could escape from his dilemma and he, together with his colleagues, readily accepted.[14] The British, in return, created the appearance of magnanimity in their offer to give a guarantee of the newly-reconstituted Czech state.[15]

The next day Chamberlain again met with the full Cabinet. He outlined the results of the Anglo-French meeting and presented the assembled ministers for the first time with the idea of cession. He cleverly made it appear as if cession were Daladier's innovation, when in reality the demand had originated with Hitler at Berchtesgaden. The Cabinet's endorsement of the Anglo-French position was, therefore, the consequence of a second deliberate deception.

A joint message was promptly dispatched to Prague calling on the Czechs to cede to Germany all Czech territory in which Germans constituted a majority of the population and offering to guarantee the remainder of the Czech state against unprovoked aggression. In the end, President Beneš had no choice but to accept the Anglo-French demands. After receiving a French warning that unless he acceded to the Anglo-French proposals France would disinterest herself in Czechoslovakia's fate, Beneš submitted to *force majeur*. On the morning of 21 September, Newton, Britain's ambassador in Prague, cabled London to inform the waiting British ministers that their proposals had been accepted. The last card had thereby fallen into place; in a matter of days Chamberlain had succeeded in persuading all the parties involved to accede in full to Hitler's demands.

It had been an amazingly rapid series of diplomatic and political maneuvers, and Chamberlain had been the pivot around which each of them revolved. He had moved through this tangle of complicated relationships with his eyes fixed resolutely on the goal without for a moment wavering from his position that Hitler's demands, no matter how unreasonable, no matter how morally contemptible, must be met. He

[14] Hoare's account of the meeting is in substantial agreement with the official records of the conference except for his observation that ". . . Chamberlain reluctantly but with the authority of the Cabinet accepted the alternative of a direct transfer of authority." Hoare's view that in accepting the idea of cession, Chamberlain was giving in to French wishes, is not supported by the evidence. Chamberlain had accepted the necessity of cession at least as early as the Berchtesgaden meeting and probably much earlier.

[15] Here, for the first time, the British were committing themselves to what they had always refused to do, namely to become involved in continental commitments which, as had so often been said, removed the decision of peace or war from the control of the British Government. That Chamberlain could accept such a commitment so easily is probably an indication of his supreme conviction that once the Sudeten issue had been resolved, the way would be open for general European appeasement and that once this happened, a British treaty commitment to Czechoslovakia would present no great problem.

It is also, however, possible that Chamberlain saw the need for something to counterbalance the great sacrifice which the Czechs were about to be asked to make. Perhaps, Chamberlain also saw the guarantee as necessary to gain acceptance by the British Government, and the public in general, of the principle of cession.

wrote to his sisters with what may have been a certain degree of unease, perhaps even of bad conscience, that his terrible apprehension had passed and that he had no regrets or self doubts. As he prepared for his second meeting with Hitler, it was with the certainty that he had done everything humanly possible to prevent another world-wide holocaust.

To Chamberlain, the intrinsic questions of the Sudeten dispute, fraught with enormous internal complexities and vast international consequences, now seemed like merely troublesome distractions which prevented progress toward the resolution of infinitely more important matters. It seemed to be just one more of those annoying minor issues like Abyssinia and Spain by which unwilling great power statesmen could be drawn down the road to general European war. The underlying tone of Chamberlain's conversations with Hitler had been one of impatience and irritation with the Czechs, who, he believed, stood between him and a new European settlement which would represent the culmination of his efforts toward appeasement, a supreme achievement by which he, like Austen, could earn a prominent place in the judgment of history. Yet the parallels between Austen Chamberlain's achievement at Locarno and what Neville Chamberlain was attempting with Hitler are easily overdrawn. In spite of his most ardent hopes, Chamberlain clearly had some doubts whether any agreement with Hitler would be kept.

Before leaving for Godesberg, Chamberlain met one last time with the Inner Cabinet. Echoing fears expressed in discussions with the French, the Inner Cabinet decided that if Hitler attempted to broaden the issue under discussion from the narrow question of the transfer of Sudeten Germans to the Reich to the broader question of self-determination for other national minorities within the multinational Czech state, then Chamberlain should break off discussions and return home. Chamberlain reaffirmed this commitment at a meeting of the full Cabinet where he promised he would break off negotiations and return for further consultation if Hitler made such demands. These pledges can only be seen as a concession to the rising feeling of apprehension, expressed in the Cabinet discussions and in the Anglo-French meetings, that there was something intrinsically repugnant about the notion of sacrificing Czechoslovakia for British security.

THE GODESBERG MEETING

On the afternoon of 22 September at the Hotel Dreesen in Godesberg, the second meeting between Hitler and Chamberlain took place. Triumphantly, Chamberlain recounted his own highly successful efforts at convincing first his British colleagues, then the French, and finally the Czechs themselves to accept the principle of cession of the Sudetenland to Germany. Hitler's Berchtesgaden demands had been acceded to in full, and now Chamberlain believed the two could get on with the really important issues between them. In fact, Chamberlain gave every appearance of offering even more than Hitler had demanded at Berchtesgaden. Not only was he accepting the idea of a quick solution to the Sudeten question, but, as he told Hitler, "The simplest method, and the one that would at the same time present least difficulty, would therefore be the attempt to manage without a plebiscite and to agree on a cession of territory by Czechoslovakia to the Reich." Hitler's interpreter Dr. Paul Schmidt later recalled that, at this point in the conversation, Chamberlain "leaned back . . . with an expression of satisfaction, as much as to say 'haven't I worked splendidly during these five days'!" Yet Hitler was unwilling to give up the prestige of an easy military victory, and Chamberlain's high hopes were immediately dashed on the hard rock of Hitler's new and obdurate demands. Not only were the proposals in which Chamberlain had placed so much confidence unacceptable to the Führer, but Hitler proceeded to make demands on behalf of the other nationalities within the Czech state. According to the German record, Hitler said:

> It was his duty . . . to remind the British Prime Minister of the demands of the other nationalities within Czechoslovakia, and added that the latter had the sincere sympathy of the German Reich, and that peace could not be established in Central Europe until the claims of all these nationalities had been settled.[16]

These were the precise demands which Chamberlain had promised the Cabinet he would not accept. The time had come to break off conversations and return home.[17]

Instead, Chamberlain merely said that he "did not wish to dissent," adding that he was "both disappointed and puzzled by the Führer's statement." Had he not succeeded in getting "exactly what the Führer wanted and without the expenditure of a drop of German blood?" Chamberlain simply could not believe that, after having granted Hitler's every demand, the German dictator could yet prefer a solution involving the use of force.

Yet this is exactly what Hitler had in mind when he outlined for Chamberlain another and more severe set of demands. The Czechs must withdraw from the Sudetenland at once and be replaced by units of the

---

[16]Hitler, it should be noted, was doing precisely what Daladier (at the London meeting) had most feared: using the issue of self-determination to make demands well beyond the claims of the Sudeten Deutsch.

[17]However, as Middlemas rightly points out, ". . . to have done so would have been taken as final, tantamount to a declaration that war was inevitable. If the assumptions behind his entire understanding of foreign policy are accepted, he was not wrong."

German army. All Czech troops, police, and State organs must immediately be removed from the German-speaking area. The Czechs would be entitled to no compensation for their losses. After German occupation was complete, Hitler said he would be willing to hold a plebiscite in the Sudetenland to determine which if any of these areas were to be returned. Hitler said that he was willing to hold the plebiscite because he had no desire to incorporate Czechs into the Reich. Responding to these new demands, Chamberlain calmly asked Hitler if he "really thought that it would be necessary to hold a plebiscite everywhere. Surely it would be necessary to hold one only in those areas where the issue was doubtful."

As the conversations proceeded, Chamberlain again began asserting himself in his role as impartial mediator between Hitler and the British Government. Chamberlain said that "he, the Prime Minister, was not a party to these negotiations, but rather a mediator seeking to achieve a peaceful solution."

> As it was, public opinion in England, was not favourably disposed towards the proposals now under consideration, and they would be less favourably disposed if it were known that Herr Hitler was increasing his pretensions. What he would like to be able to do would be to prove that the proposed solution was fair and that the plebiscite was to be held in conditions which insured freedom from military or other pressure. Again he asked why it was necessary to hold a plebiscite everywhere.

In persuading his colleagues to accept self-determination, Chamberlain said that he "had been obliged to take his political life into his hands." Clearly, Chamberlain wished to convey to Hitler the unmistakable impression that he personally had no interest in the fate of Czechoslovakia and that he was seeking to enlist Hitler's help in obtaining an orderly solution, a solution which could be cast in language acceptable to Chamberlain's critics at home and to the French. After this initial exchange of views, the meeting adjourned until the following day.

Meanwhile at home, with the prime minister out of the country, forces of opposition were gaining a new momentum. Even as Chamberlain's plane left for Godesberg, there had been boos at Heston airport. A Mass Observation poll of 22 September showed that only twenty-two percent of the British public supported Chamberlain's policy, and a full forty percent opposed it. Of the national newspapers, only *The Times* stood unequivocally behind the prime minister. Eden, Churchill, and Sinclair had made public speeches attacking the Government.

From Czechoslovakia came news that the Sudeten German Freikorps had occupied the district of Asch. In Chamberlain's absence, the Inner Cabinet met to consider whether in these circumstances Britain could still continue to advise the Czechs not to mobilize. Without Chamberlain there to prop up his resolve, Halifax was coming more and more under the influence of those in the Foreign Office who opposed further concessions. A message was sent to Godesberg informing Chamberlain that "the great mass of public opinion seems to be hardening in sense of feeling that we have gone to the limit of concession and that it is up to the Chancellor to make some contribution." Within Britain, military measures short of mobilization were taken to put the country into a state of preparedness. In the prime minister's absence, control over the machinery of state was being assumed by a bureaucracy which had long resented Chamberlain's tightfisted control and which advocated a quite different policy toward Germany.

Thus, on the evening of 22 September, as Chamberlain and Wilson contemplated the increasingly desperate situation, Chamberlain realized that to meet Hitler's demands, no matter how much he might personally be prepared to do so, was politically impossible. Wilson noted that "for the first time, Chamberlain was moved by doubt, even despair." Chamberlain ordered that a message withdrawing British objections to Czech mobilization be suspended. On the morning of the twenty-third, Chamberlain addressed a letter to Hitler stating that he was now prepared to submit Hitler's demands to the Czechs "so that they may examine the suggested provisional boundary."

Again stating his view that a plebiscite was unnecessary, Chamberlain said that the difficulty he found with Hitler's plan was in the "suggestion that areas should in the immediate future be occupied by German troops." Chamberlain said nothing to indicate that he personally found this to be objectionable, only that it would not be acceptable to the British public, the French, or the Czechs. He said that, since the principle of transfer of the Sudeten areas to the Reich had already been agreed upon, the immediate question was "how to maintain law and order pending final settlement of arrangements for transfer." Surely, there must be an alternative proposal acceptable to the Führer. Hitler's written reply left no doubt that he was not prepared to alter the original demands. Accordingly, Chamberlain had little choice but to withdraw his objections to Czech mobilization.

On the evening of 23 September, a second Anglo-German meeting took place. While granting Chamberlain certain minor changes in the wording of his proposals, Hitler refused to alter the demand for immediate military occupation of the Sudetenland. Chamberlain objected and pleaded with Hitler, while continuing to assert his impartiality as mediator, for some positive concession which he could take back to England as a sop to public opinion. In the end, Chamberlain, leaving the inescapable impression that he would work to see that Hitler's demands were met, agreed to transmit the proposals to the Czechs. On this note, the meeting adjourned. Horace Wilson noted that as Chamberlain left the conference he was "satisfied Hitler was ready (and almost eager) to march."

The following morning Chamberlain returned to Britain. At Heston airport, a weary prime minister issued a brief statement to the press in which he said, "I trust all concerned will continue their efforts to solve the Czechoslovakia problem peacefully, because on that turns the peace of Europe in our time." Clearly, Chamberlain saw the issue of Czechoslovakia as the one obstacle, a major obstacle to be sure, which stood in the way of general European appeasement. As always, he remained more or less indifferent to the wishes and aspirations of the Czechoslovakian people.

That afternoon Chamberlain met with the Inner Cabinet, telling them that Hitler would fight if his terms were rejected, that therefore the Godesberg terms should be accepted, and that "having once agreed to cession, the sooner the transfer took place the better." Even Halifax, who only the day before had shown definite signs of resolution, now joined his colleagues in concluding that Czechoslovakia was not sufficient cause for war. As usual, the Inner Cabinet meekly followed Chamberlain's lead.[18]

To the full Cabinet, Chamberlain put forward his case for what amounted to capitulation. Elaborating on the concessions he had been able to win from Hitler, Chamberlain assured the Cabinet that Hitler "would not deliberately deceive a man with whom he had been in negotiations. . . ." More than ever, he felt that the peace of Europe depended on an Anglo-German understanding. Chamberlain evoked vivid images of what would happen if such an understanding were not reached.

> That morning he had flown up the river over London. He had imagined a German bomber flying the same course. He had asked himself what degree of protection they could afford for the thousands of homes which he had seen stretched out below him, and he had felt that we were in no position to justify waging a war today, in order to prevent a war thereafter.

Chamberlain, convinced that general war would follow if the Godesberg terms were not met, sought to bring home to the Cabinet his personal sense of desperation. Although no Cabinet action, either to accept or reject the Godesberg terms, was taken, for the moment at least Chamberlain held the field.

Nevertheless, a fundamental and decisive shift of opinion was taking place within the higher levels of government. The heretofore disparate

---

[18] In his diary Cadogan said that at the meeting, the "P.M. took nearly an hour to make his report, and there was practically no discussion." Cadogan was particularly appalled at Simon's spineless acceptance of Chamberlain's point of view and that although Hoare shared Cadogan's views he was "a puny creature."

whispers of dissent were beginning to coalesce into unified opposition. With Cadogan's prompting, Halifax was beginning to lead those who were against accepting Hitler's terms.[19] Duff Cooper and others hinted that they might resign if the terms were accepted.[20] Outside the Government, Eden and Churchill were beginning to ally themselves with the Labour Opposition. While Chamberlain still retained a majority in the Cabinet, the rising forces of opposition were becoming a political barrier which he simply could not circumvent. His store of political capital was being expended at an alarming rate.

In this atmosphere of intense political debate, Chamberlain's own position was absolutely clear; the Godesberg terms must be accepted and accepted at once. Behind this policy he mustered every available argument: the anticipated destructiveness of war, Britain's military weakness, the negative attitude of the Dominions, and the uncertainty of the French. On 25 September, the French ministers once again arrived in London for conversations and appeared to be vehemently against recommending the Godesberg terms to the Czechs, but at the same time they refused to say outright that they would go to war if Germany attacked Czechoslovakia. From Paris, Phipps cabled, ". . . all that is best in France is against war almost at any price. . . ." And as Chamberlain shrewdly pointed out to the Cabinet, ". . . never once had the French put the question—if we go to war with Germany will you come too?" Whatever else may be said of these discussions, Chamberlain certainly realized that it would be impossible to unequivocally recommend to the Czechs that they accept the Godesberg proposals.

[19] Birkenhead, Lord Halifax's biographer, says that on first hearing of the Godesberg terms Halifax "had an extraordinary but fleeting moment of weakness," but that after consultations with Cadogan, Halifax decided unequivocally to reject the terms. Chamberlain wrote to Halifax that the latter's decision came as a "horrible blow to me."

In his diary of 24 September, p. 103, Cadogan wrote, on hearing of the Godesberg terms, "I was completely horrified—he [i.e. Chamberlain] was quite calmly for total surrender. More horrified still to find that Hitler has completely hypnotized him to a point. Still more horrified to find P.M. has hypnotized H[alifax] who capitulates totally.

[20] One historian, Maurice Cowling, says that at least six Cabinet members, Stanley, Winterton, Hore-Belisha, de la Warr, Eliot, and Duff Cooper were contemplating resignation if the Godesberg terms were accepted.

❧ 7 ❧

Munich

THE WILSON MISSION

TIME was running out, room for maneuver narrowing, and attitudes were hardening in favor of a firm stand against Germany. Many, if not most, British politicians now believed that the limits of tolerance and accommodation had been reached. The atmosphere in the higher reaches of the British Government was one of growing resignation to the idea that war with Germany was inevitable. In this atmosphere Chamberlain conceived still another bold initiative which he believed might yet save the peace and which would forestall, at least for the moment, rising Cabinet dissension. Invoking the authority of his personal relationship to Hitler, Chamberlain suggested to the Cabinet that he might send Horace Wilson with a personal letter to Hitler telling him that the Czechs were likely to reject the Godesberg terms and making "one last appeal" for further negotiations. If Hitler did not accept, then Wilson would deliver "a personal message from the P.M. to the effect that, if this appeal was refused, France would go to war and if that happened it seemed certain that we should be drawn in." Without objection, the Cabinet authorized Chamberlain to proceed, but in exchange for the authority to make this last direct approach to Hitler, Chamberlain agreed to accept the long-dreaded guarantee to France.[1]

It should be noted that British policy was now proceeding on two quite distinct lines. On the one hand, Horace Wilson was on his way to Berlin for a late afternoon meeting with Hitler to persuade him to accept a revision of the Godesberg demands.[2] On the other, Halifax

[1]While in the Cabinet Chamberlain had accepted the principle of a guarantee to France, it is by no means certain that he was, in his own mind, willing to go quite that far. Birkenhead quotes a note from Chamberlain to Halifax in which the former said, "If they say they will go in, thereby dragging us in I do not think I could accept responsibility for the decision." It seems likely that Chamberlain merely accepted the guarantee as the political price he had to pay for the authority to make one last approach to Hitler and that he was gambling on the success of the Wilson mission.

[2]Simultaneously, Roosevelt, acting on his own initiative, sent an appeal to the British, French, Czech, and German governments urging them not to give up their efforts at finding a negotiated settlement. In London, Roosevelt's appeal was seen as supporting Wilson's efforts in Berlin.

released a press communiqué prepared by Rex Leeper of the Foreign Office News Department stating that, ". . . if in spite of all efforts made by the British Prime Minister, a German attack is made upon Czechoslovakia the immediate result must be that France will be bound to come to her assistance, and Great Britain and Russia will certainly stand by France."[3] To communicate to Hitler the fact that Britain was unequivocally prepared to stand by France if that country became involved in a war with Germany over Czechoslovakia, from Chamberlain's point of view, did nothing to increase the chances of success for the Wilson mission. In spite of secret preparations for mobilization and the new resolve to stand by Czechoslovakia as expressed in the Leeper communiqué, the manifest message being communicated to Hitler was one of undivided support for a negotiated settlement. In sum, British policy toward Germany now barely concealed the divided strategies represented by Chamberlain and the Foreign Office. Unless Chamberlain could produce a public victory for his policy, the heretofore private differences over policy would become a public debate which might well result in the fall of the Chamberlain Government. Chamberlain was thus in the grip of a desperate last-minute gamble to save not only the peace of Europe but also his own political career.

At 5:00 P.M. on 26 September, Wilson met with Hitler and delivered Chamberlain's letter asking Hitler "to agree that representatives of Germany shall meet representatives of the Czechoslovakian Government to discuss immediately the situation by which we are confronted with a view to settling by agreement the way in which the territory is to be handed over," and offering "representation of the British Government at the discussions." Wilson found Hitler in a state of extreme agitation which left little doubt that if Czechoslovakia refused to accept his demands by 2 P.M. on Wednesday, 28 September, he would attack. In the face of this emotional outburst, Wilson declined to give the warning which was to have followed if Hitler declined Chamberlain's latest offer.

That evening Hitler delivered another of his impassioned and bellicose speeches to a cheering crowd in the Berlin Sportspalast, a speech which, in his diary, Leo Amery described as "the most horrible thing I have ever heard, more like the snarling of a wild animal than the utterance of a human being, and the venom and vulgarity of his personal vilifications of 'Beneš the liar' almost made me sick." Yet even in this torrent of venomous rhetoric, Hitler declined to close the door com-

---

[3] The so-called "Leeper communiqué" is widely discussed in the literature of appeasement. Robbins called it ". . . another example of an initiative by an official treading near to making policy." Middlemas says that Robbins's conclusion was unwarranted. If, as has been here argued, reluctant acceptance of a guarantee to France was the political price Chamberlain had to pay for the Wilson initiative, then the Leeper communiqué reflected a view which Chamberlain had unwillingly accepted but something he definitely did not want publicized. In point of fact, the Leeper communiqué was never printed in the *Times*. Whether this was by deliberate self-censorship or because the editors felt it had been superseded by subsequent events is difficult to determine.

pletely to further British efforts and made a positive reference to the role Chamberlain had played.

After hearing the speech by wireless, Chamberlain prepared a statement of his own to the British press saying that he could not abandon his efforts at peace, "since it seems to me incredible that the peoples of Europe who do not want war with one another should be plunged into a bloody struggle over a question on which agreement has already been largely obtained." Chamberlain said that the British Government felt "morally responsible" for seeing that the Czechs carried out their promise to cede the Sudetenland, and stated, ". . . we are prepared to undertake that they shall be so carried out with all reasonable promptitude, provided that the German Government will agree to the settlement of terms and conditions of transfer by discussion and not by force." Nevertheless, Wilson was not relieved of the obligation to deliver the warning to Hitler. Chamberlain, however, instructed him to deliver it "more in sorrow than in anger."

Therefore when Wilson met with Hitler on 27 September, he reluctantly delivered the warning which stated that Britain would stand by France if she became involved in a war with Germany. However, he did so only after hinting at the "many things which ought to be discussed between England and Germany to the great advantage of both countries. [including] arrangements for improving the economic position all round." Wilson was expressing Chamberlain's often repeated view that if only the two countries could get around this unpleasantness over Czechoslovakia, the way would be open for settling much more important matters. However, Hitler's adamant refusal to consider revising the Godesberg terms left very little ground for optimism or for further negotiations. Wilson returned to London having achieved no modification of the Godesberg terms.

On his return, Wilson joined a ministerial meeting then in progress. He advised the assembled ministers that the Czechs should be immediately told to accept German occupation since this was the last opportunity to avoid war. The opinions expressed by the chiefs of staff seemed to support Wilson's conclusions.[4] Having heard these and other gloomy assessments, Chamberlain, echoing the wording of the military chiefs, sent a message to Beneš informing him that unless he agreed to the terms by 2:00 P.M. the following day, it was clear to the British Government "that Bohemia would be overthrown and nothing that any other

---

[4] The views of the chiefs of staff were summarized in a later memorandum.

It is our opinion that no pressure that Great Britain and France can bring to bear, either by sea, or land, or in the air, could prevent Germany from overrunning Bohemia and from inflicting a decisive defeat on Czechoslovakia.

Dilks, in the "Cadogan Diaries," claims that these views were almost certainly aired at the Cabinet meeting of 27 September.

Power can do will prevent this fate for your country and people." The message stopped short of advising the Czechs to accept, stating only that the British Government could not take the responsibility of advising the Czechs what to do in these circumstances. The ambiguity in this statement was almost certainly intentional. Chamberlain knew that it was politically impossible for him unequivocally to advise the Czechs to accept, while at the same time, he wanted to exert maximum influence on the Czechs to do just that. In any case, it was hardly a message which would encourage Beneš to stand firm.[5]

It was early evening when the meeting in the Cabinet room of No. 10 Downing Street broke up. Chamberlain, as he later wrote to his sister, was closer to a complete emotional collapse than at any time in his career. Technicians from the BBC were beginning to prepare the room for Chamberlain's address to the nation. Cadogan, who spoke with Chamberlain that evening, said that the prime minister was "quite exhausted," and that Chamberlain had told him, "I'm wobbling about all over the place!"

It was in this state of mind that, at 8:00 P.M., Chamberlain, a tired and discouraged old man, delivered his famous broadcast to the British people:

> How horrible, fantastic, incredible it is that we should be digging trenches and trying on gas masks here because of a quarrel in a far-away country between people of whom we know nothing. It seems still more impossible that a quarrel which has already been settled in principle should be the subject of war. . . .
>
> However much we may sympathize with a small nation confronted by a big and powerful neighbour, we cannot in all circumstances undertake to involve the whole British Empire in war simply on her account. If we have to fight it must be on larger issues than that. I am myself a man of peace to the depths of my soul. Armed conflict between nations is a nightmare to me; but if I were convinced that any nation had made up its mind to dominate the world by fear of its force, I should feel that it must be resisted.
>
> Under such a domination life for people who believe in liberty would not be worth living; but war is a fearful thing, and we must be very clear, before we embark on it, that it is really the great issues that are at stake, and that the call to risk everything in their defence, when all the consequences are weighed, is irresistible.

[5] An hour later, a revised timetable for German occupation of the Sudetenland was sent to both Berlin and Prague. The plan was a last-minute attempt at compromise; part of the Sudetenland would be occupied by 1 October with the remainder of the transfer to be effected by a joint British, German, and Czech commission and it offered to send British troops as intermediaries.

Middlemas states, ". . . at 6:45 Chamberlain sent Henderson a plan offering a new timetable for occupation which he hoped would be acceptable to both sides." In his diary, Cadogan noted, "I got H[alifax] authority to send off telegrams proposing my 'timetable'." Given the tremendous pressure of events it seems quite impossible that the timetable could have been written by Chamberlain.

In sharp contrast to the rhetorical eloquence with which Churchill would later stir the hearts of his countrymen, Chamberlain's speech was not, nor was it intended to be, a resounding call to arms, but rather a statement of grim resignation. In its references to Czechoslovakia, the speech was nothing less than a repudiation of the pledge privately given to France, a pledge which Chamberlain had himself probably never fully accepted.[6] Nor for that matter, is there evidence that the French were absolutely prepared to fight, either with or without a British guarantee of support. In any case, Britain was not going to fight to preserve the territorial integrity of Czechoslovakia.

Yet Chamberlain spoke to a country preparing itself for war. The day before, evacuation of school children to safe places in the country had begun. Hospitals were being emptied to accommodate the estimated 50,000 casualties which were expected in the first few days of air attacks. Everywhere, people were being fitted with gas masks. Trenches were being dug in the parks of London. In spite of everything Chamberlain had tried to achieve, the country was preparing for a war which many believed would be more ghastly and more destructive than anything in history.

The full Cabinet convened at 9:30 P.M. shortly after the broadcast. Wilson related the long and depressing account of his meeting with Hitler to the assembled ministers, and restated his view that if Beneš would accept the new timetable, he believed that Hitler would cooperate. The beleaguered prime minister soon learned that his colleagues were no longer willing meekly to accept the Chamberlain line, including the messages which had already been dispatched to Berlin and Prague. Duff Cooper indicated that he would resign rather than submit to advising Czechoslovakia to accept Hitler's terms. Even Halifax, who only hours before had endorsed the message to Beneš, refused to accept the new plans. Wearily, Chamberlain said that "if that was the general view of his colleagues, he was prepared to leave it at that." On that note, the meeting adjourned.

Last Minute Efforts for Peace

There were now fewer than fourteen hours remaining before the expiration of the German deadline. Chamberlain had clearly reached the limit of his ability to maneuver between Hitler and the British Cabinet. It was therefore not surprising that when Joseph Kennedy, the American ambassador, met the prime minister at 10:00 P.M. that evening he found him "utterly depressed." However, just when Chamber-

---

[6]See note 15 p. 146, *supra*.

lain's options seemed to have been exhausted, there came a personal message from Hitler. Where before Hitler's attitude had been truculent and aggressive, now he seemed conciliatory and willing to negotiate. Hitler wrote, "I regret the idea of any attack on Czechoslovak territory . . . I am even ready to give a formal guarantee of the remainder of Czechoslovakia." The letter, as the historian John Wheeler-Bennett put it, was an "angel of light" to Chamberlain in his darkest hour, and he believed he saw one last chance to avert the impending catastrophe.

After reading Hitler's letter, Chamberlain decided to respond, as he had so often done in the past, with a personal initiative. Without seeking advice from anyone, he sat down at his desk and wrote letters to both Hitler and Mussolini. He showed them to no one except the ever-faithful Horace Wilson. To Hitler, Chamberlain wrote:

> After reading your letter I feel certain that you can get all essentials without war and without delay.
>
> I am ready to come to Berlin myself at once to discuss with you and representatives of Czech Government, together with representatives of France and Italy if you desire.
>
> I feel convinced we could reach agreement in a week. However much you distrust Prague Government's intentions, you cannot doubt power of British and French Governments to see that promises are carried out fairly and fully and forthwith. As you know I have stated publicly that we are prepared to undertake that they shall be carried out.
>
> I cannot believe that you will take responsibility of starting a world war which may end civilization for the sake of a few days' delay in settling this long-standing problem.

And to Mussolini:

> I have to-day addressed last appeal to Herr Hitler to abstain from force to settle Sudeten problem, which I feel sure can be settled by a short discussion and will give him the essential territory, population and protection for both Sudetens and Czechs during transfer. I have offered myself to go at once to Berlin to discuss arrangements with German and Czech representatives and, if the Chancellor desires, representatives also of Italy and France.
>
> I trust your excellency will inform German Chancellor that you are willing to be represented and urge him to agree to my proposal which will keep all our peoples out of war. I have already guaranteed that Czech promises shall be carried out and feel confident full agreement could be reached in a week.

After writing these letters, Chamberlain set to work on the speech he was to deliver next day to the Commons. At 2:00 A.M. the exhausted and depressed prime minister went to bed with only a faint glimmer of hope that this, his last initiative, might yet bear fruit.

Chamberlain's messages were dispatched to Rome and Berlin the next morning. Until a reply was received, there was little to be done but wait. Shortly before the House of Commons convened at 2:45 P.M., word came from Rome that Mussolini had succeeded in gaining a postponement of mobilization. That was the only positive news which Chamberlain carried with him that afternoon as he made his way from No. 10 Downing Street to the House of Commons.

Parliament had been in recess since the end of July and the members returned to the House in an atmosphere laden with apprehension and emotional intensity. In anticipation of an historic event, the galleries of the House were beginning to fill with dignitaries of every sort. The queen mother and other royalty were present as was Lord Baldwin, leading members of the clergy, and a full contingent of ambassadors.[7] Most of those present had some general understanding of events in Czechoslovakia but not of the prime minister's latest actions. "It was impossible" as Wheeler-Bennett has noted, "not to recall a parallel event on August 4, 1914, when Sir Edward Grey had addressed the House on a terribly similar occasion." Everyone present waited in dread anticipation that Chamberlain would deliver an ultimatum which would once again plunge the country into war.

At precisely 2:54 P.M., Chamberlain entered the House, spread his manuscript on the dispatch box before him, and began to speak in calm and measured tones. "Today," he said, "we are faced with a situation which has no parallel since 1914." Slowly, methodically, and without visible enthusiasm for his material, Chamberlain reviewed the history of British attempts to find a solution to the ever-worsening situation in Czechoslovakia; the meeting at Berchtesgaden, the Runciman mission, his second meeting with Hitler at Godesberg, and finally the ill-fated Wilson mission. Chamberlain's careful chronological recapitulation heightened the dramatic effect of his speech. As he passed from that part of the story which everyone knew to the part that had not yet been divulged, the entire House leaned forward in silent anticipation. The prime minister told the house how at 10:30 the night before he had received a letter from Hitler. The letter, he said, contained "reassuring statements," and Chamberlain said that he believed Hitler meant what he said. Finally, Chamberlain described how the letter had caused him to pen his own last-minute response to Hitler and to Mussolini, and that as a result, Mussolini had persuaded Hitler to postpone mobilization for twenty-four hours.

It was now 4:15 P.M. Chamberlain had been speaking for over an

[7]No better example of the continuity of historical analogy can be found than in the fact that among those in the galleries listening to Chamberlain's speech was John F. Kennedy, son of the American ambassador, and future president of the United States. The younger Kennedy would later write a book on Munich, *Why England Slept,* and twenty three years later would make the decision not to back down from a dictator determined to install Soviet missiles in Cuba.

hour when a sheet of Foreign Office paper was seen being passed rapidly down the Government bench to John Simon who at length gained the prime minister's attention. Chamberlain read the message. Some people believed they saw a smile cross his face and color return to his cheeks and that suddenly he looked ten years younger. "Shall I tell them now?" he asked. When Simon nodded, Chamberlain announced: "I have now been informed by Herr Hitler that he invites me to meet him at Munich tomorrow morning. Signor Mussolini has accepted and I have no doubt M. Daladier will also accept. I need not say what my answer will be." [8]

From the back benches someone said, "Thank God for the Prime Minister!" With that, a roar of approval swept over the House. A scene of near pandemonium ensued. Almost to a man, the House stood and cheered, order papers were thrown into the air, and there were tears of relief at yet another reprieve from the untold horror of war with Germany. With few exceptions, the vast majority of British subjects and people throughout the world were willing and eager to give Chamberlain his one last chance to win the peace. In such an atmosphere, few noticed that Chamberlain had asked for a five-power conference and had been invited to a gathering of four. The Czechs themselves were not invited.

Whether by coincidence or carefully premeditated design, Chamberlain had gained the initiative for one last chance to vindicate his policy. At each stage in his negotiations with Hitler: Berchtesgaden, Godesberg, the Wilson mission, and now Munich, Chamberlain had backed one step further toward the end of a political limb. If he succeeded, he would earn his place beside Austen and his father as one of Britain's pre-eminent statesmen, the man who achieved the appeasement of Europe. The dismemberment of Czechoslovakia, soon forgotten, would have been a small price to pay. If he failed, the now precarious structure

---

[8]The fact that Hitler's message was delivered to Chamberlain at the precise moment he was concluding his speech to the Commons is a coincidence almost not to be believed. Having reached the limit of the Government's willingness to meet Hitler's terms, Chamberlain had exceeded that limit and sent yet another personal appeal to Hitler, an appeal which the Cabinet would almost certainly not have approved. Once Hitler's invitation to come to Munich had been read to the Commons and following the emotional outpouring of support Chamberlain had received, it would have been impossible for the opposition within the Cabinet to repudiate Chamberlain's acceptance. All this raises the question as to whether or not the seeming coincidence was a carefully choreographed maneuver to gain for Chamberlain his one last chance at a negotiated settlement. Certainly, a man like Chamberlain was not incapable of such actions. Against this plausible explanation are the accounts left by Chamberlain himself and Cadogan, the Foreign Office official who received the message from Hitler. Cadogan vividly recalled how he received the message and then ran with it to the House of Commons where Chamberlain had already begun his speech. In a letter to his sister, Chamberlain noted that the message, coming as it did, at the very moment he was ending his speech, was a dramatic event unequaled in fiction. Yet even with such evidence, the scene seems a bit too theatrical. It is therefore possible to speculate that Chamberlain suspected or at least hoped that events would happen as they did and that he deliberately prolonged his speech in the hope that a positive reply from Hitler would arrive. Still, the author was unable to uncover any hard evidence that the event was consciously contrived.

of personal power would disintegrate and the European war which Chamberlain had desperately tried to avert would become a reality. Such was Chamberlain's understanding of the situation. In spite of moralizing objections to Chamberlain's hard-nosed pursuit of *raison d'état*, there is no evidence to suggest that he was mistaken in his political realism.

THE MEETING AT MUNICH

At 8:30 A.M. on the morning of 29 September, members of the Cabinet gathered at Heston airport to see the prime minister off for his third and final meeting with Hitler. In spite of the exhausting events of the last few days, Chamberlain appeared refreshed and in good spirits. He told his colleagues that on his return he hoped to be able to say, like Hotspur in *Henry IV*, ". . . out of this nettle, danger, we pluck this flower, safety." With that, Chamberlain boarded the plane and flew off to Munich.[9]

A few hours later the British prime minister joined Daladier for the meeting with Hitler and Mussolini. In contrast to the dictators, the British and French leaders had not met beforehand to work out a common policy. In Chamberlain's view it was unnecessary to do so since he had always assumed that the French would acquiesce to whatever position Britain took, an assumption which had always proven to be correct. In fact, had it not been for the existence of the Franco-Czech treaty, Chamberlain might well have considered French presence at Munich to be unnecessary. Although they had been hastily summoned to Munich, representatives of Czechoslovakia were not invited to take part in the negotiations.

The record of the negotiations at Munich is notable not for the intensity of deliberation, the exchange of carefully articulated points of view, but for its brevity, its almost complete lack of give and take. In sum, nothing substantial was negotiated. In short order, agreement was reached on the essential points of a plan presented by Mussolini (but drawn up by the Germans), a central feature of which was that Germany would occupy the Sudetenland in progressive stages beginning on 1 October. Britain, France, and Italy were to guarantee that the occupation would be completed by 10 October. An international commis-

---

[9]Chamberlain was accompanied by Sir Horace Wilson, Sir William Malkin, head of the drafting and legal department of the Foreign Office, and Mr. William Strang, head of the Central Department of the Foreign Office and a member of the Runciman mission. As at Berchtesgaden and Godesberg, Halifax was not asked to accompany the delegation. Hoare has suggested that this was because of Chamberlain's "reluctance to embroil one of his colleagues in what he thought would be an unpopular adventure." Several other explanations are equally plausible. In the first place, Halifax had little diplomatic or intellectual expertise of his own to contribute. More important, from Chamberlain's perspective, was the fact that Halifax had shown himself dangerously susceptible to the dissident influence of such men as Cadogan and Vansittart and therefore could not be relied upon to meekly accept Chamberlain's views.

sion composed of the four powers plus a representative of Czechoslovakia would determine the conditions of evacuation and the final boundary between Germany and Czechoslovakia. The Anglo-French offer of a guarantee to the remainder of Czechoslovakia against unprovoked aggression was included in an annex to the agreement. Once the question of the Polish and Hungarian minorities had been settled, Italy and Germany would join the guarantee. Such were the essential features of the infamous Munich agreement signed at 2:00 A.M. on the morning of 30 September 1938.

Having taken no part in the discussions over the fate of their country, the Czech ministers were advised by Chamberlain and Daladier to accept the terms of the four-power agreement. Unlike Daladier, Chamberlain had no sense of having betrayed Czechoslovakia. In fact, according to Wheeler-Bennett, he "yawned unrestrainedly throughout the interview." In Chamberlain's view, the purpose of the Munich meeting was to insure that the transfer of the Sudetenland, an issue on which agreement had already been reached, would be carried out in an orderly manner. Czechoslovakia was to be dismembered. Munich was not the place for moral handwringing, and, to the extent that he thought about it at all, Chamberlain probably saw no reason why the Czechs should not readily give their assent to the four-power agreement.

Early the following morning, William Strang, a senior member of the British delegation, was awakened by a brief message from the prime minister asking him to "draft a short statement on the future of Anglo-German relations to which he [Chamberlain] might secure Hitler's agreement." Hurriedly, Strang prepared a document for the prime minister's consideration. Chamberlain modified Strang's draft as follows:

We, the German Führer and Chancellor and the British Prime Minister, have had a further meeting today and are agreed in recognising that the question of Anglo-German relations is of the first importance for the two countries and for Europe.

We regard the agreement signed last night and the Anglo-German Naval Agreement as symbolic of the desire of our two peoples never to go to war with one another again.

We are resolved that the method of consultation shall be the method adopted to deal with any other questions that may concern our two countries, and we are determined to continue our efforts to remove possible sources of differences and thus to contribute to assuring the peace of Europe.[10]

[10]Chamberlain's insistence on including a reference to the Anglo-German Naval Treaty in the draft was probably a reference to the issues raised by Hitler at Berchtesgaden. Hitler had, perhaps only as a rhetorical device, made the treaty a central feature of the Berchtesgaden conversations. At Munich, Chamberlain was attempting to respond directly to these issues.

Chamberlain inserted the reference to the Anglo-German Naval Agreement over the objections of Strang, who felt it "was not a thing to be proud of." Chamberlain, on the contrary, felt "it was the type of agreement we should try to reach with Germany." Strang urged Chamberlain to consult with Daladier before presenting the document to Hitler, but Chamberlain would not listen, saying "that he saw no reason whatever for saying anything to the French."

That morning a private meeting between Chamberlain and Hitler took place in an atmosphere of unprecedented cordiality. Having achieved a satisfactory solution of the Sudeten question, Hitler appeared jovial and willing to compromise. Chamberlain, believing he had caught the dictator in a rare mood of conciliation, thought he saw his chance to move in one bold stroke beyond the minor but heretofore intractable problem of Czechoslovakia, to the infinitely more important questions between their two countries.

With the horrors of modern warfare always uppermost in his mind, Chamberlain said that he hoped that in the event of war between Germany and Czechoslovakia, Germany would refrain from bombing. Hitler responded by saying that "he hated the thought of little babies being killed by gas bombs." In a remarkable *tour d'horizon*, Chamberlain, moving quickly from one issue to the next, surveyed the entire range of issues separating Britain and Germany. Encouraged by what he saw as Hitler's new mood of agreeableness, Chamberlain raised the issues of Spain, air disarmament, and Anglo-German trade. On each issue, Hitler nodded in agreement until at the end of the conversation, Chamberlain produced the document he had prepared. With this, too, Hitler readily gave his consent. Without further discussion, the two affixed their signatures and with that the meeting adjourned. It was a remarkable interchange, as if Chamberlain, skeptical of Hitler's new attitude of conciliation, believed he was seizing a moment which might not come again to obtain agreement on all outstanding issues and to settle the diplomatic problems which had plagued British policy-makers since Versailles in one bold stroke. At the conclusion of the meeting, Chamberlain returned to his hotel and, patting his breast pocket, triumphantly exclaimed, "I've got it!"

To Hitler, the agreement most likely appeared to be an innocuous document and signing it meant very little, but to Chamberlain it meant a great deal. What to Hitler was an insignificant afterthought to the Munich accord was to Chamberlain nothing less than the Anglo-German understanding which he had long hoped to achieve, the foundation on which a lasting structure of peace, the appeasement of Europe, could be erected. Or, at least it was not difficult for Chamberlain to convince himself that such was the case. While critics of Chamberlain have seen the fate of Czechoslovakia as the central issue decided at Munich, this was not the meaning attached to the conference by Chamberlain himself.[11] To him, the triumph of Munich, the victory to which he attached the unfortunate phrase "peace in our time," lay not in the settlement of the Sudeten question but in the private accord he had reached with Hitler. It was this, not the four-power agreement on Czechoslovakia, which he waved to the cheering crowds at Heston airport on his return to London.

Chamberlain Triumphant

For a single brief moment, it looked as if Neville Chamberlain's dream of achieving the appeasement of Europe might be fulfilled. To the thousands who cheered and threw flowers on Chamberlain's departure from Munich and the even greater numbers who greeted him on his return to England, Chamberlain was very much the man who saved the peace.

In the aftermath of the Second World War, it is difficult, perhaps impossible, to understand the full meaning which contemporaries attached to Chamberlain's actions at Munich. As Chamberlain's car moved slowly through the cheering masses at Heston airport, at the Palace where he appeared on the balcony with the king and queen waving to the crowds below, and later when he stood at the window of No. 10 Downing Street and uttered the famous phrase, ". . . this is the second time[12] in our history that there has come back from Germany to Downing Street peace with honour. I believe it is peace for our time."[13] At these moments, Chamberlain was indeed the man who saved Europe from a repetition of the Great War. There can be no doubt that he

---

[11] Hoare, for example, said that he was "convinced that Chamberlain never regarded Munich as more than a step in his programme of peace." There were, to be sure, other reasons for Chamberlain's actions. Chamberlain's Parliamentary Secretary, Alec Douglas-Home, recalled that Chamberlain had told him, ". . . if Hitler signed it and kept the bargain well and good; alternatively that if he broke it, he would demonstrate to all the world that he was totally cynical and untrustworthy, and that this would have its value in mobilizing public opinion against him, particularly in America."

[12] This, as he made clear in a letter to his sister, was a reference to Disraeli's return from Germany sixty years earlier.

[13] There has been a great deal of discussion over the meaning Chamberlain attached to these words, and over his comment to Halifax, on leaving Heston airport for the Palace, ". . . all this will be over in three months." Chamberlain later regretted the phrase "peace with honour," telling the House not to read too much into a phrase used in a moment of some emotion. In his memoirs, Halifax explained Chamberlain's intentions:

When he said "all this will be over in three months," he was referring to the popular enthusiasm of the moment; when he spoke about "peace for our time," he was concerned with the spirit in which he believed Hitler to have signed the declaration and which at that moment he was disposed to trust.

In his memoirs, Alec Douglas-Home explained that Chamberlain first rejected any reference to "peace in our time" saying, "No, I do not do that kind of thing." A few minutes later, as Douglas-Home recalled, ". . . the next thing I knew was that he had spoken the fateful words. Somebody in the last few yards to the window must have overtaken and overpersuaded him. He knew at once that it was a mistake and that he could not justify the claim. It haunted him for the rest of his life."

expressed the hopes and aspirations of, and was supported by, the vast majority of people everywhere.[14]

The following day an exhausted prime minister left London for a weekend at Chequers. He was, as he said, on the verge of a nervous breakdown but satisfied with the fact that an unspeakably dreadful war had been avoided. At Chequers, he found time to record his private thoughts in a letter to his sisters in which he said that in the days before Munich he had lost all sense of time and that he had no wish to recall the events of that period. His most important recollection was that as time passed the inexorable pressure of history seemed to be driving them with a terrifying speed ever closer to war. He described his last letter to Hitler, the letter in which he had offered to make one final visit to Germany, as an act of sheer desperation at the very edge of the abyss. His detailed description of the events that followed left little doubt that Chamberlain believed that it was his personal accord with Hitler, and not the four-power agreement on Czechoslovakia, which was the most important achievment at Munich.

In an uncharacteristically emotional letter to Prince William of Prussia, Chamberlain wrote that for people like themselves who had lost family in the Great War there really could be no doubt that the decision to attempt a negotiated settlement at Munich was the right one. He also said that in the future such crucial decisions would be in the hands of a new generation which had no direct experience of that war, but one which would no doubt learn from the trying experiences of their elders

[14]The Chamberlain papers contain some of the more than 40,000 letters of support which Chamberlain received from people at all levels of society and from all parts of the world. Among the tributes to Chamberlain was an album of pictures from Dutch school children, a statue of Chamberlain erected in Portugal, and a street renamed in Strasbourg. The list of personal tributes to Chamberlain was, in every respect, unprecedented. Among those praising Chamberlain's actions were letters written by many of the leading academic, intellectual, and political figures of the day. The letters of Professor Temperley have been noted. Maurice Hankey, the former Cabinet secretary and veteran of many diplomatic battles, wrote, that from the time he had retired from public life until the time of Munich he had never questioned that Chamberlain would find a way to avoid going to war with Germany. The Cambridge economist A.C. Pigou wrote of his great relief that the crisis had passed. Stanley Baldwin wrote to Chamberlain on 15 September that he was greatly pleased that Chamberlain was going to meet with Hitler and stated that no matter what the outcome, Chamberlain was right "a thousand times over," to make the effort. After Munich, Baldwin again wrote to say that there was no one in England more pleased than he to see his old comrade celebrated and applauded by the entire world. Baldwin went on to say that for the time being, Chamberlain had everyone on his side and could do as he pleased. President Roosevelt wrote that he fully shared the convictions that Chamberlain had created the best opportunity in years for the creation of a new international order based on law and justice.

Prince Wilhelm of Germany wrote that he felt that at the very last possible moment, Chamberlain had saved the world from war. On the eve of Chamberlain's departure for Munich, Anthony Eden had written to wish the prime minister the very best of luck and godspeed. However much he might have differed with Chamberlain in the past, Eden was obviously not convinced that there were no hopes for success at Munich.

In sum, the least that can be said is that those who believed that the Munich agreement had at least some chance of success were not all naïve and foolish old men and that very few people accurately foresaw the future course of events. On the other hand, these letters were written in the immediate outpouring of emotion following Munich. The parliamentary debate of 3 and 6 October marked the rise of a more sober and critical attitude. Moreover, the effusive praise Chamberlain received was not so much for the Munich settlement but for averting war—two very different things.

and would as a result be able to build a world in which the terror of war would be completely eliminated. The letter is particularly revealing evidence of the degree to which historical memory colored Chamberlain's perceptions of the range of choices before him.

Over a month later, in a letter to his stepmother, Chamberlain noted that presents from all over the world were still pouring in but that no one could be as indifferent to these tributes as himself, since no one was as aware as he was that the task of peacemaking had only just begun. Yet so confident was he that the agreement with Hitler had brought about a new era in Anglo-German relations that he was able to write that he found it almost impossible to accept that another emergency as perilous as the one at Munich would happen again, at least not in the foreseeable future. With the Munich agreement behind him, Chamberlain looked forward to better days ahead when the nations of the world could return to the period of mutual trust in which rearmament would be unnecessary and in which the business of improving the human condition would be paramount. These were clearly not the sentiments of a man who believed that he had merely succeeded in "buying time" in which to rearm in preparation for inevitable war, but of a man who believed that the nadir had been reached and that better things lay ahead.

Yet to Chamberlain, the triumph of Munich, important though it was, did not mean that disarmament was a likely possibility or even that Britain would be justified in slowing down the rate of rearmament. As had always been the case, Chamberlain maintained his support for the original five-year rearmament program as expressed in the 1935 White Paper and as it had been subsequently modified. He told the House on 3 October, "Let no one think that because we have signed this agreement between these four powers at Munich we can afford to relax our efforts in regard to that programme at this moment." This, however, did not mean that Chamberlain saw the necessity for massive new increases in rearmament expenditure. On the contrary, as he told the Cabinet on 3 October:

> Ever since he had been Chancellor of the Exchequer he had been oppressed with the sense that the burden of armaments might break our backs. This had been one of the factors which had led him to the view that it was necessary to try and resolve the causes which were responsible for the armament race. He thought that we were now in a more hopeful position and that the contacts which had been established with the dictator powers opened up the possibility that we might be able to reach some agreement which would stop the armament race.

Despite his acceptance of certain modifications in the existing program, Chamberlain consistently maintained his opposition to the kind of "all out" rearmament advocated by Churchill. Indeed, much of the debate over British foreign policy in the months that followed can be seen in terms of the differing policies advocated by Chamberlain and Churchill.

Just as he had used the emotional scene in the House of Commons on 28 September to pre-empt rising Cabinet criticisms of his policy, Chamberlain now sought to use the enormous surge of popular enthusiasm for the Munich agreement to accomplish a similar end in relation to the growing opposition within Parliament. Yet the tide of public support on which Chamberlain rode so triumphantly was rapidly reaching a high-water mark; his personal power had been extended to the limit and beyond. Everything depended on whether or not the promise of Munich was fulfilled. When it became clear, or, more accurately, when people began to perceive that Hitler had no intention of honoring his promises, the overextended structure on which Chamberlain's political position was based would begin to disintegrate.

In many people's minds this process had already begun well before Munich. For others, it came with the realization that British participation in, indeed her sponsorship of, the dismemberment of Czechoslovakia might have been something less than honorable. For still others, it occurred when the promised new era of Anglo-German amity failed to materialize despite every effort on the part of the British Government. For whatever reason the underpinnings of Chamberlain's political power were beginning to collapse just at the moment of his greatest triumph.

❈8❈

The Aftermath of Munich

IN September 1938, war with Germany was still a full year away and Chamberlain would remain in office until May 1940. The final twenty months of the Chamberlain Government was a period of steady decline in the prime minister's political power. Whereas at the time of Munich Chamberlain exercised supreme control over the direction of British foreign policy, the period from September 1938 until May 1940 saw a gradual erosion of that once paramount position of influence to the point, shortly before the end, when Chamberlain was left rather desperately clinging to the formal trappings of power. Just as Munich marked the high-water mark of Chamberlain's political influence, the occupation of Prague in March 1939 was another important watershed after which the erosion of Chamberlain's power greatly accelerated.

With Hitler's armies in occupation of all of Czechoslovakia leaving Poland in a virtually defenseless position, appeasement, it would seem, had been definitively discredited. Yet Chamberlain would retain the office of prime minister for an additional eight months. It is indeed remarkable that it took so long to discredit the policy of appeasement and to remove Chamberlain from office. These facts are one indication of the unprecedented power wielded by Chamberlain at the time of Munich.

The last year of Chamberlain's Government found the prime minister caught between rising domestic opposition on the one hand, and the failure of Hitler to honor the promise of Munich on the other. At times, Chamberlain was able to intervene forcefully, even decisively, in the policy process, but in the main, British politics were returning to a more traditional balance between prime minister and Cabinet and between Government and bureaucracy. Thus, for purposes of this study, the final year of the Chamberlain Government will be discussed more in terms of the personal tragedy of Neville Chamberlain and less in terms of the events over which Chamberlain had less and less control.

DISSOLUTION OF THE MUNICH CONSENSUS

With the excitement and hysteria of the Czech crisis behind him, Chamberlain became increasingly aware of the instability of his own political position. The post-Munich debate in the House of Commons was, from the prime minister's point of view, a particularly trying time. Duff-Cooper resigned in protest over the Munich settlement and was joined by thirty Conservative MPs in abstaining in the vote following the debate. Outspoken attacks on the prime minister from the Labour and Liberal parties had been a more or less constant feature of political discussions of the period, a factor which Chamberlain had persistently and successfully ignored. However, in the aftermath of Munich, the anti-Chamberlain movement within the Tory party itself, coupled with Labour and Liberal opposition, was becoming a force which Chamberlain simply could not ignore.

The movement coalescing around the leadership of Churchill and Eden marked a decisive departure from the period in which none of Chamberlain's critics could offer a clearly articulated alternative to the course advocated by the prime minister. Chamberlain confided to his sisters that he knew that Churchill was colluding with the Czechs behind his back in an effort to discredit appeasement and his leadership. Chamberlain said that Churchill had been spreading the rumor that things were being run by the "big four" instead of the entire Cabinet, but no matter. These machinations merely showed how self-deluding Churchill could be and how gullible the Czechs were in their mistaking wish for reality.

However much he wanted to move forward with his chosen policy, Chamberlain clearly realized that the limit had, at least for the time being, been reached, since any further moves toward accommodation with the fascists would lead to further resignations from the Government. These political difficulties were beginning to bother Chamberlain a great deal and he attempted to take his mind off the critics by reading his fan mail. These letters, he said, led him to the conclusion that the entire world was on his side except for the House of Commons. Indeed, pressures were building for a restructuring of the Government to include Labour and Liberal members, but Chamberlain solidly resisted such suggestions claiming that his present Cabinet was difficult enough for him to handle—what he needed was more support from his colleagues not weak-kneed vacillation and lack of resolve.

Chamberlain's greatest concern, however, was over the question of whether or not Hitler intended to abide by the terms of the Munich agreement. In mid-October, he wrote that although the conference had succeeded in averting war, he did not believe that they were any closer to putting any ideas of war behind them and getting down to the real business of making the world a better place in which to live. He sensed that doubts were growing even within Britain over the agreement. Many thoughtless types, he said, were acting as if Munich had done nothing to avert the threat of war. He held the press largely responsible for this attitude and said that he was trying to get them back to the position that although there were still some deficiencies in Britain's military pre-paredness, there was really no need for large increases in defense spending.

Chamberlain had no intention of allowing the diplomatic initiative to slip once again from British hands. Too often at an earlier stage in his career he had had a feeling of powerlessness, that in foreign affairs things had been allowed to drift without any real direction. Now that he was prime minister he was determined not to be caught unaware. He was planning a trip to France for late November, the purpose of which was to give the French people the opportunity to vent their unex-pressed feelings of thankfulness and devotion as well as to do what he could to strengthen Daladier's political position. This was necessary, Chamberlain felt, to prepare the way for a trip to Rome which he hoped would take place in January. Chamberlain felt that at that moment, Mussolini was the dictator most amenable to negotiation. On 2 Novem-ber, he announced in the House of Commons that "the time was ripe to take a further step forward in the policy of appeasement" by bringing into effect the Anglo-Italian agreement.[1] The House supported him by a vote of 345 to 138. The fact that Chamberlain could persuade the Com-mons to bring the agreement into force despite the fact that the Italians had fulfilled none of its preconditions is an indication that Chamber-lain's political power was still relatively intact.

On 7 November, Baron von Rath, third secretary of the German Embassy in Paris, was shot and fatally wounded by a young Polish Jew. The assassination triggered a wave of officially sanctioned pogroms against the German Jews, events which would long be remembered as *Kristallnacht*, the night of shattered glass. Throughout the western world there were protestations of shock and outrage. Even Lord Londonderry, who had long been one of Britain's leading apologists for Nazi Ger-many, denounced the German action as "detestable."

Privately, Chamberlain expressed rather mild irritation that the pogroms had frustrated his hopes of moving closer toward agreement with Germany. He said that he was appalled by the Nazi action but somewhat wistfully noted that there really did seem to be a kind of predestined course to Anglo-German relations which frustrated every attempt at improvement. He supposed that he would have to make a statement about the Nazi action in the House since someone was almost

---

[1] It should be noted that this was the very day on which the Germans and Italians had forced the Czechs into granting the territorial claims of the Hungarian government.

certain to raise the matter. On 9 November, the very evening of the *Kristallnacht* atrocities, Chamberlain said in a speech at Guildhall, "Christmas is coming and I see no reason why we should not prepare ourselves for the festive season in a spirit of cheerfulness and confidence . . . political conditions in Europe are now settling down to quieter times." Such statements, coming as they did in the midst of Hitler's latest wave of persecutions, did little to stem the deterioration of the moral position on which Chamberlain had justified Munich.

In fact, Chamberlain's entire attitude toward Nazi anti-semitism as well as his attitude toward Jews seeking refuge in Britain was one of callous insensitivity. Like many if not most of Britain's ruling class, Chamberlain held attitudes which were clearly anti-Semitic in their uncritical acceptance of racial stereotypes. For example, on 30 July 1939, he responded to an article sent to him by his sister noting that he had not been aware that Jews were still being permitted to carry on in their professions and could become members of organizations like the Hitler Youth. It goes without saying that this was patently untrue and contrary to all intelligence then being received by the British Government.[2] However, Chamberlain believed that the article was proof positive that the Nazis were hypocritical in their talk of racial purity. His own analysis was that the anti-Jewish actions were motivated out of a desire to deprive the Jews of their possessions and out of envy of the Jews' wily intelligence. He went on to say that even though Jews were not a particularly likable people and indeed he didn't care for them himself, that mere racial prejudice was not a sufficient motive to explain the Nazi action. It is hard not to read such statements as springing from the same ancient racist stereotypes as those of the Nazis themselves. However even the most critical reading of Chamberlain's anti-Semitic views would not warrant the conclusion that he, like Hitler, would be prepared to pursue anti-Semitism to the level of genocide.

In spite of a clear anti-Jewish prejudice, what seems to modern readers as an unconscionable quiescence in the face of Nazi atrocities was probably much more the result of preoccupation with other matters perceived as being of far greater importance than the plight of German Jews. Among these was the alarming deterioration of Chamberlain's political position.

The prime minister was beginning to realize the seriousness and the intensity of domestic opposition to his leadership. To a great extent the post-Munich debate cut across party lines with critics agreeing that Munich had been a betrayal of Czechoslovakia. As to the future course

[2]Studies of official British attitudes toward Nazi persecution of the Jews have shown, among other things, that knowledge of German atrocities was both widespread and readily available within government circles. See particularly A.J. Sherman, *Island Refuge* (Berkeley, Univ. of California Press, 1973), and Andrew Sharf, *The British Press & the Jews Under Nazi Rule* (London, Oxford Univ. Press, 1964).

of British policy, the old debate between the left with its calls for a renewed commitment to collective security and the right demanding a great national effort was still unresolved. Perhaps the only issue on which there was reluctant agreement was on the necessity for a rapid completion of the rearmament program. As domestic political criticism became more intense, Chamberlain reacted by clinging ever more tenaciously and stubbornly to his original course.

Privately, he wrote that the only thing that really mattered to him was being allowed to continue the implementation of his policy, the correctness of which he was absolutely certain. As long as domestic criticism did not prevent him from carrying out his plans he was not bothered by it. In January, he wrote of his determination not to be deflected from his policy toward Mussolini, and he noted that the one thing Lloyd George was right about was his statement that Chamberlain had an extremely obstinate nature which refused to change. However, Chamberlain feared that if for some reason he was no longer prime minister, his successor would soon be off the track and British policy would once again be in flux with no clear direction.

Throughout December, this feeling of isolation grew, and Chamberlain became ever more embittered by the criticism leveled at him from both left and right. The visit to Paris had been something less than the public love feast he had hoped for, although it did serve to gain the reluctant approval of the French for his planned visit to Rome. The British press was becoming more and more outspoken in its criticism of the prime minister, and Chamberlain noted a wish that the British newspapers could be barred from printing material from the continental press except for accounts supportive of his position. This is what the fascists were able to do and in that they had a considerable advantage over the democracies. Chamberlain complained bitterly that Hitler refused to make even the smallest sign of goodwill toward the British. From Chequers, he wrote that he had been seeing the place with renewed interest since he had thoughts that it might not be his to enjoy in the near future. The following week, he again noted that he had had his fill of democratic processes and he sincerely doubted whether any other British prime minister had ever been subjected to such trials with even his own supporters beginning to express their misgivings about his policy. With more than a touch of self-pity, Chamberlain complained that there was no one who could give him the kind of support that he had given to Baldwin, and that as a result he had no one with whom he could share his burden. One need hardly point out that Chamberlain's political isolation was a problem of his own making, the result of his own rigidity and inability to share responsibility.

The new year brought little relief, and he noted that all the major diplomatic movements on the continent were working against the tenuous order he had been able to impose upon them. Still, he resolved not to be disheartened and to carry on as best he could. Chamberlain's letters consistently, in this period, were those of a man unable to move forward with his policy because of rising domestic criticism and because of the failure of Hitler and Mussolini to respond as he hoped they would. As a result, his letters reflected a growing frustration tempered with a faith that things were in fact getting better, or that if not, they certainly would in the near future.[3]

On 10 January, Chamberlain left Britain for his visit to Rome and a meeting with Mussolini. At the diplomatic level, the visit accomplished nothing and in the end, Chamberlain, prompted by Cadogan, reluctantly warned Mussolini that ". . . it would be a terrible tragedy if aggressive action were taken under a misapprehension as to what lengths the democracies might be prepared to go." On the other hand, Chamberlain's reception by the Italian people was for the most part positive, and he wrote to his sister that the trip had exceeded his every expectation and he was convinced that the possibilities of avoiding war were greatly enhanced. It was yet another example of Chamberlain's remarkable capacity for self-deception.

In February, he wrote that he believed at long last that they were beginning to get the best of the fascists, that Hitler had missed the bus at Munich, and that the British had recognized their own vulnerability and taken adequate steps to correct deficiencies. As a result, Britain was in a much stronger position than she had been at the time of Munich. He complained bitterly of Eden and those in the Foreign Office who were so prejudiced by their aversion to the fascists that they could not see the ultimate goal of British policy.[4]

Until the very moment of Hitler's occupation of Prague, Chamberlain maintained his faith that Hitler would honor the promises made at Munich. That Chamberlain could sustain such an attitude of unyielding optimism required a staggering act of faith and was an indication of the

---

[3] Chamberlain maintained his staggering faith in the face of what seems to be almost incontrovertible evidence to the contrary. For example, on 19 January, Halifax read to the FPC the following memo summarizing secret intelligence coming from Germany.

. . . there is incontrovertible evidence that at any rate many of the Führer's entourage are seriously considering the possibility of a direct attack on Great Britain and France during the next few months—perhaps during the next few weeks. It does not even seem to be unlikely that the Führer himself is thinking on such lines as these. At any rate all our sources are at one in declaring that he is barely sane, consumed by an insensate hatred of this country, and capable both of ordering an immediate aerial attack on any European country and of having his command instantly obeyed.

[4] During this period Chamberlain reported that from private conversations he was convinced that Eden was ready to rejoin the Government but that his followers were urging him to lead the anti-Chamberlain forces. Chamberlain said that he was unwilling to save Eden from his delicate position until the latter was willing to admit the error of his ways.

degree to which he had removed himself from the realities of German actions on the Continent. The international commission which was to have determined the final boundaries of Czechoslovakia never got off the ground. The rich industrial area of Teschen was handed over to Poland on twenty-four hours notice on 1 October, and, on 2 November, an area of Czechoslovakia was carved out to satisfy Hungarian minority claims. In sum, events in central Europe were following a course sufficient to justify Chamberlain's worst fears. Yet, on almost the eve of the German occupation of Prague, on 12 March 1938, Chamberlain wrote that like Chatham he knew that he could save the country and that no one else could, but that it would require a period of several years to do so. He believed he would have the necessary time.[5]

FALL OF PRAGUE AND THE PLEDGE TO POLAND

Only three days later on 15 March, German armies attacked and soon occupied the remainder of Czechoslovakia. The invasion came, as Wheeler-Bennett described it, "with all the suddeness of a clap of thunder in a blue summer sky." Certainly it seemed so to Chamberlain. In a matter of hours all of his well-laid plans for the appeasement of Europe lay in ruins.[6] Now no one, not even Chamberlain himself, could ignore the fact that Hitler had broken his word solemnly given at Munich.

As a result of the cries of outrage from Chamberlain's parliamentary critics, a debate on foreign affairs took place in the Commons on the very day of the occupation. The prime minister told the House what the Government proposed to do:

> In our opinion the situation had radically altered since the Slovak Diet declared the independence of Slovakia. The effect of this declaration put an end by internal disruption to the State whose frontiers we had proposed to guarantee and accordingly, the condition of affairs described by my right hon. friend the Secretary of State for the Dominions, which was always regarded by us as being only of a transitory nature, has now ceased to exist, and His Majesty's Government cannot accordingly hold themselves any longer bound by this obligation.[7]

[5] Yet only the day before Chamberlain wrote this he had received, through Cadogan, a MI 5 report indicating that Germany would invade Czechoslovakia within forty-eight hours.

[6] Years later, Chamberlain's wife would recall how, in the troubled days following the fall of Prague, Chamberlain would refer again and again to Lord Grey, the British foreign secretary in 1914. Chamberlain repeatedly expressed, to his wife, the opinion that perhaps Lord Grey hadn't been wrong about Germany after all. The statements are evidence both of the persistence of historical memory in Chamberlain's decision-making calculations and to the fundamental change in his views of Hitler brought about by the fall of Prague.

These observations were supplied to the author by the Rt. Hon. The Lord Boyle of Handsworth. Lord Boyle was a friend of Chamberlain's wife.

[7] Moreover, the British protest to Germany was watered down on Chamberlain's insistence. Apparently, Chamberlain's comments in the Commons were made on his own authority and did not reflect the views of the Foreign Office.

In an act of stubborn persistence, Chamberlain concluded by saying that British policy would remain essentially unchanged and that Britain would continue to promote the substitution of the "method of discussion for the method of force in the settlement of differences." Chamberlain may never have intended to honor the guarantee to Czechoslovakia, and the method by which Hitler had accomplished the invasion gave him a convenient way out of the dilemma.[8] Although the British were not going to fight for Czechoslovakia, the occupation of Prague caused a fundamental reorientation of their policy. Even Chamberlain later wrote that once he had time to evaluate the German action he understood that it was no longer possible to continue negotiations with Hitler.

Faced with an impending revolt in the House of Commons and within the Tory party itself, as well as a torrent of criticism from the press, Chamberlain had no choice but to reassess his position. His considered response to the German aggression was contained in a speech he delivered to a Birmingham audience on 17 March. Chamberlain said that Hitler's action in the Rhineland, in Austria, and now in the Sudetenland had shocked public opinion throughout the world. Yet however much they might disagree with the German methods there was something to be said, either out of "racial affinity or of just claims too long resisted," for their point of view. But the recent German action, in clear violation of the Munich agreements, was forcing the Government to reconsider its position "with that sense of responsibility which its gravity demands."

However, Chamberlain asserted, ". . . there is hardly anything I would not sacrifice for peace." But if such sacrifices entailed giving up the liberty which British people had enjoyed for hundreds of years, then the price was too great. Recent events in Europe had "shattered the confidence" which had been beginning to come about and sadly Chamberlain admitted that the limits of accommodation had now been reached.

> It is only six weeks ago that I was speaking in this city, and then I alluded to rumours and suspicions which I said ought to be swept away. I pointed out that any demand to dominate the world by force was one which the democracies must resist, and I added that I could not believe that such a challenge was intended, because no Government with the interests of its own people at heart would expose them for such a claim to the horrors of world war.
>
> And indeed, with the lessons of history for all to read, it seems incredible that we should see such a challenge. I feel bound to repeat that, while I am not prepared to engage this country by new unspecified commitments

---

[8] Aster demonstrates that the Foreign Office by and large accepted the view that there was no possibility of Britain's honoring the guarantee.

operating under conditions which cannot now be foreseen, yet no greater mistake could be made than to suppose that, because it believes war to be a senseless and cruel thing, this nation has so lost its fibre that it will not take part to the utmost of its power resisting such a challenge if it ever were made.

In spite of Chamberlain's public pledge not "to engage this country in new unspecified commitments," it appears he was contemplating just that. In a letter to his sisters of 19 March, he said that while the Foreign Office had as usual nothing positive to suggest, he had formulated a "bold and startling" plan for a new approach to Italy which he thought could be presented without provoking a crisis with Germany. Yet, the following day, he told the Cabinet that the particular casus belli was not important: if Germany took the offensive again, ". . . we must take steps to stop her by attacking her on all points . . . in order to pull down the bully . . . not just to save a particular victim."

The same day he wrote a letter to Mussolini deploring the new German aggression. "What above all has impressed everyone here," he said, is that "for the first time they have incorporated in the Reich a large non-German population." Chamberlain warned Mussolini that if Hitler's actions were a prelude to further aggression, "sooner or later, and probably sooner, another major war is inevitable." He called upon the Duce to do something to restore the confidence that had been shattered. A week later, taking a more rigorous line, he told the Foreign Policy Committee, ". . . our object [is] to check and defeat Germany's attempt at world domination."

Chamberlain's first idea, as he later explained it to his sister, had been to negotiate an agreement with France, Russia, and Poland that they would take joint action in case of renewed German aggression. Poland, however, refused to be associated with the Soviet Union in this type of guarantee. Chamberlain said that he understood completely the Polish objections to a four-power declaration and that therefore Britain must choose between Russia and Poland. The prime minister left no doubt which of the two he preferred. He admitted having grave misgivings about the reliability of the Russians. He had not the slightest confidence in the military capability of the Red Army to sustain an adequate offensive. But beyond that, Chamberlain was suspicious of Soviet motivation, believing that the Russians were more concerned with exploiting the situation to their advantage than they were in supporting British ideas of liberty.

Chamberlain's intensely suspicious attitude toward the Soviet Union and his offhanded rejection of proposals for Anglo-Soviet cooperation were consequences of the distrust and hostility which he had long felt. In this respect, Chamberlain's view of the Soviet Union paralleled his feelings toward the United States. In the case of Soviet Russia, however, this attitude was at least in part ideological, and Chamberlain consistently maintained that the Soviets were a military power not to be taken seriously in the making of strategic calculations.

Once it appeared to Chamberlain that the idea of a four-power guarantee was no longer viable, his next thought was a British guarantee to Rumania. He believed it to be the next target of German aggression and that Poland could be persuaded to join such a guarantee. Chamberlain concluded that if the countries of Eastern Europe would not resist German economic penetration even when supported by the British Government, then there was very little that could be done unless Britain were willing to present Germany with an ultimatum. However, in acting alone Britain did not possess sufficient military strength to make such an ultimatum credible. In such circumstances the threat could only mean war for which Chamberlain was unwilling to take responsibility.

While Chamberlain declared himself unwilling to present the Germans with an ultimatum, political pressures were building which would compel Chamberlain to take a considerably stronger line than he had taken in his Birmingham speech. These pressures originating in the Foreign Office, under Halifax's initiative, led, on 29 March, to the decision to extend to Poland a unilateral British guarantee of her territorial integrity and independence. The declaration was an "improvisation" made under considerable stress and with limited information on German intentions toward Poland.

On 31 March, in answer to a prearranged question in the Commons, Chamberlain declared:

> In order to make perfectly clear the position of his Majesty's Government . . . I now have to inform the House that . . . in the event of any action which clearly threatened Polish independence and which the Polish Government accordingly considered it vital to resist with their national forces, His Majesty's Government would feel themselves bound at once to lend the Polish Government all support in their power.[9]

In retrospect, it may well have been the most extraordinary statement of Chamberlain's career, and it certainly marked the complete reversal of the policy he had consistently pursued since becoming prime minister. Moreover, it appeared to be precisely the type of commitment which Chamberlain had vowed never to give, a commitment which, because it left for the Polish Government to determine the casus foedoris, removed the decision of peace or war from the hands of the British Government.[10]

[9] Chamberlain seems to have been personally responsible for the switch from the idea of a four-power guarantee to that of a unilateral British pledge to Poland. In a letter to Mussolini, Chamberlain explained that, in making this parliamentary statement, his "sole purpose [was] to avoid any disturbance of the peace."

[10] Hoare later denied that this was true when he wrote, "We were not giving Poland a blank cheque . . . the decision as to whether or not we should take part in a war was retained in our own hands."

Chamberlain himself believed that the pledge was not an abdication of British freedom of action. He said that the pledge applied to threats against Polish *independence*, and, therefore, a negotiated change in her borders; for example, the case of Danzig, presumably would not necessarily constitute a casus belli. In a letter to his sister, Chamberlain specifically said that it was not a question of the precise borders of a state but, rather, of threats to its independence. The Polish pledge left Britain free to determine for herself whether or not independence was threatened. Thus, to Chamberlain at least, the Polish guarantee was definitely not regarded as the giving of a blank check to that country.[11]

From Chamberlain's perspective the guarantee reflected, at least in part, his personal outrage that Hitler had broken his promise.[12] The projected guarantee to Czechoslovakia had never been brought into force, allowing Hitler to annex for the first time non-German peoples. This mistake was not going to be repeated and Chamberlain was making British intentions clear and unequivocal.

Whereas in the past Chamberlain had placed considerable trust in the special relationship he believed he had established with Hitler, now he feared that the "fanatic" might actually be contemplating a "knock out" air attack against Britain and he noted that he could never again feel secure with Hitler. For Chamberlain, the giving of a guarantee *to Poland* was not nearly as important as the message he wished to communicate to Hitler of a firm and unequivocal British stand against further German aggression and the deterrent effect he hoped to achieve.[13] Unfortunately, Hitler did not find the British guarantee credible, expecting instead another Munich.

WATCHING HITLER AND NEGOTIATING WITH RUSSIA

The British pledge to Poland, and those subsequently given to Greece and Rumania, reflected a dramatic change in British policy, but they were not, in Chamberlain's view at least, an admission that war was inevitable. It was a change from a policy based on negotiated agreements to one of deterrence, a change of tactics but not necessarily of strategy; the ultimate aim in both cases remained the preservation of peace. All through the long summer of 1939, Chamberlain continued to

[11] This runs counter to the thesis argued by Newman who maintains that the guarantee was a deliberate turning point in British policy and a commitment to war with Germany. Whatever may be said in favor of Newman's thesis, it is quite clear that Chamberlain did not personally see it as such.

[12] Hoare later wrote, "Chamberlain's swift reaction was typical of his obstinate character. Far from stunning him, the Prague *coup* made him hit back as hard and as soon as possible."

[13] As many historians have pointed out, the case for making a stand on behalf of Czechoslovakia was much stronger than the case to be made for Poland. Czechoslovakia was, after all, a reasonably democratic society, which at least had not officially persecuted its German minority. Poland, on the other hand, was seen as a semi-feudal state with little pretense to satisfying the western conception of democracy. The Danzig corridor, with its essentially German character, separated Germany from East Prussia and the demand for its return to Germany had often been regarded as one of the most justified of Hitler's demands.

hope against hope that Hitler would respond to the new policy and
retreat from the precipice beyond which lay certain and inevitable war.

Everything now depended on Hitler. There was little Chamberlain
could do beyond attempting to communicate Britain's determination to
stand by her new commitments. Since he had staked his political reputation on the achievement of negotiated settlements of German claims,
and since that policy had demonstrably failed, Chamberlain was not
the person to make the new policy credible. Yet as long as the possibility of peace remained, Chamberlain clung, with increasing desperation, to this leadership position, hoping that the future would see him
vindicated. He wrote that there were plenty of careless people who were
willing to go to war with Germany immediately but he believed that
such impulses should be resisted until the last possible moment.

Yet Chamberlain appeared anxious to take personal credit for the
pledge to Poland, and he said that the statement made in the House of
Commons was principally his idea and that he was quite pleased with
the result. He felt that the pledge had been an immediate success at
home since when the time had at last arrived to bite the bullet, there
had been hardly any dissent. He was convinced that Hitler had suffered
such a powerful blow to his position that he was no longer able to forward his colonial ambitions nor able to encourage those of Mussolini.

Although Chamberlain was disillusioned with Hitler, he continued
to place considerable hope in his relationship with Mussolini. He
admitted that the latter had failed to respond in a positive manner to
his letter.[14] Chamberlain explained this by saying that even if the Duce
were angered by Hitler's actions he could not say so publicly and it was
indeed possible that Mussolini was able to exert some moderating
influence on Hitler as a result of Chamberlain's letter. It was, however,
difficult to maintain a belief in Mussolini's pacific intentions when the
Duce's lust for empire led him to attack Albania on 7 April. In the aftermath of that action, Chamberlain showed the same sense of outrage and
personal betrayal that had characterized his reaction to the fall of Prague.
There now could be no doubt that Mussolini was not a gentleman, he
wrote, not having made the slightest gesture to preserve the prime minister's goodwill—instead, undertaking the Albanian action with total
disdain and lack of regard for British sensibilities. Just as Hitler and
Mussolini viewed their foreign policies as the quest for personal fulfillment on a monumental scale, so also did Chamberlain perceive his own
hopes and ambitions and those of the British people in personal terms.

Chamberlain believed that the attack on Albania was possibly due to
the Duce's being distracted by his latest mistress although Chamberlain
felt that the degree to which Mussolini had abdicated control over foreign policy could be easily overstated. However, Chamberlain reluc-

[14]See, p. 177, *supra*.

tantly accepted the fact that, for the moment at least, any further rapprochement with Italy was out of the question. But to Chamberlain this did not mean that his policies had been wrong, in fact, positive consequences of his policy could be seen in the emerging consensus of popular sentiment and progress in rearmament both within Britain and France. Although the positive results of appeasement, time to rearm and consolidation of world opinion, were, at least to some extent, real achievements of Chamberlain's policy, they were, as we have seen, mostly the unintended results of a policy pursued for quite different reasons.

At the end of April, Hitler sent new assurances of his peaceful intentions toward Britain and reaffirmed his allegiance to the Munich agreements. Chamberlain was not sure how these were to be interpreted but he thought that it was quite possible that Hitler had come to his senses and realized the limitations of German capabilities. But in the meantime Chamberlain believed it was best to proceed with extreme caution. He wanted very much to believe that Hitler had reached the end of his demands for *Lebensraum*, but, he noted, the problem with Hitler was his willingness to break treaties and change policies at will so that one could never take much assurance from his public statements. In fact, Hitler had made such a mess of things that further discussion would elicit no popular favor among the British people. Significantly, Chamberlain did not say that he himself would not be in favor of such conversations, only that the country would not support them.

Chamberlain simply could not and would not accept the view that war was inevitable. In a letter to his sister, of 23 April, Chamberlain wrote that he refused to be pessimistic, and that he was convinced that the passage of time lessened the possibility of an outbreak of hostilities. Further troubles were to be expected but he did not believe that Hitler would deliberately start a world war over Danzig. He felt there was reason to believe that the Germans would at least wait until spring to attempt a solution of the Danzig question, since they now knew they could not achieve their objectives without a struggle. On 28 May Chamberlain confided to his sisters that information coming from Germany and Poland indicated there was no reason to anticipate a sudden attempt to change the situation in Danzig even though he was aware of the fact that the Germans were making plans toward that end. Again he asserted his view that Hitler "missed the bus" at Munich and that Hitler's military advisers would successfully restrain their leader's reckless ambition. He could not see how a rapprochement between Germany and Britain could take place as long as the Jews stubbornly refused to assassinate Hitler.[15]

[15] Chamberlain probably intended this comment to be a bit of sardonic humor, but given the fact that reports of German persecution of the Jews were, by this time, widely circulated in Britain, Chamberlain's comment appears callous, to say the least. It is not difficult to read into such statements the

In the early months of 1939 there was a growing sentiment within the Government in favor of a rapprochement with the Soviet Union. It was an issue on which Tory dissidents could find common ground with Labour in the growing movement for a National Government. In April 1939, initial overtures toward the Soviets led by Sir William Seeds, the new ambassador to Moscow, and by Halifax and his supporters in the Foreign Office, led to the opening of negotiations between the two countries, negotiations which continued without success until Stalin decided to align the Soviet Union with Germany and concluded the infamous Nazi-Soviet Pact of August 1939. Chamberlain was forced into these negotiations quite against his will, and it is clear that in this respect at least, he had lost control over British foreign policy.

Throughout his career, Chamberlain had been intensely suspicious of the "bolshies." He consistently denigrated the military power of Soviet Russia and hence the value of an alliance with that country. As we have seen, an ideological fear of communism and what it might mean for Britain was not a particularly significant factor in Chamberlain's decision to come to terms with Hitler. To Chamberlain, reaching agreement with the dictators was a supremely important goal in its own right, and he did not need the additional ideological factor of Germany as a bulwark against communism to convince him that such agreements would be worthwhile.

In May of 1939, Chamberlain wrote that the British really did not know what they were up against when dealing with the Russians. They might be ordinary peasant folk, but he suspected that their real interest was in standing by quietly while the capitalist states tore each other apart. However, he also realized that the time was coming when the British would have to decide one way or the other if an alliance with them was in Britain's best interest. He noted that those who favored such an alliance feared that the Russians were prepared to align themselves with Germany. This view, Chamberlain thought, did not speak well for the Russians as potential allies.

In spite of his personal views of British policy toward the Soviets, Chamberlain realized that the weakness of his own political position prevented him from successfully opposing an Anglo-Soviet alliance. The press, he thought, favored it, and his refusal to negotiate further with the Russians would lead to insuperable problems in the Commons even if he could get such an idea past the Cabinet.[16] Chamberlain had by

---

view that Chamberlain, to a certain extent, believed the anti-Semitic mythology of a Jewish conspiracy manipulating the institutions of finance and government for partisan advantage. To be sure, Chamberlain had, on one or two occasions, made perfunctory comments of disapproval at the persecution of German Jews but such statements seemed to carry little conviction.

[16] In addition to the rising Foreign Office support for a Russian alliance was the suprising support for the alliance by Samuel Hoare. When even such longtime supporters as Hoare were beginning to desert him, Chamberlain knew he had no choice but bow to force majeure.

this point lost a great deal of his power to influence events. He was opposed to the idea of a Russian alliance for its own sake, but his worst fear was that such an alliance would be a lining-up of antagonistic power blocs which would make any further conversations with the Axis powers practically out of the question.[17] It was, therefore, only with the greatest reluctance and an acute sense of personal defeat that Chamberlain accepted the idea of an alliance with the Soviet Union.[18]

It is difficult to overstate the difference between the role played by Chamberlain in the negotiations with Italy and Germany in the fall of 1938 and the part he played in the negotiations with Russia in the spring and summer of 1939. In the former case, Chamberlain was the pivot on which British policy turned, shaping and controling every aspect of that policy. In the latter, it was clear that the old single-minded authority with which Chamberlain had spoken at Munich was gone. Not only was Chamberlain politically bound by the deteriorating consensus on appeasement, but also, for the first time, he was personally unsure of the proper course of action. Privately, he wrote that he couldn't decide whether the Russians were attempting to decieve the British or whether it was just the natural distrust and guile of simple country people.

Chamberlain placed little value on the Anglo-Soviet negotiations, and, at one point, admitted he would not mind particularly if the negotiations collapsed. On 15 July, he wrote that if the negotiations were successful he would not regard it as a great victory for the British. By the end of July the prospects of an Anglo-Soviet alliance dimmed, and Chamberlain noted that it was only a matter of time until the negotiations were broken off entirely. He felt that it was most unfortunate that he would have to bear responsibility for the failure since were there not political obstacles in his way, he would have settled the matter a long time ago.

Chamberlain's rising sense of uncertainty and powerlessness was also evident in his attitude toward the worsening situation in the Far East, which he blamed on the ineptitude of the Foreign Office. Again, in July, Chamberlain noted that the Japanese were causing him considerable anxiety. Thanks to the Foreign Office the British were carrying the entire burden of a policy which was of as much importance to America, France, and Germany as it was to Britain. No matter how much he might complain of Foreign Office ineptitude and the wily ways of the for-

---

[17]One reason for Chamberlain's opposition to a Soviet alliance was his fear that this would be a return to the situation which had led to the Great War. Germany would be encircled by a system of automatic alliances which, given Hitler's immoderate demands, would inevitably lead to war. On 19 May, Chamberlain said in the House of Commons, "I want to make it clear that this policy is not a policy of lining up opposing blocs of Powers in Europe animated by hostile intentions towards one another, and accepting the view that war is inevitable. . . . We are always trying to avoid this policy of what I call opposing blocs."

[18]In his diary, Cadogan notes that Chamberlain had said that "he would resign rather than sign alliance with Soviet."

eigner, it was clear that Chamberlain himself no longer had ready solutions for the intractable problems plaguing British poliicy. The period of bold and daring initiatives had passed.

Danzig and the Declaration of War

Danzig, the free city at the mouth of the Polish corridor to the sea, a corridor which separated the German Reich from its territory of East Prussia, was the trouble spot which seemed most likely to provide the occasion for German military intervention in Poland. Although the British had carefully avoided a definite commitment to maintaining the neutrality of Danzig, everyone realized that conflict between Poland and Germany over Danzig could easily escalate into a full-scale war between the two countries, a war which would involve Britain if she chose to honor her pledge to Poland.

Chamberlain's attitude toward the Danzig question was one of deepening pessimism. He doubted that any resolution short of war was possible, but if the Fascists would only have a little forbearance then he believed that a solution acceptable to both Germany and Poland was possible.

Chamberlain noted that there were rumors that Germany might be willing to delay incorporating Danzig into the Reich. However the Poles were being most uncooperative by causing unnecessary offense to officials in Berlin. From Berlin came a report that Germany was depending on Britain to pressure the Poles into submission. In Britain there were rumors that Chamberlain was prepared to sell out the Poles. All this, Chamberlain felt, made any further discussion with Germany out of the question. He believed himself to be between Scylla and Charybdis, caught between German intransigence on the one hand and domestic critics on the other, and he felt that the Germans were "utter fools" for failing to appreciate his political dilemma.

Curiously, Chamberlain maintained a distinction between Hitler on the one hand, whose pledge had been shown to be untrustworthy, and the German people on the other, with whom he continued to believe some sort of agreement might yet be reached. Chamberlain wrote of his wish to open secret lines of communication with those people in Germany who wanted an agreement with the British. However, his critics at home were, in principle, against any understanding with Germany until she had been taught a lesson on the battlefield. Obviously Chamberlain did not accept such a position, preferring instead to try to convince the Germans that a war with Britain could not be won. But to be able to do that effectively it would be necessary to convince the Germans they would receive a fair hearing for their grievances. In the unlikely event that this should happen Chamberlain believed the Germans might yet renounce the use of force to achieve their objectives.

Chamberlain continued to believe that there were moderate forces within Germany which could, even at this late date, in some way prevail upon Hitler to alter his policy. It was an attitude based more on faith than on evidence, providing yet another example of Chamberlain's capacity to manipulate his own mind so as to believe nearly anything he wanted to believe. As had always been the case, Chamberlain understood full well that Hitler was a maniac but nothing at all of the fact that the German masses shared their leader's mania.

Furthermore, Chamberlain believed that Hitler was convinced that any further aggression meant war and, as a result, had halted his plans to incorporate Danzig into the German Reich. Although Chamberlain could not dismiss the ever-present rumors of German military plans, he nevertheless felt things to be sufficiently quiet to allow him to take a badly needed holiday in the country. In August he advised his sisters not to call off their own plans for a holiday on the Continent.

Chamberlain's country vacation was cut short by ominous reports from the Continent that Hitler planned to launch an attack on Poland to begin sometime between 25 and 28 August. He returned to London fearing that war might well be imminent. Into an already tense atmosphere came news of the signing of the Nazi-Soviet Pact. What has often been referred to as the "war of nerves" had begun.

To policy-makers in London, it was supremely important that Hitler should have no doubts as to the British attitude. Therefore, on the evening of 22 August, a personal letter was dispatched from Chamberlain to Hitler. The letter stated flatly, that whatever the nature of the German-Soviet agreement, ". . . it cannot alter Great Britain's obligation to Poland which His Majesty's Government have stated in public repeatedly and plainly and which they are determined to fulfill." In this, one of the last communications with Hitler before the war, the lessons of the last war were again evoked.

> It has been alleged that, if His Majesty's Government had made their positions more clear in 1914, the great catastrophe would have been avoided. Whether or not there is any force in that allegation, His Majesty's Government are resolved that on this occasion there shall be no such tragic misunderstanding.[19]

If after all that had passed between them Hitler yet chose war, it was not to be for want of understanding the British position.[20]

---

[19] Earlier versions of this letter indicate that it was drafted by the Foreign Office and amended by Chamberlain, The above quoted passage was virtually the only passage of the draft which Chamberlain did not in some way modify.

[20] Ironically, Hitler did not, in fact, believe the British statement and the following day set the date for the invasion of Poland for 26 August. Chamberlain's letter was delivered by Henderson the following day. According to the official German record of the Henderson-Hitler meeting, Henderson did everything possible to mollify the German dictator, going beyond his official brief to tell Hitler that he believed "the hostile attitude to Germany did not represent the will of the British people. It was the work of Jews and enemies of the Nazis." This was, it should be noted, hardly a message to deter Hitler from attacking Poland!

On the twenty-fourth, Chamberlain summed up recent developments to the House of Commons and again asserted Britain's determination to stand by her commitments. His words were spoken, according to Harold Nicolson, ". . . exactly like a coroner summing up a case of murder." Only once did Chamberlain betray his personal anguish. "God knows I have tried my best," he told the House. A few days later, in a letter to his sister, Chamberlain wrote that he felt like a coachman negotiating a carriage down a difficult path on the edge of a very steep cliff. There were times when one's heart appeared to skip a beat until ultimately the crisis had passed and one was still on the road.

On Friday, 25 August, word reached London that Henderson had been summoned to yet another meeting with Hitler. Chamberlain thought it likely that the ambassador would be given his papers and told to leave the country as a prelude to a declaration of war. He described his feelings as he waited to find out the result of the Hitler-Henderson interview: he sat with his wife, being unable to do anything but await news from Germany.

As it turned out, Hitler had new proposals to make, proposals which Hitler had told Henderson might yet lead to an understanding between Britain and Germany. The Führer did not back down from his demand for a solution to the problem of Danzig and the corridor, but declared that once these issues were solved, Germany stood ready to guarantee the integrity of the British Empire, to enter into an alliance with Britain, and even to accept a limitation of armaments. Whether he realized it or not, Hitler was playing on themes close to Chamberlain's heart. He wrote that Chamberlain's speech could result in "a bloody and incalculable war between Germany and England," a war which "would be bloodier than that of 1914 to 1918," and that, because of the agreement with the Soviet Union, Germany "would no longer have to fight on two fronts." No matter how much Hitler might threaten and promise, Chamberlain clearly could not find it within himself to resurrect the trust which had been so rudely shattered by the fall of Prague. To his sisters, he wrote that anyone who had not met Hitler personally could not possibly hope to understand his behavior. In Chamberlain's view, the ease with which Hitler had concluded the Nazi-Soviet Pact had tempted the dictator into attempting a similar agreement with Britain. In his excitement Hitler had all but forgotten the Poles. Because of her new obligations, however, Britain could not forget Poland. As a result there was no question of a treaty with Germany. Thus with the greatest reluctance, Chamberlain had resigned himself to the view that if Hitler attacked Poland, Britain would go to war with Germany.[21]

---

[21]Significantly, Chamberlain seems to have given little thought to the strategic possibilities of a military campaign in Poland. If Poland were attacked it would be the occasion for a larger European war, and preserving the territorial integrity of Poland was only a secondary issue, if that. Ambassador

The flow of diplomatic proposals and counterproposals continued. Hitler responded to a firm British position by demanding that a Polish emissary be present in Berlin on one day's notice to "negotiate" a settlement. The British were determined to make a firm stand in fulfilling their guarantee to Poland. In any event the last possibility of a peaceful solution was precluded when, on the morning of 1 September, Hitler's armies attacked Poland.

The British Cabinet met that morning and were told by the prime minister that "the event against which he had fought so long and earnestly had come upon us. But our consciences were clear, and there should be no possible question now where our duty lay." That the German action meant war was generally accepted; however the manner and timing of the declaration was an issue which led to intense debate. The French did all they could to delay the declaration until the last possible moment. As a result it looked to many in the Commons as if Chamberlain were preparing another Munich. In reality, the prime minister was trying desperately to coordinate the British declaration with that of the foot-dragging French. A Cabinet revolt, including a sit-down strike reluctantly led by John Simon, was necessary to press Chamberlain into action. The Cabinet ultimately decided to declare war independently of France.

At noon on the morning of 3 September, Chamberlain told the House of Commons that no reply had been received to the British ultimatum and that consequently, "This country is at war with Germany." He added, "Everything that I have worked for, everything that I have hoped for, everything that I have believed in during my public life has crashed into ruins."[22]

THE FALL OF CHAMBERLAIN'S GOVERNMENT

Chamberlain confided to his sisters that life had become nothing short of an interminable ordeal. However, in spite of his personal anguish, he was able to summarize events with the usual methodical detachment. His analysis of the final events leading up to war was that Hitler had simply lost his head over the idea of a quick, easy victory in Poland. Chamberlain believed that Hitler had been genuinely interested in reaching an agreement with the British and had even been prepared to make new counterproposals. However, in the end, possibly under the influence of Ribbentrop, he had been overcome by the moment and put

---

Kennedy reported that Chamberlain had told him,' ". . . the futility of it all is the thing that is frightful." Kennedy added, ". . . after all they cannot save the Poles; they can merely carry on a war of revenge that will mean the destruction of the whole of Europe."

[22]The delays involved in coordinating British policy with the French postponed the declaration of war and led to a revolt in the Commons as well as in the Cabinet itself.

into operation a process which once begun could not be stopped. This, he had always known, was the basic problem of a country which had concentrated all its military power in the hands of a single paranoid leader. It was also, it might be added, a fair description of what Chamberlain believed to have been the chain of events leading up to the 1914 war.

On 10 September, he wrote that while Poland was being overrun with a speed no one had believed possible, on the western front the war had hardly begun yet. He had a feeling that it would not be a long war because there were so many people on both sides who were fundamentally opposed to war as an instrument of national policy and this desire would sooner or later find expression. Chamberlain felt that the real difficulty was Hitler himself and that until the latter disappeared, there could be no peace. What he hoped for was not a military victory but a collapse of the German home front. Regardless of the personal defeat that Chamberlain felt at the coming of war, he had no regrets about the past. He knew that through his sustained attempts at finding a peaceful solution people the world over understood that Hitler was solely responsible for causing the war. This moral rectitude, to which the British alone were entitled, would be a powerful factor insuring an allied victory.

Now that Britain was once again at war with Germany, now that his worst fears had been realized, his illusions shattered, his dreams destroyed, Chamberlain lived in the hope that this war would not be as terrible as the last. Like most people in Britain, Chamberlain feared that it would be even worse. Developments in military technology had raised the horrifying possibility of bombing attacks on British population centers and the complete devastation of entire cities. Yet as Hoare later wrote:

> Our preparations had been for Armageddon, and it had not started. We were ready with millions of gas-masks for gas attacks that had been expected in the first few days of war, and not one had been needed. A quarter of a million emergency beds were waiting in the hospitals for the casualties that did not appear.

Chamberlain, like most people in Britain, shared the feeling of relief that the airborne holocaust did not materialize, or at least did not immediately follow the outbreak of war.

Yet, to Chamberlain, the comparatively few British casualties in the first months of the war were little consolation, and he saw events as a dreadful reliving of the Great War. To him, news was good or bad depending on how it compared with his memories of the last war. On 17 September, speaking of German attacks on allied shipping, he noted that while the number of ships destroyed was nowhere near what it had been in the last war the destruction of submarines was worse and far more persistent. To Chamberlain, the German enemy was still "the Boche," and the allies still faced the enemy across a "no man's land." He expressed his conviction that the Germans were not sufficiently strong to attempt the massive trench warfare of the last war unless allied strategy forced it upon them. On 22 October, he wrote with some relief that in the opening weeks of the war, allied casualties were nowhere near what they had been in the comparable period of the Great War. In the year-end letter to his sister, Chamberlain noted that things were "all quiet" on the western front but believed this to be the calm before the storm. However he refused to be a defeatist and maintained his view that the Nazis had lost their chance of winning the war in September 1938.

For Chamberlain, a man whose public career had more than anything else been identified with preserving the peace, it would seem to have been a natural decision to resign as soon as possible after the outbreak of war. Certainly, nothing in his past experience or personal conviction had prepared him to lead a nation at war. At one point shortly after the outbreak of hostilities, Chamberlain seemed to realize this when he noted that he did not believe he had any further role to play until it came time to negotiate peace, and that that would not be for a considerable time.

When Chamberlain received news of the first British defeats he wrote that he was never cut out to be a prime minister in wartime. When he thought of all the lives lost in the sinking of the *Royal Oak* he felt like resigning. He could take no real satisfaction in the growing number of German U-boats destroyed by British forces and he mused that had these same submarines called at British ports in peacetime, their crews would have been welcomed as friends. And now these same young men were being killed just to satisfy the bloodlust of a crazed dictator. He wished that Hitler would suffer for a year the torments of hell for each life lost by his insane actions.

In December, he toured the Allied positions on the Continent, and on his return reported that it was nauseating to view the preparations for trench warfare because it reminded him of the last war. He was relieved when his tour of inspection was over.

But in spite of his privately expressed reservations, Chamberlain did not resign. Instead he held tenaciously to his office until a parliamentary rebellion forced him to step down. So difficult had been the upward climb, so staggering the view from the top, that a descent from those giddy heights proved all too difficult to contemplate. He did, however, take Churchill into his Government, and in the months that followed, the latter served a function similar to the one Chamberlain himself had played in the Baldwin Government. Churchill began gradually to assume control over the British war effort, while Chamberlain continued as the official head of government.

Increasingly Chamberlain became but a spectator to events unfolding on the Continent. One of his last major decisions, made in January 1940, was the decision to sack Leslie Hore-Belisha as minister of war. The reasons for this decision have never been made clear. Chamberlain's private papers do little to clarify matters, and in fact tend to heighten the distinct aura of anti-Semitism which has always surrounded the affair.[23]

The real control over the British war effort had, in the early months of 1940, passed to Churchill who was obviously better suited for the task. Chamberlain appeared pleased with this new relationship and wrote that Churchill's conduct was exemplary. He also reported hearing from his colleagues of Churchill's loyalty and respect for the prime minister. Churchill took to his new duties like a fish to water, and Chamberlain observed that the latter was well suited to the job. Unlike Churchill, Chamberlain had little appreciation of the importance of American involvement in the war and persistently maintained his old anti-American prejudices. He wrote that he had no desire for the Americans to fight Britain's war for them since when it came time to negotiate a peace, the price would be too high. In every respect, Chamberlain

---

[23] The usual explanation of the decision has generally been that Hore-Belisha's abrasive personality and the unpopularity of his measures for democratization of the army created dissension within the ranks, a dissatisfaction which a nation at war could ill afford. This was the explanation which Chamberlain gave when writing to his sister when he noted that for quite some time there had been discontent in the War Office. Without meaning to do so, Hore-Belisha had alienated Gort and other high ranking officials in the British expeditionary force. Chamberlain noted that while for a time he had been able to calm these troubled waters, he had felt that his solution was only temporary and that if he saw a chance to remove Hore-Belisha he should do so before another eruption occurred. This was necessary, in Chamberlain's view, because good civil/military relations were essential in time of war.

However, even Chamberlain admitted that there had been no particular charges leveled against Hore-Belisha, saying that he had accomplished more in the post than anyone since Haldane. Why, then, would Chamberlain, who of all people was not the sort of man to knuckle under to political pressure, summarily dismiss a man with whom he was so well satisfied?

Even in a letter to his sister, Chamberlain felt the need to defend Halifax's role in the affair, saying that Hore-Belisha's Jewishness had not even crossed Halifax's mind. On the question of whether to offer Hore-Belisha the Ministry of Information, Chamberlain reported that he had spoken with Simon who had expressed his reservations about the wisdom of giving such a delicate post to anyone who might use it for partisan purposes. Halifax had told Chamberlain that it would have a deleterious effect on opinion in neutral countries to have a Jew as minister of information, and that Hore-Belisha's style would be bad for British status. Chamberlain himself believed that appointing a Jew to this post would not be favorably received by the Americans.

In a letter of 27 December 1939, Gort wrote to Chamberlain that any bad feeling that had once existed toward the minister had now completely disappeared and he expressed his willingness to continue working with Hore-Belisha. If this truly represented the sentiments of the military why then, we are entitled to ask, was Hore-Belisha sacked?

It is perhaps significant that Gort prefaced his letter to Chamberlain by saying that he had burned Chamberlain's "secret and personal" letter and that he had told no one what it contained. We of course will never know the contents of the letter to which Gort referred. It should, however, be noted that in all of Chamberlain's long correspondence, this kind of secrecy was totally unprecedented. Likewise, we shall probably never know the full reasons for Hore-Belish's dismissal, but the charge of anti-Semitism at the highest levels of British government can certainly not be dismissed. It does seem likely that anti-Jewish prejudice had something to do with Chamberlain's decision.

had become an anachronism, an exhausted old man whose day had passed.

Yet he refused to give up the office which he had fought so hard to obtain. While he admitted his inadequacy to conduct the war and repeatedly stated his desire to step down, Chamberlain was convinced that he was yet indispensable. He felt it would not be a bad thing if he were compelled to resign, except for the fact that it was by no means clear that anyone else could do a better job. Suggestions in the press calling for a restructuring of the Government along the lines of the Lloyd George War Cabinet led him to write that it was ridiculous to assert that allied victory in the 1914 war had been in any way due to the way Lloyd George had formed his Government and that it could not be demonstrated that that Government had been any more effective than Chamberlain's own. In any case, Chamberlain said, circumstances were completely different from the last war in that this time Britain had an efficient planning staff and closer liaison with the French. On 27 April, he wrote that he had a powerful desire to give up his office. However, he knew he could not do so and therefore he had to continue as best he could to do his duty.

All through the early months of 1940, Chamberlain refused to believe the rumors of an impending German offensive in the West, placing blind faith in the effectiveness of economic warfare. He believed that it was a lack of petroleum, not the lack of men or machines which kept the Germans from attacking. Chamberlain further believed that Mussolini would do everything he could to help the Germans but that he would not allow the Italians to become involved in the war. Even as late as 4 May 1940, he wrote that it was a cruel, evil world but that he didn't believe his enemies would succeed in overthrowing the Government.

The illusions of his own indispensability and that of Hitler's relative weakness were rudely shattered with the defeat of allied forces in Norway. It was a grave national humiliation and there were charges of gross bumbling and incompetence. In Parliament the call for new leadership and a National Government was being sounded with new and bitter intensity. Chamberlain turned the parliamentary debate on the conduct of the war into a test of his personal leadership, calling on "my friends in the House—and I have friends in the House" for support. In the last great parliamentary speech of his career Lloyd George said, ". . . the Prime Minister should give an example of sacrifice because there is nothing which can contribute more to victory in this war than he should sacrifice the seals of office." It was somehow appropriate that the end of Chamberlain's parliamentary career should find him pitted against his ancient enemy Lloyd George. The House divided, and although the Government retained an eighty-one-vote majority, the prime minister was clearly shaken.

The next day Chamberlain resigned and a Government was formed with Churchill as prime minister. Less than twenty-four hours later, Hitler launched the blitzkrieg which led in short order to the occupation of Belgium, Holland, and France.

The Second World War now entailed a total commitment of men and resources. Chamberlain wrote that he found little satisfaction in being relieved of the responsibilities of high office and that his private defeat seemed insignificant in the face of this great national peril. But at the same time he could not unconditionally support the new Government. Churchill, he noted, had formed a Government with a quite different style of leadership, one that reminded him of the old Lloyd George days. Chamberlain suspected that the latter was deliberately separating himself from the Churchill Government in order to assume a leadership position once Germany had won the war.

Even in his final defeat, Chamberlain saw the old enemies of 1916 come back to haunt him. It may well have seemed to him not only as if the horrors of the last war were repeating themselves but that his personal defeat as minister of national service was happening again, a defeat suffered at the hands of the same enemy, Lloyd George.

In these very grim days for the allied cause, Chamberlain wrote that his entire world had fallen apart but that his personal tragedy paled before the great national peril, and that as a result no personal animosity remained. He said that he had known all along that he was not cut out to lead a nation at war since he could not bear to make decisions which would bring death and destruction to so many thousands of people. However, once the war came, it had been so unlike what he had expected that he had found himself able to carry on. Perhaps it was an act of fate that his final defeat should coincide with the beginning of the real war. He was glad to be out of office but he could not dismiss from his mind the terrible path that lay ahead.

At Churchill's insistence, he stayed on in the Government in the sinecure position of lord president and retained his leadership of the Tory party. His new duties unofficially included looking after domestic aspects of the war effort, and he reported that he felt he was still able to make a contribution which would allow Churchill to devote himself exclusively to winning the war. But, he noted, he could take no satisfaction in this new role. In spite of everything, he never admitted that his policy had been a mistake, and, as late as 17 October, wrote to Baldwin that he had not for a moment questioned the decisions he had taken at the time of Munich nor did he believe he could have done more to prepare the country for war after Munich.

Chamberlain's tenure in the Churchill Government was short-lived, and in July, after complaints of severe stomach pain, he was hospitalized. Medical examination revealed that he was suffering from cancer.

Yet, the day before his operation Chamberlain had spent ten hours inspecting coastal defenses at Norfolk. He emerged from the operation knowing he had terminal cancer but determined to return to public life. Even in his illness, he never forgot his enemies and noted that he suspected Lloyd George of having plans to become Britain's Marshal Pétain. He never forgot the personal agony of lives lost in a war for which he bore a certain responsibility. From his sickbed, Chamberlain occupied himself with letters of condolence to the families of men lost in the war. It is simply too much to bear, he said, to be forced to do this twice in a single lifetime. How much he hated Hitler! Yet, it must be noted, that what he felt for the nameless thousands who were dying in war was something he had never felt for those closer to him, and herein lay the great personal tragedy of his life.

Even as the battle of Britain raged around him, Chamberlain never abandoned his belief in the Victorian ideal of progress. On 11 October he ended his last broadcast to the British people saying, ". . . it is not conceivable that human civilization should be permanently overcome by such evil men and evil things, and I feel proud that the British Empire, though left alone, still stands across their path, unconquered and unconquerable."

His return to public life was cut short, and in less than a fortnight he returned to his bed with the certain knowledge that his illness was entering its final phase. In what was to be his last letter to his sister, Chamberlain wrote that he had lost all interest in life, even the small pleasures of country living were denied him. He had nothing left to anticipate. He had no doubt that Britain could do nothing but continue to fight in the conviction that eventually the Germans would give in. Still, he knew that soon there would be another budget before the Government and it would be a crushing burden to bear, and with that, the letter ended. He died on 9 November 1940.

ℵ 9 ℵ

Conclusion

VIEWED as it were from Chamberlain's own perspective, there is no doubt a great deal of tragedy in the events leading up to the British involvement in a second great war with Germany. His death from cancer was an ignominious end to a career marked by a tragedy that was both personal and national in scope. Chamberlain had staked everything on a policy aimed not only at preventing another war in Europe but also at achieving a peaceful settlement of all the issues which had plagued European diplomacy since the signing of the Versailles treaty, a policy of European appeasement. Now, with German bombs falling on London, that policy was manifestly a failure.

Viewed from the outside, with as much objectivity as we can muster, those events reveal not so much a personal tragedy as a profound paradox; a paradox which is both methodological and substantive. On the one hand, Neville Chamberlain appears as a political figure wielding much more control over the machinery of state and over the course of events than has heretofore been assumed. Thus the traditional method of biography by which the British have chosen to understand their national past appears to be vindicated. Yet if we seek to remove ourselves from the details of Chamberlain's life history in seeking the general causes of the Second World War, then the inherent limitations of the biographical method become immediately apparent. Clearly, much of what historians have identified as the policy of appeasement was Chamberlain's policy, particularly the decisions leading to the Munich Conference, and our analysis of Chamberlain can explain a great deal. But the term "British policy" is, of course, merely a convenient abstraction which conceals a multiplicity of forces; some individual, some social, and some material, of which the particular desires and influence of Neville Chamberlain was but one. There were, in sum, a variety of British policies, many of them in conflict, and we have merely demonstrated how, for a brief period in British history, the specific personal policy of Chamberlain came to dominate all others. When one considers the full range of social and material causes of the Second World War, the Munich Conference and the events leading up to it appear, at least to a degree, epiphenomenological, but they were epiphenomena of profound and disastrous consequences for the Czechoslovakian people. Whether or not the general course of events would have been significantly different without Chamberlain as head of the Government or whether a different policy could have averted war with Germany are questions on which we can only speculate.

As we trace the history of Chamberlain's rise within the ranks of the British governing hierarchy, we find a man whose determined and at times ruthless pursuit of personal political power presents a portrait quite at odds with the traditional genteel notion of collective cabinet responsibility. In this respect Chamberlain was a political leader who would have understood the dynamics of, and have been perfectly at home in, the American political setting which he so ardently detested. Politics was thus and continues to be a kind of personal warfare waged for the most part by pacific means. It is this aspect of Chamberlain's personal history which clearly emerges from an examination of his private papers, and it is a dimension which is rather sharply at odds with the traditional view of Chamberlain as a well-intentioned but hopelessly naïve man of peace.

Chamberlain was much more actively involved in the policy process and was, in general, a much more powerful political figure than has heretofore been indicated. His extraordinary influence behind the scenes in the Baldwin Government, his intolerance of dissenting colleagues, and his role in the confusing events leading to Eden's resignation are all at odds with the traditional view. Still, as one reviews the literature on Neville Chamberlain and appeasement and compares it with the new material available in the Chamberlain papers, the general conclusion which emerges is not so much that previous judgments are mistaken, although some clearly are, but that they are incomplete.

Certainly there is a great deal to be said for the traditional defense of Chamberlain and appeasement, which claims that Chamberlain's policy was a judicious response to the British problem of limited resources and dangerously overextended commitments. When compared to the self-righteous moralism exhibited by members of the parliamentary opposition, there is indeed much to be said in Chamberlain's defense. Once Germany had made clear her intention to rearm, no one saw more clearly than Chamberlain the conflict between extolling the virtues of the League and at the same time refusing to support the armaments without which collective security was but an empty slogan.

In the mid-thirties no one was more active than Chamberlain in promoting the rearmament effort, although he can be rightly criticized for viewing the program specified in the 1935 White Paper as a one-shot effort which would leave Britain adequately armed. In the late 1930s the inadequacy of Britain's military preparations was certainly a powerful reason for avoiding a confrontation with Hitler. Significantly, however, Chamberlain used the argument of military inadequacy only as an ex post facto justification of policies he had pursued for other reasons. From the time he became prime minister until the fall of Prague, Britain's military inadequacy apparently played almost no part in Chamberlain's decision to seek a negotiated agreement with Hitler. It was only after he became convinced Hitler could not be trusted that Chamberlain began to cite military inadequacy and the need to buy time as justifications for his policy. Likewise, it cannot be denied that when war eventually came in 1939, Chamberlain led a country unquestionably united in opposition to fascism in a way which would never have been possible in an earlier period. But here again, uniting Britain against the German enemy was the unintended consequence of policy pursued for other reasons. It was events in Europe, and not a conscious policy on Chamberlain's part, which eventually convinced the British public that war was inevitable. Chamberlain himself did nothing to prepare the British people for war, and, in fact, felt that a public which believed that war could be avoided was itself a factor in maintaining the peace. One of the lessons he drew from the Great War was that war was, in part, caused by a kind of mass hysteria leading men to flock mindlessly to national banners. To avoid this sort of thing happening again, Chamberlain deliberately sought to substitute reason for national passion. This is one explanation of the fact that his policy utterances were so devoid of stirring emotional appeals.

On the other hand, Chamberlain's critics, the proponents of the "guilty men" view of appeasement, have also made arguments of irrefutable validity. Certainly, Chamberlain was naïve in believing that the pledged word or the signing of a document irrevocably bound Hitler in the same way that an agreement bound Birmingham businessmen. Also, he never understood the degree to which Hitler was the leader of a mass political movement rather than a crazed tyrant of a more traditional sort. In this sense, Chamberlain most certainly did, as one of his critics has alleged, see events in Europe through the wrong end of a municipal drainpipe. Nowhere was this naïveté more abundantly, and in the end tragically, demonstrated than at Munich. Chamberlain did not sign an agreement which meant the end of Czechoslovak sovereignty because he wanted to buy time or because he felt Britain was too weak militarily to do otherwise, but because he believed that the dismemberment of Czechoslovakia was the price which had to be paid if another world war was to be avoided. He unquestionably believed that the private accord which he and Hitler had signed at Munich would usher in a whole new era of Anglo-German relations, that it was in fact "peace in our time." From this perspective, the view that Chamberlain was never prepared to allow any real changes in the status quo in Eastern Europe is no longer tenable.

Nor is it true that Chamberlain was prepared to give the Nazis a free hand in Eastern Europe. If the price of appeasement was the transfer of certain African real estate to German sovereignty, it was a price which certainly would be paid. Since Hitler was never really interested in Africa, then the incorporation of the ethnic Germans of the Sudetenland into the German Reich was, in Chamberlain's view, a reasonable substitute. But the wholesale annexation by force of vast numbers of Slavic people was surely too high a price even for Neville Chamberlain.

It is thus, in a sense, true that Chamberlain's world view was essentially parochial, but it was surely the parochialism of an entire ruling class rather than simply the provinciality of a Birmingham merchant. He believed that a nation's strength lay in its fiscal stability, that economic vitality was Britain's secret weapon, which, when weighted in the balance of war, would ultimately tip the scales in Britain's favor. Therefore, in the rearmament effort nothing should be done to jeopardize the nation's economic vitality on which everything depended. This was the basis for his decision to impose on the services a rationed budget to insure that rearmament did not damage Britain's economic strength. To be sure, the limits of what Britain could afford were continually pushed backward as the national peril increased, but, in the mid-thirties, Chamberlain's view of economic orthodoxy was widely, if not universally, shared. It is worth noting that even today, economic "science" provides no sure answer to the question of how far a nation can spend beyond its capacity to produce.

In the end, however, the portrait of Chamberlain which emerges is neither that of the "guilty men" school nor an affirmation of the views held by those have poignantly asked, "What else could he have done?" Nor does it lie conveniently between what have been perceived as the polar extremes of Chamberlain scholarship. In fact, the arguments of Chamberlain's hagiographers and those of his detractors present partial views of Neville Chamberlain. Each is to a limited extent valid, and they need not be seen as contradictory.

What is, however, necessary to complement the older views is a psychological understanding of Chamberlain's behavior, some notion of the passions to which the reasonableness of more public explanation was the slave. A concept of power thus becomes central to an understanding of both the politics of psychology and the psychology of politics of public personalities. In the end, Chamberlain and others like him can perhaps be best understood in terms of political power defined as the ability to coerce, manipulate, and intimidate. For Chamberlain and others like him, political power was, and is, the major currency of human relations. His personality was such that he could not conceive of any human interaction except on the basis of power, and his leadership rested ultimately on his ability to coerce. It was bolstered by the fact that few around him could offer an alternative either to his leadership or to the policy he advocated. The emotional emptiness of his early years produced a man of singularly passionless austerity, a man for whom the silent masses rather than the individual were the dominant objects of concern.

Chamberlain's personal development was thus a classic example of what Harold Lasswell has described as the "displacement of affects on to public objects." In part because his private emotional world was an arid wasteland devoid of personal satisfaction of emotional need, he sought in the public sphere what he could not find within. It was for this reason that his experience and memories of the Great War took on such staggering proportions that he could see policy toward Hitler only in terms of his overwhelming need to avoid another Great War.

There were at least two specific experiences in the Great War which became crucial determinants of Chamberlain's policy as prime minister. In the first place, there was the personal tragedy of the loss of his cousin, Norman Chamberlain, who, from all existing evidence, seems to have been one of the very few persons with whom Chamberlain had established relations of personal intimacy. Although we can never prove it to be the case, it would seem reasonable to conclude that Norman Chamberlain's death drove Neville ever more fiercely into the public arena to seek satisfaction of emotional need. There can be no doubt that, in his later career, Chamberlain often saw his relationship to "the masses" as one of personal involvement and identification. Secondly, the Great War was inextricably associated in Chamberlain's mind with his political humiliation at the hands of Lloyd George during his brief tenure as minister of national service. The evidence that Chamberlain carried this painful memory with him into his later career can be found in the almost pathological hatred and scorn which Chamberlain never tired of heaping on Lloyd George.

One objection to such an interpretation is the fact that psychoanalytic explanations of political behavior are conventionally based on establishing connections between early childhood psychosexual experiences and adult behavior. However, we know that Chamberlain's childhood was one of extreme deprivation and austerity and that his career as a young adult was a series of frustrations and failures as witnessed by the Andros experience and his general failure to live up to parental expectations in the world of business. These experiences, we might well argue, resulted in an emotionally immature adult. Moreover, the death of Norman Chamberlain and Neville's own failure as minister of national service came at precisely the point in Chamberlain's psychological development when he was for the first time beginning to overcome, in the business world and as lord mayor of Birmingham, the debilitations of early failure. This explanation accounts for the powerful connection between personal affect and public policy which we see so clearly at the time of Munich. Thus it was that at every moment of important political decision, his mind tended toward memories of the past, thoughts about what father would have done, and memories of the 1914 war.

Chamberlain's cognitive rigidity was bolstered by the fact that he entered national public life at such a late age and retained his position of power well beyond the normal age of retirement. In terms of developmental psychology in the tradition of Erik Erikson,[1] Chamberlain's political career illustrates the disruption of generational continuity which results when a particular leader refuses to relinquish authority at an appropriate age. In this sense, Chamberlain belongs to a category of leaders which includes Mao Tse-tung, de Gaulle, Ben-Gurion, Churchill, and John D. Rockefeller, all of whom accomplished much in their public careers but ended as overaged leaders out of touch with their constituencies and alternatively hated and idealized by them. That the politicians who led Britain into a second war with Germany should have been a group of almost exclusively elder statesmen was perhaps an inevitable demographic consequence of the loss of life in the First World War, but it was none the less unfortunate as a result. Parenthetically, it ought to be noted that generational problems resulting from an overaged leader is a phenomenon not without relevance for observers of the contemporary American political scene.

There is, moreover, another more public and more rational level on which we can examine the politics of history in the making of public policy. Those who make political decisions see before them a range of choice, an array of options, from which one must be chosen which best maximizes the values held to be desirable. One of the factors which makes this range of choice seem more narrow than it in fact is, often to the point where alternatives seem not to exist at all, is the perception that past mistakes must not be repeated, that the lessons of history must be learned and acted upon. One of the functions of retrospective analysis is to demonstrate the general proposition that things need not have been as they in fact were, but not necessarily to specify precisely the nature of what could have been.

The lessons of the past, both the political actor's particular past and the larger national past, are the baggage which every statesman brings

---

[1] Erikson's view of the problem of generativity in the life cycle is found in his *Childhood and Society* (New York-Norton, 1950), and "Identity and the Life Cycle" in *Psychological Issues*, 1959. More recent examples of work in this tradition include Daniel J. Levinson, *The Seasons of a Man's Life* (N.Y.: Ballantine Books, 1978), and George E. Valliant, *Adaptation to Life* (Boston: Little, Brown 1977).

with him to every decision he makes. They are like the blinders used to keep a plowhorse from seeing anything but a limited range of what lies ahead. So too, the statesman can never see the entire panorama of possibilities before him. Yet somewhere within the perceived range of choice, the statesman must make a decision, whether it be to move somewhere slightly to the left or slightly to the right of the path directly ahead.

There are, however, decisions in which the blinders of history seem to have been all encompassing and in which the available options have been reduced to one: all history seems to point to a single course of action. For the scholar conducting his researches at some future date, the range of choice appears considerably broader than it did to the person making the decision. Yet, the judgment that a particular statesman could have seen more than he did is a difficult judgment to make for the historian who has entered into the lives of his subjects and has seen events through their eyes. Nevertheless, it seems reasonable to conclude that public policy formulated on the basis of a single analogy, an analogy applied uncritically and without reference to other possibilities, is fundamantally untenable.

Such was surely the case for Neville Chamberlain and appeasement. At no point does he seem to have questioned seriously the appropriateness of the historical analogies he so uncritically and persistently applied. Hitler was not the kaiser, and at some level Chamberlain recognized that he was dealing with a man who did not fit the mold of the more traditional European statesman. But that awareness never translated itself into a recognition that different tactics might be necessary to cope with what was in fact an unprecedented threat to British security. Chamberlain was in this respect the captive rather than the master of events, like a fly caught in the web of history. Therefore, if we credit the quality of creativity, the ability to respond to the unique aspects of a given historical situation, with an independent role in the shaping of events, then we would certainly not place Chamberlain very high in the ranks of world historical figures.

But the sun has not yet set on the horrible events of the Second World War and Minerva's owl is only beginning to take flight. Perhaps, future students of the interwar years will see them as but a long cease-fire between two periods of total war, an era in which the advanced industrial societies turned to autarchy, when the regimes of the United States, Germany, Britain, Italy, and the Soviet Union were but variations on a common theme rather than distinct categories to which the labels fascism, communism, and democracy can be easily, meaningfully, and unproblematically applied. While it is perhaps too early for such questions to be productively explored, this study of Chamberlain points toward a diminution of the heretofore unbridgeable gap between our conception of political leadership in the West, in Britain, France, and the United States on the one hand, and that of Germany, Italy, and Soviet Russia on the other. Such is not, of course, to argue that there were no important differences among these regimes but to suggest that personal political leadership in each of these countries was marked by unmistakable commonalities of method which differ fundamentally from the norms established by the liberal Anglo-American tradition of political theory.

If such is the case, then it becomes important to answer the question of whether the type of leadership represented by Neville Chamberlain was a consequence of the need to deal effectively with the totalitarians or whether it was more a manifestation of social and material conditions shared to a greater or lesser extent by all the advanced industrial societies. Certainly, we have seen how Chamberlain perceived that the diffuse political structure of liberal democracy, with its relatively free press and need for consensus, put him at a distinct disadvantage in negotiating with Germany. But whether the resulting autocratic style of political decision-making was merely imitative or a result of deeper social forces and conditions is a question which has yet to be answered. Perhaps, then, the apparent paucity of "charismatic" larger-than-life political leaders in our own time is a denouement to be applauded rather than lamented.

Notes

PREFACE

Ian Macleod's study of Chamberlain and Alan Beattie's chapter on Neville Chamberlain in John P. Mackintosh (ed.), *British Prime Ministers in the Twentieth Century*, should also be included in a list of biographical works utilizing Chamberlain's private papers. Beattie, like Feiling and Macleod before him, writes from the Tory point of view and is concerned with rehabilitating Chamberlain from the popular left-wing vilifications. Steven Roskill, *Hankey: Man of Secrets*, Maurice Cowling, *The Impact of Hitler*, and Keith Middlemas, *The Strategy of Appeasement* (originally published in England as *The Diplomacy of Illusion*) should also be mentioned as works apparently utilizing at least part of the Chamberlain papers for purposes other than biography.

The reference to Erik Erikson is from his *Life History and the Historical Moment*, (New York: Norton, 1975). See particularly the chapter entitled "On the Nature of 'Psycho-Historical' Evidence."

INTRODUCTION

For Martin Gilbert's distinction between appeasement in general and Munich see his *The Roots of Appeasement*, introduction and pp. 175–76.

Churchill's warning about the Soviet Union is from *The Gathering Storm*, p. 38. Eden's statement with respect to Suez is from his *Full Circle*, p. 578.

For a discussion of the influence of the Munich analogy on American decision-makers in the postwar period see Ernest May, *"Lessons" of the Past* (New York: Oxford University Press, 1973), pp. 50–51.

Forrestal's comment is from *The Forrestal Diaries* (New York: Viking, 1951), p. 128. Donovan's statement is from his book *The Cold Warriors* (Lexington; Ma.: D.C. Heath, 1974), p. 2.

Truman's statement is from his *Memoirs*, Vol. II (Garden City, New York: Doubleday, 1955), p. 82. See also Glenn Paige's, *The Korean Decision*, p. 114, and May, p. 83.

George Ball's statement is from *State Department Bulletin*, LI, 7 June 1965 as quoted by May, pp. 112–13.

Trevor-Roper's view of the "lessons" of appeasement is from his article in Francis L. Lowenheim, ed., *The Historian and the Diplomat* (New York: Harper and Row, 1967), p. 157. Gabriel Almond's view is from his classic, *The American People and Foreign Policy* (New York: Praeger, 1960), p. 220. The American studies of appeasement referred to are Arthur Furnia, *The Diplomacy of Appeasement,* and Keith Eubank, *Munich.* Ernest May's suggestion is from his "A Case For Court Historians," in *Perspectives in American History,* Vol. II, pp. 413–34.

CATO's *Guilty Men* is perhaps the most famous contemporary condemnation of appeasement. Also in this category are such works as A.L. Rowse, *Appeasement—A Study in Political Decline,* and Labour memoirs such as Hugh Dalton's *The Fateful Years.*

The two major biographies of Chamberlain by Sir Keith Feiling, 1946, and Iain Macleod, 1961 are more or less explicit efforts at vindicating Chamberlain. Other Tory memoirs such as Viscount Templewood (Samuel Hoare), *Nine Troubled Years,* 1954, and Lord Halifax, *Fulness of Days,* 1957, also serve this function. David Dilks, "Appeasement Revisited," 1972, and Alan Beattie, "Neville Chamberlain," in *British Prime Ministers* Vol. I, 1977 are recent statements of the Tory position.

For a general discussion of the literature of appeasement see D.C. Watt, "Appeasement: the Rise of a Revisionist School?," 1965, and Robert Skidelsky's "Going to War With Germany Between Revisionism and Orthodoxy," 1972.

John Wheeler-Bennett, *Munich: Prologue to Tragedy,* 1948, Sir Lewis Namier, *Europe in Decay,* 1950, and W. N. Medlicott, *Britain and Germany the Search for Agreement 1933–37,* 1969, are examples of the view which attempts to judge appeasement on the basis of what could have been known about Hitler. It is a view which survives in such works as Keith Middlemas, *The Strategy of Appeasement,* 1972.

A.J.P. Taylor, *The Origins of the Second World War* is the most well known example of a revisionist view but is by no means the first nor the only book to take such a position.

For examples of works which attempt to transcend the old stereotypes of appeasement see Simon Newman, *March 1939; The British Guarantee to Poland,* 1976, and Telford Taylor, *Munich: The Price of Peace,* 1979. Unfortunately, neither Simon nor Taylor were apparently able to utilize the Chamberlain papers and as a result tend to underplay the importance of the prime minister in the making of policy and to see British policy as much more uniform and uncontested than it actually was.

For the more recent Tory revisionism see for example Alan Beattie, "Neville Chamberlain," and J.H. Grainger, *Character and Style in English Politics.*

Two very different works which deal with the questions of unspoken assumptions and bounded rationality are James Joll, *1914: the Unspoken Assumption* (London: Weiderfeld & Nicolson, 1968), and Leon Festinger, *A Theory of Cognitive Dissonance* (Evanston, Ill.: Row Peterson, 1957).

For a discussion of the human consequences of the Great War see Francis Hirst, *The Consequences of the War to Great Britain* (New York: Greenwood Press, 1968), p. 270, and Samuel Dumas, *Losses of Life Caused by War* (Oxford: The Clarendon Press, 1923) particularly the Prfeace by Harold Westergaard.

Two recent works dealing with the effect of the First World War on postwar British politics are Phillip Knightly, *The War Correspondent as Hero* (New York:

Harcourt Brace Jovanovich, 1975), and Paul Fussell's *The Great War and Modern Memory* (London: Oxford University Press, 1976). See Charles Loch Mowat, *Britain Between the Wars*, for a general discussion.

Churchill's view is from *The Aftermath* as quoted in *The Gathering Storm*, pp. 36–37.

CHAPTER I FATHERS AND SONS

The Chamberlain Family in Politics: For an adequate, though somewhat sycophantic discussion of the place of the Chamberlain family in British society see Charles Petrie, *The Chamberlain Family in Politics.*

On the question of the Chamberlain's so-called parochialism see H.R. Trevor-Roper, "Munich—Its Lessons Ten Years Later," in Francis Loewenheim, ed., *Peace or Appeasement*, pp. 150–57.

The excerpts from Chamberlain's "official" biographer are from Sir Keith Feiling, *The Life of Neville Chamberlain*, p. 3, p. 43, and p. 234.

Joseph Chamberlain's statement on the Jews is from W. Wickham Steed, *Through Thirty Years*, p. 163 quoted by Julian Amery in Vol. IV, pp. 256–57 of *Joseph Chamberlain*, a six-volume biography the first three volumes of which were written by J.L. Garven, (1932–34) and the remaining three by Julian Amery (1951–69). The biography is hereafter cited as "Garvin/Amery."

See Garvin/Amery, Vol. IV, Ch. 87, *passim*, for information on Joseph Chamberlain's attitudes toward Zionism. The quoted sentence on Joseph Chamberlain's aim with respect to an Anglo-German alliance is from Garvin/Amery, Vol. IV, p. 145. For a general discussion of Joseph Chamberlain's German initiative see Garvin/Amery, Vol. IV, Ch. 71, *passim*.

On Neville Chamberlain's early childhood see Feiling, pp. 3–10. Chamberlain's reverent attitude toward his father is noted by, among others, Middlemas, p. 45.

Neville Chamberlain's statement to the House on the passage of the tariff bill is from 261, *H.C. Deb.*, 5th Series, col. 296.

Joseph Chamberlain's motives for sending his son to Andros are from Garvin/Amery, Vol. II, p. 499. Neville Chamberlain's letters from Andros are found under the heading NC 1/16/1/54–1/16/2/21 in the Neville Chamberlain papers. See also Austen Chamberlain to Mary Endicott Chamberlain, 25 December 1892, quoted in Sir Charles Petrie, *The Life and Letters of the Right Hon. Sir Austen Chamberlain*, Vol. I, p. 38, hereafter cited as "Petrie."

Joseph Chamberlain's thoughts on the Andros venture are from Garvin/Amery, Vol. II, p. 500. Neville Chamberlain's feeling of responsibility for the experiment's failure are from Neville to Joseph Chamberlain, 28 August 1896. Austen's 1935 letter is from Austen to Neville Chamberlain, 15 January 1935 in the Neville Chamberlain papers.

Neville Chamberlain's Early Career: Neville's 1902 letter is in Neville Chamberlain to Alfred Greenwood, 7 October 1900, found in the Neville Chamberlain papers.

For Chamberlain's thoughts on marriage see Neville to Ida Chamberlain, 8 January 1911. Two characteristic letters to his wife are Neville to Annie Chamberlain, 14 May 1918, and 9 August 1918. For further information see Feiling, pp. 49 and 124 and Macleod, p. 40.

The quoted material on Chamberlain's plans for Birmingham civil defense is from Feiling p. 59 and 61. For material on Neville's relations with his half brother see particularly, Petrie, Vol. I, p. 356.

Austin's thoughts on the ministry of national service are from Petrie, Vol. II, p. 64. Neville's comments are from Feiling, p. 62. Lloyd George's comment is from his memoirs, pp. 283–84. Chamberlain's diary entry is from Feiling, p. 71.

Norman Chamberlain's letter is from Neville Chamberlain's biography of him, *Norman Chamberlain*, pp. 142–43. Macleod's statement is from his biography pp. 46–47 and p. 74. Neville's feelings about his cousin are from the biography of Norman, p. v in the introduction and p. 140 and p. 160 in the text. Chamberlain's diary entry is from Feiling p. 84. Further citations from *Norman Chamberlain* are from the introduction p. vi, p. 141, p. 159, and p. 35 respectively. The citations from Chamberlain's diary are quoted by Feiling, p. 76 and 78. The citation from Chamberlain's first parliamentary speech is also from Feiling, p. 82.

The excerpt from the *Daily Mail* is from an article written by Rev. E.L. Macassey which appeared on 9 April 1938.

Chamberlain as a National Politician: Chamberlain's private feelings on entering Parliament are from Neville Chamberlain to Mary Endicott Chamberlain, 14 August 1917, and from Neville to Hilda Chamberlain, 23 February 1918.

Amery's comment is from *My Political Life*, Vol. III, p. 225. See also Vol. II, pp. 100–1.

On Chamberlain's initial acquaintance with Halifax and Hoare see Lord Birkenhead, *The Life of Lord Halifax*, p. 147. On Chamberlain's growing rift with Labour see Macleod pp. 119–20 and Feiling, p. 142.

Chapter II The Struggle For Power: 1931–35

Information on Chamberlain's attempted coup is from Ann Fagan, unpublished manuscript, Chapter I, pp. 12–15, Robert Rhodes James, *Memoirs of a Conservative*, pp. 857–61, and T. Jones, *A Diary With Letters*, pp. 4–6 and p. 52.

For Chamberlain's scorn of Baldwin see, for example, Neville to Hilda and Ida Chamberlain, 9 December 1934, and Neville to Hilda Chamberlain, 14 July 1935. His frustration with his behind-the-scenes role is expressed in Neville to Hilda Chamberlain, 23 March 1935, and Neville to Hilda Chamberlain, 17 October 1936. For further information see Middlemas, p. 44.

Chamberlain's Views on Foreign Affairs: Macleod's view that Chamberlain was an "intellectual" is found in his biography of Chamberlain, pp. 202–3.

Halifax's assessment of Chamberlain is from his memoirs, *Fulness of Days*, p. 231. One example of a historian who criticizes Chamberlain's application of business methods to foreign affairs is Hugh Trevor-Roper in Loewenheim, *Peace or Appeasement*.

Chamberlain's April 1938 statement is from the *Times*, 15 April 1938.

Arnold Wolfer's views are found in his book *Discord and Collaboration*.

Chamberlain's views on war as an instrument of policy are from the introduction to *In Search of Peace*. His statement on the morality of war is quoted by Feiling, p. 320.

Beginning of Active Participation in International Politics: Chamberlain's private views on the Lausanne Conference are from Neville Chamberlain to Mary Endicott, 13 July 1932. See Feiling, p. 208 and Macleod, p. 159 for further discussion.

The decision to abandon the ten-year rule is found in Cab 23/70, March 1932. See also CID, 1087-B, 17 March 1932. For further discussion see M.M. Postan, *British War Production*, pp. 1–9, and Robert Shay, *British Rearmament in the Thirties*, pp. 23–24.

Chamberlain's statement to the CID is from Cab 2/6, 261(1), 11 September 1933. The DRC report is in Cab 24/247, C.P. 64(34), 5 March 1934. Chamberlain's January 1934 statement on rearmament is from Feiling, p. 251.

On Churchill's views as chancellor of the Exchequer see Telford Taylor, *Munich*, pp. 202–4. Cf. Churchill's *The Gathering Storm*, pp. 21–25.

Chamberlain's statement to the House of 25 April 1933 is from 277 *H.C. Deb.*, 5th Series, cols. 60–61.

For a general discussion of the positions taken during these years by the various segments of the labor movement see John Naylor, *Labour's International Policy*, Ch. III, *passim*. Cf. Hoare's memoirs, *Nine Troubled Years*.

The DRC report is in Cab 24/247, C.P. 64(34), 5 March 1934. See also Middlemas and Barnes, *Baldwin*, p. 764. Chamberlain's attitude toward the report is discussed in Macleod, p. 178, Keith Robbins, *Munich 1938*, p. 99, and Feiling, p. 258. For the final report see Cab 24/250, C.O. 203(34), 1 July 1934. Chamberlain's private views are in Neville to Hilda Chamberlain, 12 May 1935.

For an assessment of Chamberlain's role in the modification of the DRC report see Shay, pp. 19–47, and Roskill, *Hankey: Man of Secrets*, Vol. II, pp. 110–14, and p. 119. Cf. Middlemas and Barnes, p. 718, *et. seq.* and Middlemas, p. 1.

Chamberlain's private views on his modification of the DRC report are from Neville to Hilda Chamberlain, 28 July 1934. The same letter contains his views on the Austrian assassination. Churchill's similar reaction is from *The Gathering Storm*, p. 96.

Chamberlain's Cabinet proposal is in Cab 53/23, C.O. 328, 27 March 1934. See also Feiling, p. 252, quoting Chamberlain's diary of 25 March 1934.

Chamberlain's views on the new budget are from Neville to Ida Chamberlain, 6 August 1934.

Chiefs of staff discussion is in Cab 53/4. Minutes of the 123rd meeting of the chiefs of staff, 17 April 1934. Their report to the Cabinet is in Cab 53/23, C.O.S. 329, March 1934.

Chamberlain reported on his discussion with Flandin in Neville to Ida Chamberlain, 20 August 1934. His proposal is in *DBFP*, Second Series, Vol. 13, p. 26, a memo entitled, "Naval Conference and Relations with Japan." His private thoughts on the plan are in Neville to Hilda Chamberlain, 27 August 1934. Chamberlain's memorandum as presented to the Cabinet is in C.P., 223(34) and was discussed by the Cabinet on 24 October. See "Memorandum by the Chancellor of the Exchequer and the Secretary of State for Foreign Affairs on the

Future of Anglo-Japanese Relations," in *DBFP,* Second Series, Vol. 13, pp. 61–65.

Chamberlain's report on the negotiations with Japan is in Neville to Hilda Chamberlain, 17 November 1934. See also Neville to Hilda Chamberlain, 29 September 1934. The letter comparing himself with his father is Neville to Ida Chamberlain, 13 October 1934.

Rearmament, the League, Anglo-German Naval Treaty, Hoare-Laval Pact: The quotation from Chamberlain's biographer is by Feiling, p. 234.

The White Paper on Defense is in Cmd. 3827, 1935, "Statement Relating to Defence." Chamberlain's private thoughts on the White Paper are in Neville to Hilda Chamberlain, 9 March 1935, which contains a reference to Simon. Other criticism of the foreign secretary and the meeting with Hitler are in Neville to Ida Chamberlainn 16 March 1935, and Neville to Ida Chamberlain, 30 March 1935. The latter contains a reference to the Stresa Conference. Other references to Stresa are in Neville to Hilda Chamberlain, 6 April 1935, and Neville to Hilda Chamberlain, 23 February 1935.

Chamberlain's comments on Lloyd George and Churchill as well as his criticism of the prime minister are in Neville to Hilda Chamberlain, 9 March 1935, and Neville to Hilda Chamberlain, 23 March 1935. Churchill's comment is from Feiling, p. 275.

The reference to Simon's challenge to Chamberlain's position is from Neville to Hilda Chamberlain, 22 May 1935. His attitudes toward "the foreigner" are in Neville to Hilda Chamberlain, 12 May 1935.

Feiling's assessment is from his biography pp. 257 and 268. Chamberlain's attitude toward the upcoming meeting with Hitler is in Neville to Hilda Chamberlain, 18 March 1935, and Neville to Ida Chamberlain, 16 March 1935.

Hoare's view of the Anglo-German Naval Treaty is from his memoirs, p. 142. See also Martin Gilbert, *The Roots of Appeasement,* p. 150, and Keith Middlemas, *The Strategy of Appeasement,* note p. 8. Chamberlain's view of the treaty is in Neville to Ida Chamberlain, 30 March 1935. Hoare's statement is quoted by Churchill in *The Gathering Storm,* pp. 127–28. The citation by Keith Robbins is from his book, p. 144.

Chamberlain's views on Eden's mission are in Neville to Hilda Chamberlain, 22 June 1935, and Neville to Ida Chamberlain, 6 July 1935. His speculations on a possible approach to France are in Neville to Hilda Chamberlain, 14 July 1935. His views on Italy and rearmament are from Neville to Ida Chamberlain, 25 August 1935. Chamberlain's thoughts on the possibility of avoiding war are in Neville to Ida Chamberlain, 5 October 1935.

Chamberlain's diary entry on the future of the League is from 5 July 1935. His letter on the same subject is Neville to Ida Chamberlain, 19 October 1935. On the question of Mussolini's intentions and British rearmament see Neville to Ida Chamberlain, 8 December 1935.

Chamberlain's thoughts on the Hoare-Laval affair are in Neville to Hilda Chamberlain, 15 December 1935.

Greenwood's criticism of Chamberlain is from Robbins, p. 133, that of Herbert Morrison is from Macleod, p. 184.

Chamberlain's thoughts on the election are from Neville to Hilda Chamberlain, 7 September 1935, and Neville to Ida Chamberlain, 17 November 1935. His comments on the terrible costs of rearmament are from Neville to Ida Chamberlain, 8 December 1935, and Neville to Hilda Chamberlain, 9 February 1936.

Chapter III Chamberlain in Control: 1936–37

Herbert Samuel's comment is from W.P. Crozier's interview of Samuel in A.J.P. Taylor, ed., *Off the Record*, p. 50.

Reoccupation of the Rhineland: Taylor's position is from his book, *The Origins of the Second World War*, p. 99. Churchill's view is from *The Gathering Storm*, p. 177.

Chamberlain's comments on allied policy in the wake of the German action are from Neville to Ida Chamberlain, 14 March 1936. Chamberlain's account of the conversations with Flandin is from his diary of 12 March 1936.

Baldwin's statement is from Flandin's memoirs, *Politique Française, 1919–1940*, as quoted by Churchill, p. 177. Dalton's statement is from 310, *H.C. Deb.*, 5th Series, col. 1454.

Chamberlain's report of his activities in the Cabinet and his thoughts on the future are from Neville to Hilda Chamberlain, 21 March 1936. His comments on Abyssinia are from Neville to Ida Chamberlain, 12 April 1936, and from Neville to Hilda Chamberlain, 2 May 1936. His thoughts on a colonial settlement in Africa are in Neville to Ida Chamberlain, 13 April 1936. Chamberlain discussed his request for a Cabinet committee on the League in Neville to Ida Chamberlain, 25 April 1936.

The citations from his 1900 Club speech are from the *Times*, 10 June 1936. Eden's comment is from his memoirs, p. 385. Lloyd George's comment is from Middlemas and Barnes, p. 940. Baldwin's letter to Chamberlain is in the Chamberlain papers NC 7/11/30/23.

Eden's admission is from Middlemas, p. 50. See also Macleod, p. 194.

See Naylor, p. 137, for a discussion of Labour's attitude toward lifting of sanctions.

Chamberlain's private feelings on his speech and its reporting by the press are from Neville to Hilda Chamberlain, 14 June 1936, and Neville Chamberlain to Mary Endicott, 15 June 1936.

Domestic Political Maneuvering: Chamberlain's comments on his brother's flirtation with the Churchill faction are in Neville to Ida Chamberlain, 4 July 1936. Cabinet discussion of Austen Chamberlain's proposal is in Cab 23/85, 48(36), 6 July 1936. Chamberlain's afterthoughts on the affair are in Neville to Hilda Chamberlain, 11 July 1936.

Chamberlain's attitude toward meeting Churchill in parliamentary debate is discussed in Neville to Hilda Chamberlain, 25 June 1936 and in other similar letters.

Baldwin's letter is from Middlemas and Barnes, p. 929.

Chamberlain's thoughts on Baldwin's competence are in Neville to Ida Chamberlain, 20 June 1936, and Neville to Hilda Chamberlain, 27 June 1936. For further discussion of Baldwin's mental state see Middlemas and Barnes, p. 963, Tom Jones, pp. 209–68, *passim,* and James, p. 412.

For Chamberlain's private criticism of Baldwin's leadership see Neville to

Hilda Chamberlain, 17 October 1935: Neville to Ida Chamberlain, 19 July 1936; and Neville to Hilda Chamberlain, 14 November 1936. See Middlemas and Barnes, *passim* for a very different assessment of Baldwin's leadership.

Economics and the Nazi Threat: Chamberlain's private assessment of German intentions is from Neville to Ida Chamberlain, 20 June 1936; Neville to Hilda Chamberlain, 27 June 1936; and Neville to Ida Chamberlain, 19 July 1936.

The 1937 White Paper is in Cmd. 5374, "Statement Relating to Defence Expenditure," 16 February 1937. Duff Cooper's statement is from his memoirs, *Old Men Forget,* p. 200.

Chamberlain's warning to Baldwin is in Neville to Hilda Chamberlain, 9 February 1936. Material on Chamberlain's relations with Maurice Hankey is from Roskill, Vol. III, pp. 191–208.

Chamberlain's assessment of the lessons of the last war is in Neville to Hilda Chamberlain, 9 February 1936. For a discussion of British army doctrine see the Liddell Hart *Memoirs,* Vol. II, Ch. I, *passim.* Chamberlain's conversation with Inskip is from Neville to Ida Chamberlain, 10 October 1936.

Duff Cooper's memorandum is in Cab 24/265, C.P. 326(36), 3 December 1936. Cabinet discussion is in Cab 23/86, 73(36), 9 December 1936. The 1936 White Paper is in Cmd. 7107, "Statement Relating to Defence," 3 March 1936. Chamberlain's argument for a restricted role for the army is in Cab 24/265, C.P. 334(36), "The Role of the Army," 11 December 1936.

Chamberlain's views on Inskip's appointment are in Neville to Ida Chamberlain, 4 March 1936. Churchill's comment is in *History of the Times,* Vol. IV, p. 902. See also CATO, *Guilty Men,* p. 46, for a critical view of Inskip and Roskill, Vol. III, p. 20, for a more favorable assessment.

Chamberlain's view of the role of the minister for coordination of defense is from Neville to Hilda Chamberlain, 14 November 1936. Cabinet discussion of the role of the army is in Cab 23/86, 75(36), 16 December 1936. The chiefs of staff report on the role of the army is in C.P. 41/37, the conclusions of which are reprinted in Ian Colvin, *The Chamberlain Cabinet,* pp. 24–25.

Duff Cooper's plan for resolution of the issue of the role of the army is in Cab 23/87, 2(37), 20 January 1937, and Cab 23/87, 5(37), 3 February 1937. See also Shay, pp. 137–40, for a discussion of Chamberlain's attempt to postpone a decision on the equipping of the territorial army. Inskip's proposal is in C.P. 46/37.

Chamberlain's report on the outcome of the deliberations on the role of the army is from Neville to Ida Chamberlain, 6 February 1937. For further discussion see Middlemas and Barnes, p. 1026, and the Liddell Hart *Memoirs,* Vol. II, pp. 6–10.

Duff Cooper's recollections are from his memoirs pp. 199–200. Hore-Belisha's statement is from A.J.P. Taylor, ed., *Off The Record,* p. 47. Chamberlain's comment on Duff Cooper is in Neville to Hilda Chamberlain, 1 June 1936.

Chamberlain as de facto *Prime Minister:* Davidson's comment is Robert Rhodes James, *Memoirs of a Conservative,* p. 417.

See Middlemas and Barnes, p. 1019 for discussion of Baldwin's last few months as prime minister.

Chamberlain's plans for the transition of power are in Neville to Ida Chamberlain, 16 January 1937. His warning to the Cabinet on the question of rearmament spending is in Cab 23/88, 19(37), 28 April 1937. Chamberlain's proposal for increasing the public debt to pay for rearmament is in Cab 23/87, 7(37), 10 February.

A discussion of the National Defence Contribution is found in Shay, pp. 147–48. Public reception of the NDC is discussed in Mowat, p. 571. See also the *Manchester Guardian,* 21 April 1937.

Chamberlain's discussion of the NDC is in Neville to Hilda Chamberlain, 25 April 1937. The citation assessing Chamberlain's failure with respect to NDC is from Shay, p. 153.

Chamberlain's comparison of himself with his father and Austen is in Neville to Ida Chamberlain, 21 March 1937.

Chapter IV The Fall of Avalanches

Chamberlain's comments on kissing hands are in Neville to Hilda Chamberlain, 30 May 1937.

The Formation of the Chamberlain Government: Extracts from Churchill's speech are from the *Times,* 1 June 1937, p. 18. On the question of Churchill's relationship to Chamberlain, cf. Neville Thompson, *The Anti-Appeasers,* p. 137.

Eden's retrospective comment on Chamberlain's becoming prime minister is from an interview with Eden (Lord Avon), 25 October 1974, by Kenneth Harris. A transcript of the interview was supplied to the author courtesy of Lord Avon, Mr. Harris, and the BBC. Cf. Eden's memoirs, *Facing the Dictators,* p. 502.

Hankey's views are from Roskill, *Hankey: Man of Secrets,* Vol. III, p. 264. Hore-Belisha's views are from an interview by Crozier in Taylor, ed., *Off The Record,* p. 63. See also Davidson, p. 418. The views of Attlee and Sinclair are from the *Times,* 1 June 1937, p. 9.

The excerpt from Chamberlain's speech on election to the party leadership is also from the *Times,* 1 June 1937. His personal views are from Neville to Hilda Chamberlain, 30 May 1937.

On Leo Amery and his relations with Chamberlain see Neville to Hilda Chamberlain, 10 April 1937; Chamberlain to Amery, 30 May 1937; and Amery to Chamberlain, 4 June 1937, all of which are found in the Neville Chamberlain papers.

Chamberlain's thoughts on the process of Cabinet making are from Neville to Hilda Chamberlain, 30 May 1937.

For Duff Cooper's reaction to being offered the Admiralty see his memoirs, p. 206.

On Hore-Belisha's appointment to the War Ministry see, the Liddell Hart *Memoirs,* Vol. II, p. 10.

Swinton's comment is from his memoirs, *Sixty Years of Power,* p. 114. Middlemas's comment is from his *The Strategy of Appeasement,* p. 60.

Chamberlain's idea of an Inner Cabinet is from his diary, 5 May 1937. On the question of the competence of the new Cabinet, cf. Gilbert & Gott, p. 61. Birkenhead's comments are from his *Life of Lord Halifax,* p. 362.

Italian Initiatives: For Chamberlain's assessment of his first few months in office, see Neville to Ida Chamberlain, 6 June 1937; Neville to Ida Chamberlain, 21 June 1937; Neville to Hilda Chamberlain, 26 June 1937; and Neville to Hilda Chamberlain, 18 July 1937.

Extracts from Chamberlain's first parliamentary speech as prime minister are from 325. *H.C. Deb.*, col. 1549, 25 June 1937. See Eden, pp. 446–47, for a discussion of the *Leipzig* cruiser incident.

Excerpts from his Birmingham speech are from, *In Search of Peace*, pp. 14–16.

Chamberlain's private thoughts on German and Italian intentions are from Neville to Ida Chamberlain, 4 July 1937.

For the background to the Grandi-Chamberlain meetings see particularly, Telford Taylor, pp. 556–57. Chamberlain's thoughts on the Italian initiative are from Neville to Ida Chamberlain, 24 July 1937. Eden's reflections on the Grandi-Chamberlain meeting are from his memoirs pp. 508–10.

Chamberlain's letter to Mussolini is in PREM 1/276, Chamberlain to Mussolini, 27 July 1937. His private comments on it are in Neville to Hilda Chamberlain, 1 August 1937. The February 1938 comment is from Chamberlain's diary of 19 February 1938. Eden's recollections are from his memoirs, p. 510 and from the Crozier interview cited above.

Chamberlain's views on Halifax and on relations with Italy are from Neville to Ida Chamberlain, 8 August 1937.

Chamberlain's private views on his accomplishments with respect to Italy are in Neville to Hilda Chamberlain, 29 August 1937.

The Role of the Army: For further information on the question of the role of the army and rearmament including material on the views of the military, see Peter Dennis, *Decision by Default*, pp. 100–26.

The proposal for a rationed budget is in Cab 24/270, C.P. 165(37), "Defence Expenditure," 25 June 1937. Cabinet discussion of the proposal is from Cab 23/88, 27(37), 30 June 1937.

For material on Hore-Belisha's appointment to the Ministry of War see Feiling, p. 317, and R.J. Minney, *The Private Papers of Leslie Hore-Belisha*, p. 14. Chamberlain's comments on Hore-Belisha are in Neville to Hilda Chamberlain, 1 August 1937.

Chamberlain's letter to Hore-Belisha is from Minney, p. 54. For the relevant part of Liddell Hart's analysis see *Europe in Arms*, p. 150. Chamberlain's letter to Liddell Hart is in the latter's memoirs, Vol. I, p. 386. Hore-Belisha's letter to Chamberlain is in the Chamberlain papers, Hore-Belisha to Chamberlain, 1 November 1937. Cf. Middlemas, p. 125.

Chamberlain's letter to Hore-Belisha on the role of the army is from Minney, p. 66. Liddell Hart's recollections are from his memoirs, Vol. II, p. 53. The Hore-Belisha/Liddell Hart memo is in NC7/11/30/77 and in Minney, p. 66.

Chamberlain's satisfaction with Hore-Belisha is from Liddell Hart's memoirs, Vol. II, p. 56. Chamberlain's note on the Hore-Belisha/Deverell controversy is from Minney, p. 68. See also Liddell Hart, Vol. II, p. 56. Hore-Belisha's letter of thanks to Chamberlain is in Hore-Belisha to Chamberlain, 3 December 1937 in the Chamberlain papers. See Minney, pp. 51 and 68–71 on Hore-Belisha's view of Gort. Chamberlain's private reaction to Hore-Belisha's action is in Neville to

Hilda Chamberlain, 5 December 1937. Hore-Belisha's diary entry is found in Minney, p. 69.

The citation from the CID memorandum is from CID, 1366B as embodied in C.P. 295(37) and summarized by Chamberlain in Cab 23/90, 46(37), 8 December 1937. See also Middlemas, pp. 121–22. Chamberlain's report of private talks with colleagues on the question of the role of the army is in Neville to Hilda Chamberlain, 5 December 1937.

Inskip's memo is in C.P. 316/37, discussed in the Cabinet on 15 and 22 December. See Cab 23/90, 47(37), 48(37), and 49(37). See also Colvin, *The Chamberlain Cabinet*, pp. 72–81. Hore-Belisha's comments on the Inskip memo are in Cab 23/90, 49(37), 22 December 1937. Chamberlain reported these arguments to the Commons during the debate over the 1938 White Paper. See 332, *H.C. Deb.*, 5th Series, col. 1561–66.

Chamberlain's comments to the Committee of Imperial Defence are in PREM 1/308, Committee of Imperial Defence, Draft minutes of a Conference of Ministers held 14 February 1938. Simon's statement is from the same source.

The paper containing the new role for the army is in Cab 24/275, C.P. 26(38), "The Organization of the Army For its Role in War."

The Halifax Visit: For further discussion of the invitation to Neurath see Toynbee, *Survey of International Affairs, 1933–39,* Vol. I, pp. 327–28 and Henderson, *Failure of a Mission,* p. 64.

For a discussion of the events surrounding Halifax's invitation to visit Germany see Schwoerer, "Lord Halifax's Visit to Germany November 1937," pp. 354–58. For Hoare's assessment of Chamberlain's intentions see his memoirs, pp. 282 and 258. Halifax's views are from his memoirs, p. 184.

Chamberlain's thoughts on Eden and the Foreign Office are from Neville to Hilda Chamberlain, 24 October 1937; Neville to Ida Chamberlain, 30 October 1937; and Neville to Hilda Chamberlain, 6 November 1937. Eden's views are from his memoirs, pp. 506–8 and 578.

Eden's recollection of his meeting with Chamberlain is from his memoirs, p. 580. His letter to Chamberlain is in PREM 1/330, 16 November 1937.

Chamberlain's private views on the Halifax instructions are from Neville to Ida Chamberlain, 14 November 1937. Eden's views are from his memoirs, p. 577.

Halifax's letter to Eden is in PREM 1/330. See also Birkenhead pp. 369–72. Halifax's views on the meeting are from "Halifax's Notes on Berchtesgaden," in PREM 1/330.

Chamberlain's private views on the accomplishments of the Halifax visit and his ideas for a colonial settlement are from Neville to Hilda Chamberlain, 21 November 1937. Eden's very different view is from his memoirs, pp. 513–16. Hoare's assessment is from his memoirs, p. 282. See also Schmidt's transcript of the Halifax-Hitler meeting in *DGFP*, Series D., Vol. I, pp. 62–63.

Chamberlain's view of the future course of Anglo-German negotiations is from Neville to Ida Chamberlain, 26 November 1937.

A report of the Anglo-French meeting is in Cab 23/90, 45(37), 1 December 1937. His private views on the meeting are from Neville to Hilda Chamberlain, 5 December 1937.

Chamberlain's statement to the Cabinet is in Cab 23/90, 43(37), 24 November 1937. His statement to the House of Commons is 329, *H.C. Deb.*, 5th Series, cols. 1877–78, which contains the communiqué. Chamberlain's private comments are from Neville to Hilda Chamberlain, 5 December 1937. See also Schwoerer, p. 374.

Purging the Dissidents: Chamberlain's thoughts on resuming conversations with Italy are from Neville to Hilda Chamberlain, 29 August 1937. His views on Eden and the Foreign Office are in Neville to Ida Chamberlain, 7 September 1937, and Neville to Hilda Chamberlain, 12 September 1937.

On the Nyon Conference see particularly, Eden, pp. 518–38, and Cowling, pp. 167–69. Chamberlain's thoughts on the Conference are from Neville to Ida Chamberlain, 19 September 1937.

For Chamberlain's attempt to control Eden see *The Diplomatic Diaries of Oliver Harvey*, 22 September 1937, p. 47.

His plans to get rid of Vansittart are in Neville to Hilda Chamberlain, 5 December 1937, and Neville to Ida Chamberlain, 12 December 1937. Eden's views on Vansittart are in his memoirs, p. 591. See also Colvin, *Vansittart in Office*, p. 148, and Neville Thompson, *The Anti-Appeasers*, pp. 140–41. For a discussion of public knowledge of the affair see Ian Colvin, *None So Blind*, pp. 172–73. Eden's belated realization is from his memoirs, pp. 653–54.

Chamberlain's thoughts on Duff Cooper are in Neville to Hilda Chamberlain, 17 December 1937. The letters exchanged between the two men are in the Chamberlain papers, NC7/11/30/39–40.

Roosevelt's Initiative, Eden's Resignation: For a copy of the Roosevelt initiative as Sumner Welles had submitted it for presidential approval see *FRUS*, 1938, Vol. I, pp. 115–18. On Chamberlain's contempt for the Americans see Neville to Ida Chamberlain, 28 September 1936; Neville to Ida Chamberlain, 10 October 1936; and Neville to Hilda Chamberlain, 14 November 1936.

On the reasons for Chamberlain's declining the invitation to visit the United States see Neville to Ida Chamberlain, 4 July 1937; Neville to Hilda Chamberlain, 29 August 1937; and *FRUS*, 1937, Vol. I, p. 113.

For Chamberlain's reaction to Roosevelt's quarantine speech see Neville to Hilda Chamberlain, 9 October 1937. His further thoughts on American policy are from Neville to Ida Chamberlain, 16 October 1937; Neville to Hilda Chamberlain, 17 December 1937; and Neville to Hilda Chamberlain, 9 January 1938.

Chamberlain's claim that he had no time to consult Eden on the American initiative is from his diary, 19–27 February 1938. Cf., Eden, p. 627.

Chamberlain's reply to Roosevelt is in Chamberlain to Roosevelt, 14 January 1938, *FRUS*, 1938, Vol. I, pp. 118–20. Churchill's comment is from, *The Gathering Storm*, p. 254. See also Hoare, pp. 263–68 and Langer and Gleason, *Challenge to Isolation*, p. 32.

Roosevelt's response is in *FRUS*, 1938, Vol. I, pp. 120–22. Eden's views are in his memoirs, p. 695.

Chamberlain's discussion of the American time bomb is from Neville to Ida Chamberlain, 16 January 1938; Neville to Ida Chamberlain, 23 January 1938; Neville to Hilda Chamberlain, 30 January 1938; and Neville to Hilda Chamberlain, 6 February 1938.

Chamberlain's feelings about Eden are from Neville to Ida Chamberlain, 16 January 1938. Eden's letter to Chamberlain of 9 January is in the Chamberlain papers, NC7/11/31/100.

See Macleod, p. 212 for the full citation of Chamberlain's diary entry concerning the Roosevelt initiative. Eden discussed his telegram to Lindsay in his memoirs, p. 628. See the same volume, p. 565 for Eden's statement about resignation.

Chamberlain's protestations that he and Eden were in complete agreement is from Neville to Hilda Chamberlain, 13 February 1938. His view that he had no notion that Eden would resign is from Neville to Hilda Chamberlain, 27 February 1938.

Swinton's comment is from his memoirs, *Sixty Years of Power*, p. 166.

Chamberlain's letter to Halifax of 7 August 1937, is in PREM 1/276. See "Notes on Anglo-Italian Discussions" by Neville Chamberlain in PREM 1/276 for a discussion of the question of *de jure* vs. *de facto* recognition. This file also contains letters between Chamberlain and Eden on this matter. See also Eden's memoirs, p. 569. Roosevelt's letter disapproving of *de jure* recognition is in *FRUS*, 1938, Vol. I, Roosevelt to Chamberlain, 17 January 1938.

On the role of Ivy Chamberlain see *Ciano's Hidden Diary*, pp. 57–68. Eden's letter of protest is in PREM 1/276, which also contains Chamberlain's response. See also Eden's memoirs, p. 653 and Appendix D, pp. 705–9.

Readers wishing an account of the last-minute attempts to compromise the Eden-Chamberlain differences are directed to Eden's own account, pp. 666–84, David Carlton, *Anthony Eden*, pp. 100–31, Middlemas, pp. 151–54, and Rock, *Appeasement on Trial*, pp. 28–31. Cabinet discussion is from Cab 23/92, 7(38), 20 February 1938.

For the view that Chamberlain had always intended to replace Eden see, for example, Margaret George, *The Warped Vision*, p. 176.

On the question of Eden's reputation see, for example, A.J.P. Taylor, *English History*, p. 423. See also Roskill, Vol. II, p. 304.

Chapter V The Anschluss and Beyond

Chamberlain's private views on Eden's resignation can be found in Neville to Hilda Chamberlain, 27 February 1938.

An Overture to Germany: FPC discussion of the colonial question can be found in Cab 27/622, FP (36) 27 July 1936, Cab 27/622, 18 March 1937, and Cab 27/623, FP (36), 24 January 1938. For Chamberlain's thoughts on the plan for a colonial settlement see Neville to Ida Chamberlain, 23 January 1938, and Neville to Hilda Chamberlain, 30 January 1938.

The German record of the Henderson-Hitler meeting can be found in *DGFP*, Series D, Vol. I, No. 138. With respect to the colonial question, the German document is in substantial agreement with Henderson's report to the British Cabinet and the record found in his memoirs. Henderson's account can be found in Henderson, 113–18. See also *The Diaries of Sir Alexander Cadogan*, p. 58, and *The Diplomatic Diaries of Oliver Harvey*, pp. 107–9, hereafter cited as "Cadogan Diary" and "Harvey Diary" respectively. See also Birkenhead, p. 385.

Cabinet discussion of the Hitler-Henderson meeting is in Cab 23/92, 2 March

1938 and Cab 23/92, 9 March 1938. See Telford Taylor pp. 574–78 for further discussion. Chamberlain's personal views are in Neville to Hilda Chamberlain, 6 February 1938, and Neville to Hilda Chamberlain, 13 March 1938.

For Cabinet discussion of Austria prior to the Anschluss see Cab 23/92, 19 February 1938. Anglo-German documents regarding the Anschluss can be found in *DGFP*, Series D, Vol. I, Nos. 150 and 151 as well as *DBFP*, 3rd Series, Vol. I, No. 46.

On the Chamberlain-Ribbentrop meeting see Neville to Hilda Chamberlain, 13 March 1938. Cabinet reaction to the Anschluss can be found in Cab 23, 9 (38), 9 March 1938.

Reactions to the Anschluss: Cabinet discussions following the Anschluss can be found in Cab 23/92, 12 March 1938. Chamberlain's original pledge, as well as FPC discussion on the question of Italian negotations is contained in Cab 27/623, 15 March 1938.

Churchill's statement to the House is in 333 *H.C. Deb.*, 5th Series, cols. 99–100. For further discussion see Marion Kenney, "The Role of the House of Commons in British Foreign Policy during the 1937–38 session."

See Middlemas, p. 184n for a discussion of the origins of Halifax's important FPC memo of 18 March 1938 the text of which is found in Cab 27/923, 18 March 1938, Appendix I, Memo by Lord Halifax, "Possible Measures to Avert German Action in Czechoslovakia." See also the general FPC discussion of the memo in Cab 27/623, 18 March 1938 from which excerpts are quoted. See also Middlemas, p. 192.

The views of the military chiefs of staff can be found in CP (36) 57, cited in Cab 23/93, 22 March 1938 which contains Cabinet discussion of the strategic significance of Czechoslovakia to Britain.

Chamberlain's statement to the House of Commons is in 33 *H.C. Deb.*, 5th Series, Colm 1042.

The official British rejection of the Soviet offer was given to the Soviets on 24 March. See *DBFP*, 3rd Series, Vol. I, No. 116. The British message to France is found in *DBFP*, 3rd Series, Vol. I, 106.

Chamberlain's private views on his speech in the Commons are found in Neville to Hilda Chamberlain, 27 March 1938. His plans for dealing with Czechoslovakia are found in Neville to Ida Chamberlain, 20 March 1938.

Anglo-Italian Agreement and the Acquiescence of France: The record of Cabinet meetings in this period is contained in Cab 23/93, 6, 13; and 22 April 1938.

Chamberlain's private views on the Anglo-Italian agreement are contained in Neville to Ida Chamberlain, 16 April 1938.

The record of Anglo-French meetings is contained in *DBFP*, 3rd Series, Vol. I, No. 164, from which excerpts are quoted.

Chamberlain's private assessment of the meeting is in Neville to Ida Chamberlain, 1 May 1938. His views on domestic opposition to his policy are found in Neville to Hilda Chamberlain, 8 May 1938.

The May Crisis: Many of Chamberlain's speeches from this period are contained in *Search For Peace*. The first excerpt is from "The Fear Over Countless Homes," speech to Women's Conservative Association, 12 May 1938. The second is from "The Meaning of War," Speech to a National Government Rally, 2 July 1938. See also his speech to a Birmingham Unionist meeting, 8 April 1938, "To Make Gentle the Life of the World."

Chamberlain's statement to Goeffrey Dawson is found in *The History of the Times*, Vol. IV, Part 2, p. 919, and to Halifax in *DBFP*, Vol. I, Nos. 134 and 140.

On the matter of Lady Astor's luncheon see 333 *H.C. Deb.*, 5th Series, Col. 1540–41, Wheler-Bennett, *Munich*, p. 52, and Middlemas, p. 231. See also Cab 23/93, 25 May 1938.

Chamberlain's assessment of the diplomatic situation at the time is found in Neville to Ida Chamberlain, 13 May 1938.

For a discussion of the May crisis see Middlemas, p. 234, Robbins, pp. 219–71, and W.F. Wallace, "The Making of the May Crisis of 1938," as well as Telford Taylor, pp. 390–95 and 654–55.

The British message to Germany is found in *DBFP*, 3rd Series, Vol. I, No. 250. The warning followed the formula agreed upon at the Anglo-French meeting of 28 and 29 April, the official record of which may be found in *DBFP*, 3rd Series, Vol. I, No. 164. See also Wallace, p. 377 and Middlemas, pp. 237–38. See also cable to Phipps, 22 May 1938, appended to Cab 23/93, 22 May 1938.

Chamberlain's private reflections on the May Crisis are found in Neville to Hilda Chamberlain 22 May 1938, and Neville to Ida Chamberlain, 28 May 1938.

Chapter VI Berchtesgaden and Godesberg

The Sudeten Crisis Worsens: Chamberlain's private views on the May Crisis are found in Neville to Ida Chamberlain, 28 May 1938.

FPC discussion of economic policy toward southeastern Europe can be found in Cab 27/623, 1 June 1938. See also Newman, pp. 33–53.

The French rejection of the Halifax plan is in *DBFP*, 3rd Series, Vol. II, no. 601.

Chamberlain's views on Spain and Italy are found in Neville to Ida Chamberlain, 18 June 1938; Neville to Hilda Chamberlain, 9 July 1938; and Neville to Hilda Chamberlain, 6 August 1938. His attitudes on the Sudeten question are found in Neville to Ida Chamberlain, 18 June 1938, and Neville to Hilda Chamberlain, 25 June 1938.

Material on Chamberlain's understanding of German attitudes is from Neville to Hilda Chamberlain, 9 July 1938; Neville to Ida Chamberlain, 16 July 1938; Neville to Hilda Chamberlain, 13 August 1938; Neville to Ida Chamberlain, 21 August 1938; and Neville to Ida Chamberlain, 3 September 1938.

On the Weidemann meeting, see Harvey Diary, 18 July 1938, pp. 163–64, Cadogan Diary, pp. 87–88, *DGFP*, Series D., Vol. VII p. 628, and Neville to Hilda Chamberlain, 24 July 1938. Mason-Macfarlane's report is from the Cadogan Diary, pp. 87–88.

Cowling, p. 183, and the *Observer*, 31 July 1938, both refer to the Runciman mission as "the original and hearty idea of the Prime Minister." An examination of the Cabinet papers indicates that the intial planning was done by Wilson, Halifax, and Vansittart. See J.W. Bruegel, *Czechoslovakia Before Munich*, pp. 228–42, for a detailed discussion of the Runciman mission.

Documents cited on the Runciman mission include; *DBFP,* 3rd Series, Vol. II, No. 558, p. 21 from which the quoted material is taken; No. 575, pp. 44–45; No. 577, pp. 46–47; No. 590, pp. 58–60; No. 608, pp. 78–80; and No. 661, pp. 127–28, as well as *DGFP,* Series D, Vol. II, No. 379, pp. 559–601.

On Chamberlain's attitudes toward the worsening state of continental affairs, see particularly Neville to Hilda Chamberlain, 13 August 1938; Neville to Ida Chamberlain, 21 August 1938; and Neville to Ida Chamberlain, 3 September 1938.

Plan Z: Chamberlain's statement to the Cabinet is from Cab 23/94, 30 August 1938.

The correspondence with Temperley is in Temperley to Chamberlain, 24 July 1938, NC7/1131/286, and Temperley to Chamberlain, 10 November 1938, NC7/11/31/269. See also Neville to Ida Chamberlain, 11 September 1938.

The Cabinet decision not to issue a warning to Hitler is in Cab 23/94, 3 August 1938. The Wilson Memorandum on Plan Z is discussed by Middlemas 300–33. See also Cadogan Diaries, 9 September 1938, p. 96.

Halifax note to Ribbentrop is in *DBFP,* 3rd Series, vol. II, No. 815.

Chamberlain referred to the possibility of implementing Plan Z in Neville to Hilda Chamberlain, 6 September 1938, and Neville to Ida Chamberlain, 11 September 1938. See also *DBFP,* 3rd Series, Vol. II, No. 862, p. 314n2.

Henderson's message is in *DBFP,* 3rd Series, Vol. II, no. 819. See also Hoare, p. 31. Henderson's warning is in *DBFP,* 3rd Series, Vol. II, No. 849. See also Neville to Ida Chamberlain, 19 September 1938.

Chamberlain's note to Hitler is in *DBFP,* 3rd Series, Vol. II, No. 862. Cabinet discussion of Plan Z is in Cab 23/95, 14 September 1938.

The Berchtesgaden Meeting: The record of Chamberlain's last meeting with the Cabinet before Berchtesgaden is in Cab 23/95, 14 September 1938.

Readers interested in a fuller discussion of the meetings are referred to Wheeler-Bennett, *passim,* and Robbins, pp. 268–358. There exist three separate documentary accounts of the Hitler-Chamberlain meeting. The first is that of Dr. Schmidt, Hitler's interpreter, found in *DGFP,* Series D, Vol. II, pp. 786–98. The second is Chamberlain's own notes of the meeting found in *DBFP,* 3rd Series, Vol. II, No. 895, pp. 339–41, from which the quoted material is extracted. The third is Chamberlain's private account of the meeting as he wrote it a few days later found in Neville to Ida Chamberlain, 19 September 1938. For Hitler's attitude see Bullock, pp. 454–57.

Chamberlain's statement to the Commons is in 339, *H.C. Deb.,* 5th Series, col. 15.

Persuading the French: Readers interested in a discussion of the negotiations between Britain and France and the messages exchanged with the Czechs in the period between Berchtesgaden and Godesberg are referred to F.S. Northedge, *The Troubled Giant,* pp. 529–32, and Middlemas, pp. 346–64.

Cabinet discussion of the Berchtesgaden is in Cab 23/95, 17 September 1938. The record of the Anglo-French meeting is in *DBFP,* 3rd Series, Vol. II, No. 928, from which the quoted material is taken. Hoare's account of the meeting can be found in his memoirs, *Nine Troubled Years,* pp. 305–8.

Cabinet discussion of the Anglo-French meeting is in Cab 23/95, 19 September 1938. The Anglo-French message to the Czechs is in *DBFP*, 3rd Series, Vol. II, No. 937. Ambassador Newton's response is in *DBFP*, 3rd Series, Vol. II, No. 993.

Chamberlain's private feelings on the matter of cession of the Sudetenland are in Neville to Ida Chamberlain, 19 September 1938.

Chamberlain's final words to the Cabinet before leaving for Godesberg are in Cab 23/95, 21 September 1938. See Middlemas, pp. 362–63, for further discussion.

The Godesberg Meeting: The German record of Chamberlain's meeting with Hitler at Godesberg is in *DGFP*, Series D, Vol. II, No. 562. The British account is in *DBFP*, 3rd Series, Vol. II, no. 1033. Schmidt's account is in his book, *Hitler's Interpreter*, p. 96.

The account of British public opinion at the time of Godesberg is from Madge and Harrison, *Mass Observation*, pp. 4–5, and Middlemas, p. 370.

The Halifax message to the British delegation at Godesberg is in *DBFP*, 3rd Series, Vol. II, No. 1058. Wilson's comments are from the Wilson Memorandum as cited by Middlemas, p. 366. The message withdrawing British objections to Czech mobilization is in *DBFP*, 3rd Series, Vol. II, No. 1035. Chamberlain's message to Hitler is in *DBFP*, 3rd Series, Vol. II, No. 1048. Hitler's reply is in No. 1053.

The record of the FPC meeting after Godesberg is in Cab 27/646, 24 September 1938. Chamberlain's subsequent statement to the Cabinet is from Cab 23/95, 24 September 1938. See also Hoare p. 312, Middlemas, pp. 365–66, Cadogan Diaries, 24 & 25 September 1938, Birkenhead, pp. 399–400, and Cowling p. 198, n115.

Ambassador Phipps's message is in *DBFP*, 3rd Series, Vol. II, No. 1076. Chamberlain's statement to the Cabinet on the question of the French position is in Cab 23/95, 25 September 1938.

Chapter VII Munich

The Wilson Mission: Cabinet discussion of Chamberlain's proposal of the Wilson mission and Wilson's instructions are in Cab 23/95, 25 September 1938. See also Birkenhead, p. 400. Roosevelt's initiative is in *FRUS*, 1938, Vol. I, pp. 657–58.

The "Leeper communiqué" is found in *DBFP*, 3rd Series, Vol. II, No. 111. See also, Robbins, p. 297, Middlemas, p. 338n, and Wheeler-Bennett, *Munich*, pp. 149–50.

The record of Wilson's conversations with Hitler is in *DBFP*, 3rd Series, Vol. II, No. 1097, and No. 1118. Amery's comment is from Birkenhead, p. 403. Chamberlain's statement to the press is in *DBFP*, 3rd Series, Vol. II, No. 1121. Wilson's warning is in *DBFP*, 3rd Series, Vol. II, No. 1129.

FPC discussion of the above is in Cab 27/646, 27 September 1938. The views of the chiefs of staff are in C.O.S. 765, 4 October 1938. See also Cadogan Diaries, p. 108.

Chamberlain's message to Beneš is in *DBFP*, 3rd Series, Vol. II, No. 1140.

Chamberlain's private thoughts at the time are in Neville to Hilda Chamberlain, 2 October 1938. Cadogan's comment on Chamberlain's emotional state is in Cadogan Diaries, 27 September 1938, p. 107. Chamberlain's radio message to the British people is in *Search For Peace,* pp. 174–75.

The account of British preparations for war is based on Wheeler-Bennett, pp. 158–59.

Cabinet discussion of the results of Wilson's mission is in Cab 23/95, 27 September 1938. See Middlemas, pp. 396–97 for further discussion.

Last Minute Efforts for Peace: Joseph Kennedy's observation is from *FRUS,* 1938, Vol. I, No. 1144.

Hitler's message to Chamberlain is in *DBFP,* 3rd Series, Vol. II, No. 1133. See also Wheeler-Bennett, p. 164. Chamberlain's messages to Hitler and Mussolini are in *Parliamentary Papers,* 1937–38, Vol. XX, Cmd. 5848, No. 1 and 2 respectively. See also Feiling, p. 372.

The description of the atmosphere in the House of Commons is based on Wheeler-Bennett, p. 168. See also Nicolson Diaries, 28 September 1938, pp. 368–71; Cadogan Diaries, 28 September 1938; and Neville to Hilda Chamberlain, 2 October 1938.

The Meeting at Munich: Hoare's comment is from his memoirs, p. 379. The text of the Munich agreement is in *DBFP,* 3rd Series, Vol. II, No. 1224. See also Wheeler-Bennett, p. 180.

William Strang's account is from his memoirs, pp. 146–47.

Hoare's comment on the Munich agreement is from his memoirs, p. 378, that of Douglas-Home from his otherwise uninteresting memoirs, *The Way the Wind Blows,* p. 66.

Chamberlain Triumphant: Chamberlain's private recollection of the Munich meeting is in Neville to Hilda Chamberlain, 2 October 1938.

On the question of the meaning of the phrase "peace with honour" see Feiling, p. 381, Halifax, p. 199, and Douglas-Home, p. 67.

Many of the letters of support Chamberlain received on his return from Munich are found in the Chamberlain papers. Those cited include: Hankey to Chamberlain, 30 September 1938, NC13/11/675; A.C. Pigou to Annie Chamberlain, 30 September 1938, NC13/11/749; Baldwin to Chamberlain, 15 & 30 September 1938, NC13/11/618–19; Prince Wilhelm to Chamberlain, 24 October 1938, NC13/11/798; and Eden to Chamberlain, 28 September 1938, NC13/11/655.

Additional material on the thesis that Chamberlain believed his greatest achievement at Munich was not the four-power accord but the personal agreement with Hitler is found in a letter to his stepmother, Chamberlain to Mary Endicott, 5 November 1938.

Chamberlain's letter to Prince Wilhelm is in Chamberlain to Prince Wilhelm of Prussia, 10 November 1938, NC7/11/31/291. His statement to the House of Commons is in 339, *H.C. Deb.,* 5th Series, Cols. 49–50 and that to the Cabinet in Cab 23/95, 3 October 1938.

CHAPTER VIII THE AFTERMATH OF MUNICH

Dissolution of the Munich Consensus: Chamberlain reported his domestic political troubles in Neville to Ida Chamberlain, 9 October 1938, and Neville to Hilda

Chamberlain, 15 October 1938. His thoughts on internal affairs are in Neville to Ida Chamberlain, 22 October 1938, and Neville to Hilda Chamberlain, 6 November 1938.

Chamberlain's statement to the Commons is in 340, *H.C. Deb.*, 5th Series, col. 332.

See Wheeler-Bennett, pp. 297–98, for a contemporary discussion of allied reaction to *Kristallnacht*. Chamberlain's private reaction is from Neville to Ida Chamberlain, 13 November 1938.

Chamberlain's Guildhall speech is in *Search For Peace*, pp. 231–36.

The letter cited with respect to Chamberlain's anti-Semitism is Neville to Hilda Chamberlain, 30 July 1939.

Material on Chamberlain's growing despair is from: Neville to Ida Chamberlain, 4 December 1938; Neville to Hilda Chamberlain, 11 December 1938; Neville to Ida Chamberlain, 17 December 1938; and Neville to Ida Chamberlain, 8 January 1939.

The FPC memo of 19 January is from Cab 27/627, 19 January 1939, as quoted by Aster, p. 47. See also Aster pp. 38–59 for a general discussion of British intelligence reports in the period.

Chamberlain's warning to Mussolini is in *DBFP*, 3rd Series, Vol. II, No. 500, p. 529. See also Cadogan Diaries, p. 137.

Chamberlain's comments on his visit to Rome are in Neville to Hilda Chamberlain, 15 January 1939. His optimism with respect to continental affairs and his comments on Eden are found in Neville to Hilda Chamberlain, 5 February 1939, and Neville to Ida Chamberlain, 12 February 1939.

For additional material on Chamberlain's steadfast optimism see Neville to Ida Chamberlain, 12 February 1939, and Chamberlain to Henderson in *DBFP*, 3rd Series, Vol. IV, Appendix I, pp. 59–92. See also Neville to Ida Chamberlain, 26 February 1939, and Neville to Ida Chamberlain 12 March 1939.

See Middlemas, p. 434, for details on the Polish and Hungarian action against Czechoslovakia.

The MI 5 report is discussed by Aster, p. 22 and in Cadogan Diaries, 11 March 1939, pp. 60–61.

Fall of Prague and the Pledge to Poland: Chamberlain's statement to the House is from 345, *H.C. Deb.*, 5th Series, cols. 437–40. A discussion of the attitudes of Halifax, Cadogan, and Vansittart toward the German action can be found in Aster, pp. 33–35.

Chamberlain's reassessment of the diplomatic situation and his plan for a new approach to Italy is in Neville to Hilda Chamberlain, 19 March 1939.

His Birmingham Speech is in *Search For Peace*, pp. 274–75. Churchill's comment is in *The Gathering Storm*, p. 308. Chamberlain's subsequent comments to the Cabinet are in Cab 23/98, 20 March 1939.

The letter to Mussolini is in *DBFP*, 3rd Series, Vol. IV, No. 448. His comment to the FPC is in Cab 27/624, 27 March 1939.

Chamberlain's distrustful attitude toward the Soviets and his position on Eastern Europe is in Neville to Ida Chamberlain, 26 March 1939.

For material on the British pledge to Poland see Newman, pp. 183–84, Eubank, p. 344, Cadogan Diaries, p. 165, and Lord Strang, p. 161. For a general discussion see R. Rock, "The British Guarantee to Poland, March 1939."

Chamberlain's statement to the Commons is in 345, *H.C. Deb.*, 5th Series, 31 March 1939, col. 2415.

Material on Chamberlain's role in the pledge to Poland is in Aster, p. 89. The reference to Chamberlain's letter to Mussolini is from *DBFP*, 3rd Series, Vol. IV, No. 581, pp. 551–52.

Hoare's interpretation of the pledge to Poland is in his memoirs pp. 348–49.

Chamberlain's interpretation of the Polish pledge is from Neville to Hilda Chamberlain, 2 April 1939, and in Cab 23/98, 31 March 1939. Simon Newman's thesis is from pp. 174–204 and p. 218 of his book.

Hoare's opinion is from his memoirs, pp. 347–48.

Chamberlain's fear of a knock-out blow is found in Neville to Ida Chamberlain, 26 March 1939.

For a discussion of Hitler's perceptions see Eubank, p. 348.

Watching Hitler and Negotiating with Russia: Material on Chamberlain's views on the situation in Poland is from: Neville to Hilda Chamberlain, 2 April 1939; Neville to Ida Chamberlain, 9 April 1939; Neville to Hilda Chamberlain, 15 April 1939; Neville to Ida Chamberlain, 23 April 1939; Neville to Hilda Chamberlain, 29 April 1939; Neville to Hilda Chamberlain, 14 May 1939; and Neville to Hilda Chamberlain, 28 May 1939.

For a discussion of the negotiations with the Soviet Union see L.B. Namier, *Diplomatic Prelude*, pp. 143–210, and Aster, pp. 152–87.

Chamberlain's views on the Anglo-Soviet negotiations are from Neville to Ida Chamberlain, 21 May 1939; Neville to Hilda Chamberlain, 28 May 1939; Neville to Ida Chamberlain, 10 June 1939; Neville to Hilda Chamberlain, 2 July 1939; Neville to Hilda Chamberlain, 15 July 1939, and Neville to Ida Chamberlain, 23 July 1939. See also Aster, pp. 93–94, and pp. 179–85 as well as Cadogan Diaries, pp. 180–87. Chamberlain's parliamentary statement of 19 May is from Aster, 179–80.

For Chamberlain's views on the situation in the Far East see Neville to Ida Chamberlain, 25 June 1939, and Neville to Hilda Chamberlain 15 July 1939.

See Aster, pp. 204–5, for Chamberlain's scheme for mediation by the Scandinavian countries.

Danzig and the Declaration of War: Chamberlain's views on the situation in Danzig are found in: Neville to Hilda Chamberlain, 15 July 1939; Neville to Ida Chamberlain, 23 July 1939; Neville to Hilda Chamberlain, 30 July 1939; and Neville to Ida Chamberlain, 19 August 1939.

Chamberlain's letter to Hitler is in *DBFP*, 3rd Series, Vol. VII, No. 145. Earlier drafts of the letter can be found in PREM, 331A. An account of Henderson's presentation of the letter to Hitler is in *DGFP*, Vol. VII, No. 200.

Nicolson's comments are from his diary, Vol. I, p. 413. Chamberlain's statement to the House is in 352, *H.C. Deb.*, 5th Series, cols. 3–10.

Chamberlain's sense of the delicacy of foreign affairs is from Neville to Hilda Chamberlain, 27 August 1939.

Hitler's letter to Chamberlain is in *DBFP*, 3rd Series, Vol. VII, No. 283. Ambassador Kennedy's comments are in *FRUS*, 1939, Vol. I, p. 355.

Chamberlain's statement to the Cabinet after the invasion of Poland is in Cab 23/100, 1 September 1939.

The events leading to the declaration of war are graphically described by Aster, pp. 368–90.

Chamberlain's statement to the Commons declaring war on Germany is in 351, *H.C. Deb.*, 5th Series, cols. 291–92. See also Neville to Ida Chamberlain, 10 September 1939, and Aster, pp. 368–90.

The Fall of Chamberlain's Government: Chamberlain's thoughts on the coming of war are in Neville to Ida Chamberlain, 10 September 1939. Hoare's comments are from his memoirs, p. 399.

Chamberlain's letters comparing the initial stages of the war with that of World War I include: Neville to Hilda Chamberlain, 17 September 1939; Neville to Ida Chamberlain, 8 October 1939; Neville to Ida Chamberlain, 22 October 1939; and Neville to Ida Chamberlain 10 September 1939. His thoughts on the initial British setbacks are from Neville to Hilda Chamberlain, 15 October 1939, and Neville to Ida Chamberlain, 20 December 1939.

Material on the Hore-Belisha affair is from Neville to Ida Chamberlain, 7 January 1940, and from Gort to Chamberlain, 27 December 1939, in the Chamberlain papers NC7/11/32/77. Hore-Belisha loyally refused to divulge anything he may have known on this matter.

Chamberlain's attitudes toward Churchill and the question of resignation are in Neville to Ida Chamberlain, 27 January 1940; Neville to Ida Chamberlain, 30 March 1940; Neville to Hilda Chamberlain, 6 April 1940; Neville to Hilda Chamberlain, 20 April 1940; Neville to Ida Chamberlain, 27 April 1940; and Neville to Hilda Chamberlain, 4 May 1940.

The parliamentary debate which led to Chamberlain's defeat is in 360, *H.C. Deb.* 5th Series, cols. 1266–83, which contains Lloyd George's denunciation.

Chamberlain's thoughts after resignation are from Neville to Ida Chamberlain, 11 May 1940, and Neville to Hilda Chamberlain, 17 May 1940.

See Feiling p. 454 for an account of Chamberlain's last radio broadcast from which the quoted material is excerpted. See also Neville to Hilda Chamberlain, 15 June 1940; Neville to Ida Chamberlain, 21 June 1940; and Neville to Hilda Chamberlain, 14 July 1940, for material on Chamberlain's thoughts in the last weeks before his death.

Selected Bibliography[*]

I. Unpublished Sources
  A. British Government Archives, Public Record Office London.
    Cabinet:
      Minutes and Conclusions, (CAB 23), 1936–39.
      Cabinet Committees, (CAB 27), 1936–39, particularly minutes of the
        Foreign Policy Comm.
      Cabinet Papers, (CAB 24), 1936–39.
    Committee of Imperial Defence:
      Minutes and Reports, (CAB 2).
      Reports of Chiefs of Staff, (CAB 50).
    Prime Minister:
      Prime Minister's Papers, (PREM 1).
    Foreign Office:
      General Correspondence and Minutes, particularly FO 371.
      Confidential Prints.
  B. Neville Chamberlain Papers, Birmingham University, Birmingham
    England.
    Chamberlain letters, particularly those to his sisters, Hilda and Ida, 1893–
      1940. Also of interest are Chamberlain's letters to and from Winston
      Churchill, Leopold Amery, and others.
    Diaries, 1893–1938.
  C. Interviews:
    Various members of the Chamberlain, Kennrick, and Beale families, Bir-
      mingham, England.
    The Rt. Hon. The Lord Boyle of Handsworth, Leeds, England.
    Professor David Dilks, The University of Leeds, Leeds, England.
    Mr. Kenneth Harris, British Broadcasting Corporation, London, England.
    British Broadcasting Corporation, Anthony Eden interview by Kenneth
      Harris, "Facing the Dictators, An Account of the Years Up Till 1939,"
      transmitted on BBC–1, 25 October 1974. Transcript made available to
      author courtesy of the BBC.

---

*This selected bibliography only includes works relevant to Neville Chamberlain. For citations relevant to particular theoretical questions see notes in text.

II. Published Documents

Czechoslovak Republic and the Union of Soviet Socialist Republics, *New Documents on the History of Munich*, Prague, Orbis, 1958.

Documents on British Foreign Policy 1919–1939, Third Series, London, HMSO.

Documents on German Foreign Policy 1919–1939, Series D, London, HMSO.

Foreign Relations of the United States, Washington D.C., U.S. Government Printing Office.

Parliamentary Debates, London, House of Commons.

Parliamentary Papers, London, House of Commons.

Royal Institute of International Affairs, *Documents on International Affairs, 1938*, Vols. I and II, London, 1942–43.

Various Newspapers and Periodicals, particularly:
Daily Herald
Daily Telegraph
Manchester Guardian
the *Spectator*
the *Times*

III. Memoirs and Biographies

Amery, Leopold S. *My Political Life*. 3 vols. London: Hutchinson, 1953–55.

Amery, Julian, *see* Garvin, J.L.

Avon, the Earl of (Anthony Eden). *The Eden Memoirs*. 3 vols. *Facing the Dictators, The Reckoning, Full Circle*. London: Cassell, 1962–65.

Beattie, Alan. "Neville Chamberlain," in John P. Mackintosh, ed. *British Prime Ministers in the Twentieth Century*. London: Weidenfeld & Nicolson, 1977–19—).

Bowle, John. *Viscount Samuel, A Biography*. London: Gollancz, 1957.

Birkenhead, the Earl of. *The Life of Lord Halifax*. London: Hamish Hamilton, 1965.

Butler, James Ramsay. *Lord Lothian*. London: Macmillan, 1960.

Cadogan, Sir Alexander. *The Diaries of Sir Alexander Cadogan 1938–45*. Edited by David Dilks. London: Cassell, 1971.

Carlton, David. *Anthony Eden: A Biography*. London: Allen Lane, 1981.

Chamberlain, Neville. *Norman Chamberlain, A Memoir*. London: John Murray (for private circulation), 1923.

———. *In Search of Peace*. New York: M.G.P. Putnam's Sons, 1939.

———. *The Struggle for Peace*. London: Hutchinson & Co., 1939.

Churchill, Sir Winston. *The Gathering Storm*. Boston: Houghton Mifflin, 1948.

Ciano, Count Galeazzo. *Hidden Diary, 1937–38*. Translated by Andreas Mayor. New York: Dutton, 1953.

Colvin, Iain. *None So Blind*. New York: Harcourt, Brace & World, 1965.

Cooper, Alfred Duff. *Old Men Forget*. New York: Dutton, 1954.

Craig, Gordon & Felix Gilbert. *The Diplomats, 1919–1939*. Princeton: Princeton University Press, 1963.

Dalton, Hugh. *Memoirs, 1931–1945*. 3 vols. *The Fateful Years*. London: F. Miller, 1953–62.

Douglas-Home, Alec. *The Way the Wind Blows*. New York: Quandrangle, 1976.

Eden, Anthony, *see* Avon, the Earl of.

Feiling, Keith. *The Life of Neville Chamberlain*. London: Macmillan, 1946.

Garvin, J.L. *The Life of Joseph Chamberlain*. 4 vols. (Volume IV by Julian Amery). London: Macmillan, 1932–51.

Halifax, the Earl of. *Fulness of Days*. London: Collins, 1957.

Harvey, Oliver. *The Diplomatic Diaries of Oliver Harvey*. London: Collins, 1970.

Henderson, Sir Neville. *Failure of a Mission*. New York: G.P. Putnam's Sons, 1940.

———. *Water Under the Bridges*. London: Hudder & Stoughton, 1945.

Hoare, Samuel, *see* Templewood, Viscount.

Hodgson, Stuart. *The Man Who Made The Peace: Neville Chamberlain*. London: Christophers, 1938.

Ironside, Edmund. *The Ironside Diaries, 1937–1940*. London: Constable, 1962.

James, Robert Rhodes. *Memoirs of a Conservative: J.C.C. Davidson's Memoirs and Papers, 1910–1937*. London: Weidenfeld & Nicolson, 1969.

Johnson, Alan Campbell. *Viscount Halifax*. London: Robert Hale, 1941.

Jones, Thomas. *A Diary With Letters, 1931–1950*. London: Oxford University Press, 1954.

Kirkpatrick, Sir Ivone. *The Inner Circle; Memoirs*. London: Macmillan, 1959.

Liddell Hart, B.H. *The Memoirs of Captain Liddell Hart*. 2 vols. London: Cassell, 1965.

Lloyd George, David. *War Memoirs of David Lloyd George: 1916–1917*. Boston: Little, Brown & Co., 1934.

Macleod, Iain. *Neville Chamberlain*. London: Frederick Muller, 1961.

Middlemas, Keith and John Barnes. *Baldwin: A Biography*. London: Weidenfeld & Nicolson, 1969.

Minney, R.J. *The Private Papers of Hore-Belisha* London: Collins, 1960.

Nicolson, Sir Harold. *Diaries and Letters*. 3 vols. New York: Atheneum, 1966–68.

Petrie, Sir Charles. *The Chamberlain Tradition*. New York: Frederick A. Stokes, 1938.

———. *The Life and Letters of the Rt. Hon. Sir Austen Chamberlain*. 2 vols. London: Cassel, 1940.

Pyper, C.B. *Chamberlain and His Critics: A Statesman Vindicated*. London: L. Bishop, 1962.

Reith, J.C.W. *Into the Wind*. London: Hudder & Stoughton, 1949.

Rock, William R. *Neville Chamberlain*. New York: Twayne, 1969.

Roskill, Stephen W. *Hankey: Man of Secrets*. 3 vols. London: Collins, 1970–74.

Schmidt, Paul. *Hitler's Interpreter*. Edited by R.H.C. Steed. New York: Macmillan, 1951.

Simon, John. *Retrospect*. London: Hutchinson, 1952.

Skidelsky, Robert. *Oswald Mosely*. New York: Holt, Rinehart & Winston, 1975.

Strang, William. *Home and Abroad*. London: A. Deutsch, 1956.

Swinton, The Earl of. *I Remember*. London: Hutchinson, 1952.

———. *Sixty Years of Power*. London: Hutchinson, 1966.

Steed, Henry Wickham. *Through Thirty Years, 1892–1922*. Garden City, New York: Doubleday, 1924.

Templewood, Viscount. *Nine Troubled Years*. London: Collins, 1954.

Vansittart, Lord. *Lessons of My Life*. London: Hutchinson, 1943.

———. *The Mist Procession*. London: Hutchinson, 1958.

IV. Secondary Sources

Aster, Sidney. *1939: The Making of the Second World War*. New York: Simon & Schuster, 1973.

Bruegel, J.W. *Czechoslovakia Before Munich, The German Minority Problem and British Appeasement Policy*. Cambridge: Cambridge University Press, 1973.

Byrd, Peter. *Britain and the Anschlus 1931–1938, Aspects of Appeasement*. Unpublished dissertation, University College, University of Wales.

Carr, E.H. *The Twenty Years Crisis, 1919–1939*. New York: St. Martin's Press, 1966.

CATO [pseud., Frank Owen] *Guilty Men*. New York: Frederick A. Stokes, 1940.

Cole, G.D.H. *A History of the Labour Party from 1914*. London: Routledge & Kegan Paul, 1948.

Colvin, Ian. *The Chamberlain Cabinet*. New York: Taplinger, 1971.

Cowling, Maurice. *The Impact of Hitler, British Politics and British Policy 1933–1940*. Cambridge: Cambridge University Press, 1975.

Dennis, Peter. *Decision by Default*. Durham: Duke University Press, 1972.

Einzig, Paul. *Appeasement Before, During and After the War*. London: Macmillan, 1942.

Eubank, Keith. *Munich*. Norman: University of Oklahoma Press, 1963.

Furnia, Arthur H. *The Diplomacy of Appeasement*. Washington D.C.: Georgetown University Press, 1960.

Fussell, Paul. *The Great War and Modern Memory*. New York: Oxford University Press, 1975.

Gannon, Frank Reid. *The British Press and Germany*. Oxford: Clarendon Press, 1971.

George, Margaret. *The Warped Vision: British Foreign Policy 1933–1939*. Pittsburgh: University of Pittsburgh Press, 1965.

Gilbert, Martin. *The Roots of Appeasement*. London: Weidenfeld & Nicolson, 1966.

Gilbert, Martin & Richard Gott. *The Appeasers*. London: Weidenfeld & Nicolson, 1963.

Grainger, J.H. *Character & Style in English Politics*. London: Cambridge University Press, 1969.

Graves, Robert & Alan Hodge. *The Long Week-end A Social History of Great Britain 1918–1939*. London: Faber and Faber, 1940.

Hardie, Frank. *The Abyssinian Crisis*. Hamden Conn.: Archon Books, 1974.

Hoggan, David. L. *Der erzwungene Krieg, Die Ursachen und Urheber des 2. Weltkriegs*. Tubingen: Verlag der Deutschen Hochschullehrer Zeitung, 1964.

Kennedy, John F. *Why England Slept.* New York: W. Funk Inc., 1964. Originally published 1940.

Langer, William and S. Everett Gleason. *The Challenge to Isolation.* New York: Harper, 1952.

Liddell Hart, B.H. *Europe in Arms.* London: Faber and Faber, 1937.

Loewenheim, Francis L., Ed. *Peace or Appeasement? Hitler, Chamberlain, and the Munich Crisis.* Boston: Houghton Mifflin, 1965.

McElwee, William. *Britain's Locust Years.* London: Faber & Faber, 1962.

Medlicott, William N. *British Foreign Policy Since Versailles.* London: Methuen, 1940.

———. *The Coming of War in 1939.* London: The Historical Association, 1963.

Middlemas, Keith. *The Strategy of Appeasement: The British Government and Germany, 1937–1939.* Chicago: Quadrangle Books, 1972.

Mowat, Charles. *Britain Between the Wars, 1918–1940.* Chicago: University of Chicago Press, 1955.

Namier, Sir Lewis. *Personalities and Powers.* New York: Harper and Row, 1965.

———. *Diplomatic Prelude 1938–1939.* London: Macmillan, 1948.

———. *Europe in Decay, a Study in Disintegration, 1936–1940.* London: Macmillan, 1950.

National Declaration Committee (Great Britain). *The Peace Ballot, The Official History.* London: Gollancz, 1935.

Naylor, John. *Labour's International Policy.* Boston: Houghton Mifflin, 1969.

Newman, Simon. *March 1939: The British Guarantee to Poland.* London: Oxford University Press, 1976.

Nicoll, Peter H. *Englands Krieg gegen Deutschland. Die zweite Weltkrieg und die Kriegsschuldfrage (die Hoggan Kontroverse).* Wurzburg, 1965.

Northedge, F.S. *The Troubled Giant, Britain Among the Great Powers, 1919–1939.* New York: Praeger, 1966.

Parkinson, Roger. *Peace For Our Time: Munich to Dunkirk—the Inside Story.* London: Rupert Hart-Davis, 1971.

Postan, M.M. *British War Production.* London: HMSO, 1952.

Reed, Franklin. *The British Press and Germany.* New York: Oxford University Press, 1971.

Robbins, Keith. *Munich 1938.* London: Cassell, 1968.

Rock, William. *Appeasement on Trial.* Hamden, Conn.: Archon Book, 1966.

Rowse, A.L. *Appeasement: A Study in Political Decline 1933–1939.* New York: Norton, 1961.

Seton-Watson, Robert William. *From Munich to Danzig.* London: Methuen, 1939.

Shay, Robert Paul, Jr. *British Rearmament in the Thirties: Politics and Profits.* Princeton: Princeton University Press, 1977.

Taylor, A.J.P. *English History 1914–1945.* London: Oxford University Press, 1965.

———, ed. *Off The Record: Political Interviews.* London: Hutchinson, 1973.

———. *The Origins of the Second World War.* London: H. Hamilton, 1961.

Taylor, Telford. *Munich: The Price of Peace.* New York: Doubleday & Co., 1979.

Thompson, Laurence. *The Greatest Treason: the Untold Story of Munich.* New York: William Morrow, 1968.

Thompson, Neville. *The Anti-Appeasers: Conservative Opposition to Appeasement.* London: Oxford University Press, 1971.

Watt, Donald Cameron. *Personalities and Policies.* London: Longmans, 1965.

Wheeler-Bennett, Sir John W. *The Nemesis of Power.* New York: St. Martin's Press, 1964.

———. *Munich: Prologue to Tragedy.* New York: Duell, Sloan and Pierce, 1948.

Wiskemann, Elizabeth. *Europe of the Dictators, 1919–1945,* New York: Harper and Row, 1966.

Wolfers, Arnold. *Britain and France Between Two Wars.* New York: Harcourt, Brace & World, 1940.

V. Articles

Burn, W.L. "Neville Chamberlain." *The Nineteenth Century and After.* Vol. 141, February 1937.

Craig, Gordon A. "High Tide of Appeasement: The Road to Munich, 1937–1938." *Political Science Quarterly.* Vol. 65, 1950.

Dilks, David. "Appeasement Revisited." *University of Leeds Review.* Vol. 15, May 1972.

Eubank, Keith. "The British Pledge to Poland: Prelude to War." *Southwestern Social Science Quarterly.* Vol. 45, March 1965.

Germains, V.W. "Military Lessons of the War." *Contemporary Review.* Vol. 158, 1940.

———. "Some Problems of Imperial Strategy." *National Review.* Vol. 110, 1938.

Kenny, Marion L. "The Role of the House of Commons in British Foreign Policy during the 1937–38 Session." In Nortown Downs, Ed. *Essays in Honor of Conyors Read.* Chicago, 1953.

Lammers, Donald. *Explaining Munich.* Stanford, The Hoover Institution on War, Revolution, and Peace. Hoover Institution Studies No. 16, 1966.

Moorehead, Alan. "Munich in the Light of Today." *New York Times Magazine.* Vol. 28, September 1958.

Mowat, C.L. "Baldwin Restored?" *Journal of Modern History.* Vol. 27, 1955.

Northedge, F.S. "Freedom and Necessity in British Foreign Policy." An inaugural lecture delivered on 14 October 1954.

Rock, William R. "The British Guarantee to Poland, March 1939: A Problem in Diplomatic Decision-Making." *South Atlantic Quarterly.* Vol. 65, Spring 1966.

Sancourt, Robert E., (pseud.) "The Foreign Policy of Neville Chamberlain." *Quarterly Review.* Vol. 600, April 1954.

———. "How Neville Chamberlain Fought Hitler." *Quarterly Review.* Vol. 602, October 1954.

Schmidtt, Bernadotte E. "Munich." *Journal of Modern History.* Vol. 25, June 1953.

Schwoerer, Lois G. "Lord Halifax's Visit to Germany: November 1937." *The Historian.* Vol. 32.

Skidelsky, Robert. "Going to War With Germany." *Encounter.* Vol. 39, July 1972.

Sontag, Raymond J. "The Origins of the Second World War." *Review of Politics.* Vol. 24, October 1963.

Ratcliffe, S.K. "The Chamberlain Family in British Politics." *Current History.* Vol. 37, January 1933.

Taylor, A.J.P. "The Myths of Munich." *History of the Twentieth Century.* Vol. 59, March 1969.

Templewood, Viscount, (Samuel Hoare). "The Lessons of Munich." *The Listener.* Vol. 40, December 1948.

Wallace, W.V. "The Making of the May Crisis of 1938." *Slavonic and East European Review.* Vol. 41, June 1963.

Watt, D.C. "The Anglo-German Naval Negotiations on the Eve of the Second World War." *Journal of the Royal United Service Institution.* Vol. 103, 1955.

———. "The Reoccupation of the Rhineland." *History Today.* Vol. 6, 1956.

———. "Appeasement: The Rise of a Revisionist School?." *Political Quarterly.* April-June, 1965.

Webster, Sir Charles. "Munich Reconsidered: A Survey of British Policy." *International Affairs.* Vol. 37, 1961.

Weinberg, G.L. "The May Crisis, 1938." *Journal of Modern History.* Vol. 29, 1957.

Index

abdication crisis (1936), 30, 64, 70–71
Abyssinia:
  Chamberlain's position on, 55, 61–62, 102–3
  Italian aggression in, 41, 45–46, 55, 56–58
  League involvement in, 45, 46, 47, 55, 56
  recognition of Italian rule in, 84, 95, 102–3, 122
Africa, imperial view of, 55–56
air force, British, 36, 37–38, 52, 64, 121, 122–23
Albania, 180
Alexander, king of Yugoslavia, 38n
Almond, Gabriel, 4n
Amery, Leo, 24, 78, 154
Anglo-German Naval Treaty (1935), 44–45, 142, 162–63
Anglo-Italian agreement (1938), 122, 125, 128, 133, 171
Anglo-Japanese alliance (1902), 14
Anschluss, 110–14
  Anglo-Italian relations affected by, 113–14
  British opposition to, 125
  Cabinet meeting on, 112–13
  Chamberlain's position on, 111–12
  crisis leading to, 110–11
  rearmament accelerated after, 121
anti-Semitism:
  in Hore-Belisha's dismissal, 190n
  of Joseph Chamberlain, 13
  in Nazi Germany, 171–72
  of Neville Chamberlain, 13, 172, 182n, 190n
appeasement policy:
  Anglo-German Naval Treaty in, 44
  Chamberlain's pursuit of, 2, 58, 104–5, 107
  Chamberlain's view of, x, 3–4, 10, 32–33, 38

Czechoslovakian occupation as dis-crediting of, 169, 175
determinants of, 10
"guilty men" view of, 197, 198
historical lesson of, 4
as ill-defined goal, 89–90
Italian applications of, 82, 84, 95
literature on, 4–5
as metaphor for weakness, 2
in Munich meeting, 164
as overdetermined, 7
positive results of, 181
as response to limited resources, 196–97
symbolic meaning of, 2–4, 5
Tory position on, 75, 77
as tragic failure, ix, 195
Army, British, 84–89
  air force funding vs. funding for, 121
  Chamberlain's position on, 84, 85–87, 88–89
  debate on role of, 84, 85–87
  Inskip's memorandum on, 88, 89
  Territorial, 65–66, 67, 68, 69
Aster, Sidney, 176n
Attlee, Clement, 77
Austria:
  Chamberlain's view of, 38, 93
  German invasion of, 110–11
  Hitler's plans for, 93
  in interwar years, 38

Baldwin, Stanley:
  in abdication crisis, 71
  in Abyssinian dispute, 47
  Chamberlain's relations with, 29, 30, 34, 43, 48–49, 60–61, 71
  conflicting strategies pursued under, 52
  coup against, 29, 69n
  first Government of, 25
  ineffectiveness of, 43, 61